# CANAL HOUSE
# COOK
# SOMETHING

Voracious / Little, Brown and Company
Hachette Book Group
1290 Avenue of the Americas, New York, NY 10104
littlebrown.com

First Edition: September 2019

Voracious is an imprint of Little, Brown and Company, a division of Hachette Book Group, Inc.
The Voracious name and logo are trademarks of Hachette Book Group, Inc.

The publisher is not responsible for websites (or their content)
that are not owned by the publisher.

The Hachette Speakers Bureau provides a wide range of authors for speaking events.
To find out more, go to hachettespeakersbureau.com or call (866) 376-6591.

ISBN 978-0-316-26825-7
LCCN 2016934518

10 9 8 7 6 5 4 3 2 1
IM
Printed in China

CANAL HOUSE

# COOK

## SOMETHING

*recipes to rely on*

hirsheimer & hamilton

**VORACIOUS**

Little, Brown and Company
New York   Boston   London

*We dedicate this book to everyone who likes to cook and eat, as well as those who haven't yet awakened to the enjoyment of the kitchen and table. The everyday practice of simple cooking and the enjoyment of eating are two of the greatest pleasures in life.*

# RECIPES BY CHAPTER

## EGGS

# GOOD BEGINNINGS

# SOUP

*continued*

## SALADS

*Clockwise from top left: esteemed editor Judith Jones kept her apron on the back of her kitchen door;*
*a bunch of beets pulled from the garden; our beloved inherited Le Creuset pot*

## ITALIAN GEMS

## FISHIES

# CHICKEN & OTHER BIRDS

# BRAISES & STEWS (and a few roasts)

# GROUND MEAT

# GRILLING

# VEGETABLES

# SWEETIES

## Equipment

- wooden spoon
- whisk
- metal mixing bowl
- fish spatula
- microplane
- grater
- tongs
- rubber spatula
- large sieve
- rolling pin
- big metal spoon
- measuring spoons
- dry measuring cups
- glass liquid measuring cup
- Japanese suribachi (ceramic mortar & wooden pestle)
- swivel blade vegetable peeler
- pastry brush
- paring knife
- chef's knife
- serrated knife
- cutting board
- non-stick skillet(s)
- sauté pan(s)
- saucepan
- enameled cast-iron Dutch oven
- large soup/pasta pot
- roasting pan
- baking sheet pan
- gratin pan
- scale
- cast-iron skillet

## Pantry

- Kosher salt * sea salt
- finishing salt
- black peppercorns
- extra-virgin olive oil
- really good extra-virgin olive oil
- red wine vinegar
- anchovies packed in oil
- crushed red pepper flakes
- tomato paste
- spices * harissa
- pasta * rice *
- onions * garlic

## Fridge

- butter * eggs * bacon
- heavy cream * mayonnaise
- lemons * Dijon mustard
- ketchup * parmesan cheese

*Above: the Canal House suggested equipment and pantry list (desert island must-haves highlighted in yellow). Facing page: top, a well-stocked Irish kitchen; bottom, the Canal House minimalist kitchen*

# introduction
(why we wrote this book)

*We cook to feed ourselves. We cook to celebrate. We cook to honor. We cook to bring people together. We cook to satisfy our cravings. We cook to remind ourselves who we are. We cook to give. We cook to feed the ones we love. We cook to nourish. We cook because we have to. Go ahead, please cook something.*

THIS IS A BOOK ALL ABOUT HOME COOKING. It is how, with nearly a century of experience between us, we cook. Everyone needs a small cache of classic recipes: everyday recipes, weekend meals (when you have a little more time to cook), some special dishes for those big deal dinners, and of course, a way to tackle a holiday turkey. But you also need a helping hand to guide you through the process. Home cooking should be simple, but for too many people (especially young people), it seems intimidating. We love to share our kitchen knowledge. In fact, both of us have daughters, nephews and nieces, and many friends, young and old, who ask us kitchen/cooking questions all the time. We always take a work break, dry our hands, and answer them. We want to pass along what we have learned and encourage everyone to cook. It is our mission. Wholesome, healthy home cooking feeds both the body and the spirit.

What is it that gets in the way of cooking at home, even something simple on a weeknight? Everyone works and work now absorbs a lot more time, even after we "punch out". Add in a couple of kids with soccer games and piano lessons, and you can see how cooking can fall by the wayside. Most of us think we don't have an hour or two to spare each day to prepare a meal and sit down at the table to eat. How do you even begin? Dashing home in the evening, we all face the daily dilemma, "What's for dinner?" Too often, it is easier to grab ready-made food, or shop one meal at a time with no strategy or planning. We both grew up in big families that always gathered together for dinner at the end of the day. The table was set, and the meal was

*Christopher, left, and Melissa, right, in the Canal House kitchen*

served on platters that were passed from one person to the next. That's where we were enlightened to the art of conversation and civilized table manners. So often memorable moments are celebrated at the table. These meals humanize us.

Good cooking begins with good shopping. Fresh, wholesome food is the starting point for any recipe, so find a really good grocery store. You want helpful service, fair prices for quality goods, and management that is willing to bring in what shoppers want to buy. After all, it's the place we rely on when the garden has gone to sleep and it's too cold for farmers' markets. We keep things very simple and return to flavors that feel familiar. Our kitchens are stocked with a good supply of olive oil and Irish butter; parsley, chives, and other fresh herbs; bacon and pancetta; Parmigiano-Reggiano; good anchovies; canned tomatoes and tomato paste. We follow the seasons and look forward to their flavors as the year rotates: slicing, tossing, and grilling in the summer and braising and roasting in the winter. We anticipate asparagus and strawberries in spring, tomatoes in the summer, beets and squash in the fall.

There is good thrift in shopping once or twice a week. Then use what you have in your pantry of provisions to make what you want. Shopping every day can break the bank. Some weeks we might buy a big fat chicken. We cut it up, then use the parts to make weeknight meals like chicken soup (legs, back, and wings), chicken breasts poached in cream, and chicken thighs with kale and golden raisins. Or we cook pots of beans on Sunday to use in different ways throughout the week. Remember, leftovers are often the basis for the next night's dinner.

We learned to cook first by watching, then doing. If you grow up in a house where someone is cooking, the kitchen is filled with indelible sights, sounds, and smells. These early experiences remain in our memories and become a collection of maps that help us navigate through our culinary lives. Real recipes are usually attached to stories of people and place. They can reawaken a memory or create something you've never experienced. If a recipe is good, it will keep the story and the people associated with it alive for a long time. We rely on recipes as they hold the nuts and bolts of cooking. But there is no such thing as a foolproof one, there are just too many variables in the whole process of cooking. That's where your senses come in.

With enough experience you can almost learn to cook "by ear". It happens all the time to us. Before the timer rings, a waft of vanilla and cardamom will float through the studio, then we'll both look up at the same time and say, "The pound cake's ready"; a stir with a wooden spoon can determine the tenderness of a pot of cannellini beans; and gentle pressure on a steak or piece of fish will tell us if it is done.

It's good to remember that home kitchens don't have the rigor of professional ones. It always strikes us as curious that novice cooks set such store in honing their knife skills and/or mastering techniques that you rarely use, like tempering chocolate. Chefs are überskilled with their knives, but they might face chopping bushels of onions or cutting up hundreds of ducks. They need to be Olympians. For home cooking you'll need sharp knives; they are safer, and you'll find the more you use them, the better your slicing and dicing will get. We don't worry too much about special tools and intricate techniques. We focus our attention on the process: what are we making, what should it look and taste like, what is it supposed to be when it's finished. Then we work toward that vision. Should the onions be sliced so they offer texture, or do we want them minced so they offer flavor? Is the flavor delicate or full and rich, straightforward or complex? We watch, taste along the way, fuss, or leave things alone, but we are always paying attention.

Every morning when we come to the studio, the first one there starts the coffee or puts the kettle on for tea. If it is cold, we light a fire and if it's hot, we go outside to gather a few herbs or flowers. There is so much comfort in these rituals. In the past we traveled the world to eat, but now it's our studio and its little garden that give us our center. We prefer to go slower, paying attention to simple moments often involving food: cream biscuits slathered with butter and apricot jam with a cup of strong black China tea on a rainy morning; a bowl of thick, soft noodles curling in golden chicken broth; cold leftover spaghetti bolognese for breakfast straight from a plastic container; or eating fat asparagus spears bathed in lemon butter with our fingers. Every day we stop to cook and eat lunch together. It's usually simple, often leftovers, but always delicious and satisfying. Then at the end of each day we both go home to our families to cook and share a meal with them. Because after all, they are the ones that really matter.

And that's what we hope for you, that you'll find many things to cook in this book and eventually you'll make those recipes your own. The everyday practice of simple cooking and the enjoyment of eating are two of the greatest pleasures in life. Eat well, be happy!

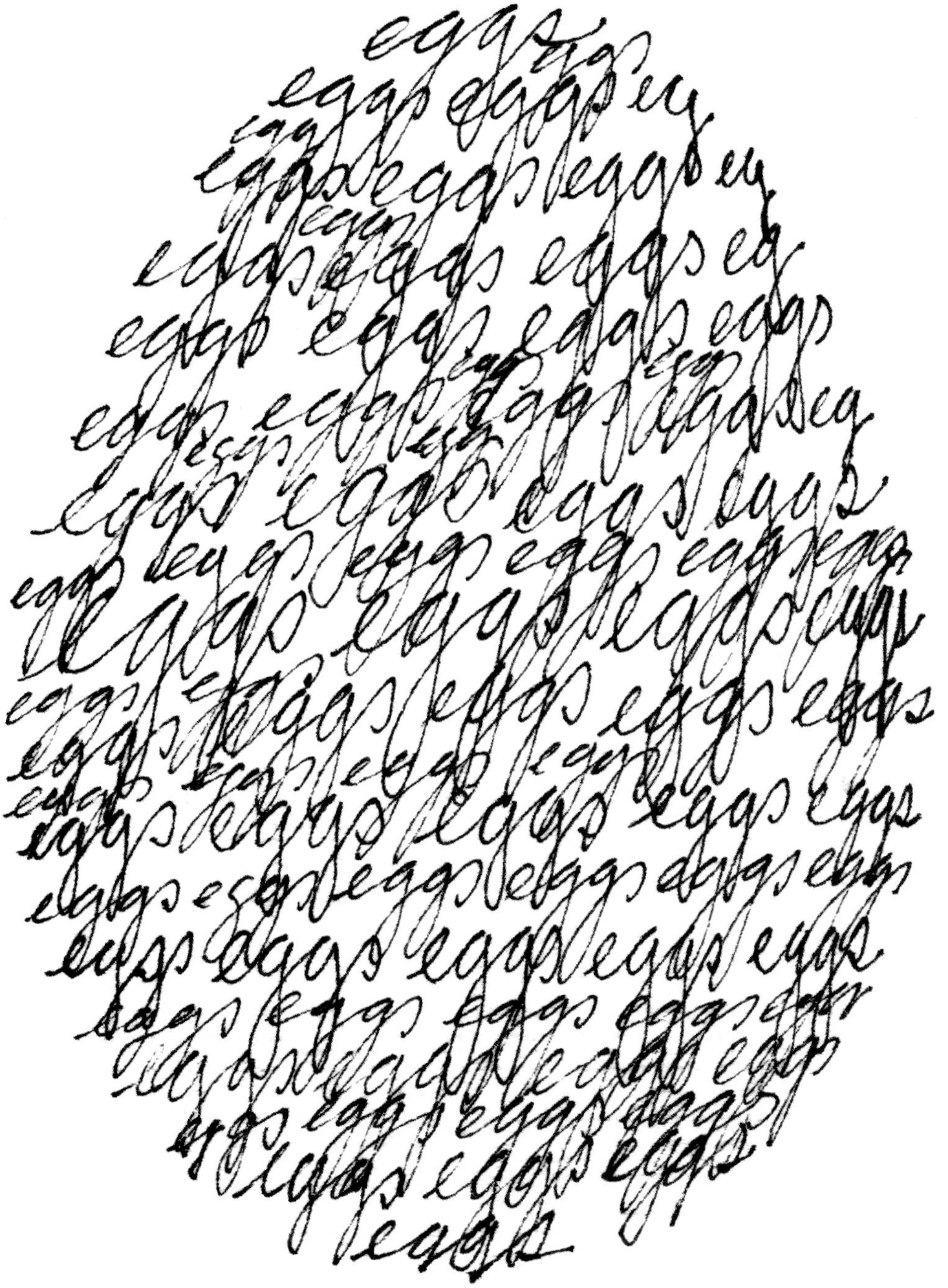

# Our Favorite Fallback

*Probably one of the most private things in the world is an egg before it is broken.*—M.F.K. Fisher

IT WASN'T STARTING WELL. OUR PLANE ARRIVED LATE. It was raining hard. All the shops and cafés were closed, and we were hungry. We drove through the dark streets, each of us silently wondering why we had left our homes to go on this adventure.

The house was remote, but the thoughtful landlady had left us a bottle of red and breakfast makings—a slab of butter, a wedge of cheese, a loaf of bread, cream for our morning coffee, and a carton of eggs. One lit a fire to warm up and cheer up, one opened the wine, poured two glasses, then cranked up the music—Van Morrison. We knew how to cure this homesick feeling—we'd make a breakfast dinner. The eggs were farm-fresh, we could see by their thick, clear whites and firm yolks as we cracked them into a bowl, then scrambled them together with heavy cream. Soon butter foamed, then sizzled in a slope-sided pan, the audible cue to add the eggs. A shower of grated cheese, a nudge and fold with a spatula, and two lovely omelets emerged. We sat in front of the fire in this new place, eating the familiar taste of buttery eggs, and felt at home. That's the power of food.

Usually we eat eggs in the morning at breakfast, the most private of meals. It is the bridge between our state of sleep and our reentry into the conscious world. From dark to light, from dream to awake.

An egg is a sacred thing. The beginning of something, a symbol of the cycle of life. To break an egg into a saucer and slide it into gently simmering water is sacramental. How did anyone venture to eat an artichoke? It seems almost a challenge to nature. But the egg; this is an obvious gift.

We both come from big families, but neither of us ever experienced the pageantry of a Cleaver breakfast with June in pearls, heels, and an apron serving up pancakes and eggs. Instead, our family members, then and today, wander or rush downstairs to grab a cup of coffee to slosh on the ride to work or to sip quietly while reading the paper. But we love eggs for breakfast, and we both have childhood memories of eating eggs in an eggcup, almost a lost art. We used a small spoon to tap the fat round end of the egg, circumnavigating the shell, then lifted off the top to reveal a soft-boiled yolk and white. We plunged in with a small spoon or dipped toast soldiers into the runny yolks. Then there were Sunday breakfasts after church, with slices of fried ham with a golden crust topped with two fried eggs. Everyone loved the salty sweetness of the meat, the yolk like golden velvet, and the slightly metallic taste of the edge of the egg white. The best part: mopping up the drippings with slices of buttery toast.

We both love to poach eggs in simmering salted water, lifting and draining them with a slotted fish spatula, before placing them on buttered, toasted English muffins. Add a baste of butter on each egg, salt, and a few grinds of pepper. There is nothing better—except maybe the time we were on a truffle hunt near Aix and stopped by a farmhouse for lunch. We watched a woman sit at the hearth as she scrambled eggs in a big seasoned steel pan over the fire. When they were barely set, she shaved a shower of black truffles over them. The warmth of the eggs released their sensual perfume, infusing the eggs and the air around us.

The preparation—scrambled, poached, soft-boiled, coddled—is a preference most likely tied to childhood. We are no exception. We each like our egg cooked in a particular way. Take scrambled eggs: barely mixed eggs, streaked with yellow and white versus well-beaten eggs, pure pale yellow. Then the matter of consistency: very soft, barely cooked is loved by one but intolerable to the other, who prefers still soft but completely cooked. It's a visceral thing.

One of our friends explains patiently whenever she orders eggs, "I would like my eggs fried hard. I mean really hard." They rarely get them right. She just can't eat them any other way. And we know a man who we would call a *gourmand* if that word didn't sound so poncy. He's forgotten more about food and wine than most people will ever know. But he won't touch an egg. Maybe someday he will sit at our table and we will win him over with spoonfuls of delicately scrambled eggs. But we may have to throw in a truffle.

## JUST THE FACTS, MA'AM...

THE COLOR: An eggshell's or yolk's color has nothing to do with its nutritional value, quality, or flavor. Hens with white feathers and white ear lobes lay white eggs; hens with red feathers and red ear lobes lay brown eggs.

THE SIZE: It hardly matters! Most recipes are written for large eggs. They are interchangeable with extra large eggs until you get to 5 eggs. Then for every 5 large eggs, use 4 extra large eggs; for every 6 large eggs, use 5 extra large eggs.

BUYING: Egg cartons from packaging plants that produce eggs graded by the U.S. Department of Agriculture (USDA) must display a Julian date, the date the eggs were packed. Although not required, egg cartons may also carry an expiration (sell by) date and/or a best by (use by) date. Expiration dates are included on some egg cartons, ensuring that retailers do not keep eggs on shelves past a certain date. However, eggs can be safely eaten 2 to 3 weeks beyond the sell by or expiration date. Look for the Certified Humane label which ensures the best practices for raising birds.

STORING: Under normal refrigeration (35F°–40°F), eggs can be kept for 4 to 5 weeks beyond the pack date or about 3 weeks after purchase. Store the eggs in their carton inside the refrigerator (rather than on the door, which may be slightly warmer). Eggs have 7,000 to 17,000 pores that (unfortunately) allow them to absorb other odors in the fridge.

FRESH TEST: Though the yolk takes center stage, it is really the quality of the albumen surrounding it that determines freshness. Thick albumen holds the yolk up, round and proud, right in the center of the egg. An off-center, flattish yolk surrounded by watery albumen is a good indication that the egg isn't fresh.

1. SALTED WATER ⊙ Very fresh eggs are tricky to peel when hard-boiled. The shell clings so tightly, it often tears and pockmarks the surface. Storing eggs in the fridge for a week or two before boiling them makes slipping off their shells easier. However, to peel very fresh eggs easily, we've come to rely on this trick: Add ⅓–½ cup salt to a pot of water (6–8 cups) and bring to a gentle boil.

2. BOILING WATER ⊙ Adding eggs to gently boiling water takes the guesswork out of determining just when to begin timing your eggs. It also makes peeling them easier. Use a slotted spoon to carefully lower large eggs straight from the fridge into the gently boiling water. Boil the eggs in a single layer covered by at least 1 inch of water.

3. COLD WATER ⊙ Unless you are making soft-boiled eggs, you need to quickly stop hard-boiled eggs from cooking beyond the desired doneness. Drain the eggs, then immediately submerge them in cold running water until they are cool to the touch.

4. CRACKING & PEELING ⊙ Tap eggs on a hard surface, cracking them all over. Peel off the shell, starting at the fatter end (where the air sac is). Dipping eggs under water will help. If not using uncracked, unpeeled eggs within 4 hours, keep them in the fridge.

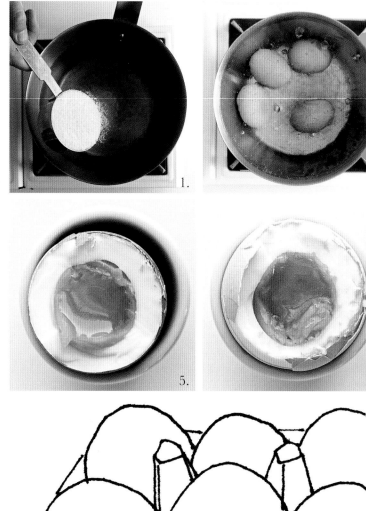

1.

5.

JR PERFECT BOILED EGGS

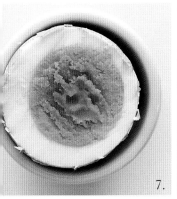
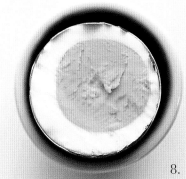
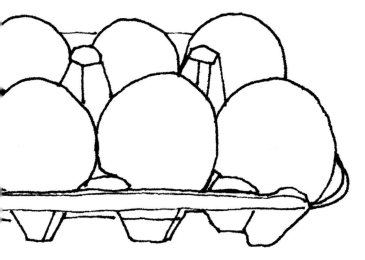

### 5. THE 5-MINUTE SOFT-BOILED EGG

A perfect soft-boiled egg is a matter of taste. How soft or firm you like the yolk to be when you spoon into it will determine how long to boil the egg. A large egg straight from the fridge, submerged into gently boiling water and cooked for 5 minutes, produces a soft-boiled egg with a firm white and a warm, runny yolk that is just set around the outside. A perfect soft-boiled egg for some, just a minute shy of perfection for others.

### 6. THE 6-MINUTE SOFT-BOILED EGG

If you want a soft-boiled egg with a firm white and a warm, jammy yolk just a bit runny in the center, this one will suit your taste. Submerge a large egg straight from the fridge into gently boiling water and cook for 6 minutes.

### 7. THE 11-MINUTE HARD-BOILED EGG

We like the texture and flavor of hard-boiled eggs with a just-firm yolk, still moist in the center. Boiling large eggs for eleven minutes gives us these—our all-purpose hard-boiled eggs.

### 8. THE 12-MINUTE HARD-BOILED EGG

We boil large eggs for 12 minutes when we want firm, dry yolks without the dreaded green ring (which indicates an over-cooked egg). We use these to make deviled eggs. The yolks pop out of the whites easily and make the fluffiest filling.

## HARD-BOILED EGGS ☞ makes as many as you like

Before we started writing cookbooks, we simply boiled eggs by ear. Our instincts became so acute that we could "feel" when they were done. But then we needed times and temperatures, so we started paying attention to what we were actually doing. Here's what we found: Keep the water at a gentle boil or vigorous simmer, as a hard boil may cause the eggs to crack. Older eggs peel more easily, so it's best to use eggs that are about a week old. And, we have a trick! Add lots of salt to the cooking water, then douse the cooked eggs in cold running water, and the shells will peel off easily.

⅓–½ cup salt
Large eggs, any number

Choose a saucepan large enough to accommodate the eggs in a single layer. Add water to cover the eggs by about 1 inch (well submerged). But don't put the eggs in just yet. Depending on the size of the pan, use part or all of the salt. Bring the water to a gentle boil over high heat.

Reduce the heat until the water is just bubbling. Give the water a stir to be sure the salt has dissolved. Use a large spoon and lower the eggs into the simmering water. Start the timer and cook until the eggs are done to your preference (see page 9).

Drain the eggs in the sink and immediately start running cold water in the pot to cool down the eggs. You can add ice cubes to really cool them down. Drain the eggs when they are cool enough to handle. Now they are ready to peel if you are going to eat them in the next few hours.

Tap the eggs all over on the kitchen counter, then peel off the shell starting from the fatter end of the egg (where the air sac is). This is easier to do under cold running water (see page 8).

Keep the uncracked, unpeeled hard-boiled eggs in a covered container in the refrigerator if you are not going to use them within 4 hours.

SOFT-BOILED EGGS TWO WAYS ☞ makes as many as you like

As a rule of thumb, start with the best ingredients you can find. Eggs are no exception. A "farm-raised" egg with a sturdy shell, tight thick white, and deep yellow-orange yolk is not only a thing of beauty; its flavor is rich and round. Good markets, farmers' markets, and roadside farmstands sell eggs worth gathering.

There are two ways we like to eat soft-boiled eggs, neither one better than the other. It just depends on the weather, or what we're in the mood for that day.

In an eggcup—Place a just-cooked, still warm, soft-boiled egg (page 9) into an eggcup, fat end up (where the air sac is). Using a spoon or dinner knife, tap around the top third of the egg, cracking the shell as you go, and lift off the top, revealing the cooked white and soft yolk. Scoop out the white and pop it in your mouth. Eat the rest of the egg, spooning it straight from the shell, seasoned with salt and freshly ground black pepper, and with warm buttered toast cut into narrow strips (called "soldiers") for dunking into the soft yolk.

In a bowl—Using a dinner knife, cut off the top third of 1–2 still warm, soft-boiled eggs (page 9). Run a spoon between the egg and the shell, scooping the egg out and into a bowl with warm buttered toast cut into bite-size squares. Add a knob of soft butter to the eggs and season with salt and freshly ground black pepper.

## DEVILED EGGS ☞ makes 12

These deviled eggs stand on their own but we often embellish the tops with a dab of harissa (Tunisian chile-spice paste), a fat cooked asparagus tip, shards of crisp bacon, chopped ham, prosciutto, a small spoonful of salmon roe, or a thin slice of cornichon (see page 14). We're sure you will think of your own combinations.

12 twelve-minute hard-boiled eggs, peeled (page 9) and halved lengthwise
½ cup mayonnaise
2 tablespoons sour cream
2 teaspoons Dijon mustard
Salt and freshly ground black pepper

Pop the egg yolks out of the whites into a fine sieve set over a bowl. Set the whites upside down on a paper towel to drain before filling. Use a wooden spoon or spatula to press the yolks through the sieve. Fold in the mayonnaise, sour cream, and mustard. Season with salt and pepper. (Or alternately use a food processor to purée everything together until smooth.) Place plastic wrap directly on the surface of the filling until ready to fill the eggs.

Use two small spoons to fill each egg white with the filling. Garnish the eggs simply with fresh tarragon leaves or finely chopped fresh chives, or as you like.

## "BUTTERED" EGGS

Anyone who knows us can tell you that we always start off a gathering—large or small—with either our deviled eggs (see above) or these delicious buttered-with-mayonnaise beauties. We simply "butter" the cut sides of peeled hard-boiled eggs with mayonnaise. The creamy yolks of 11-minute hard-boiled eggs (page 9) have the best texture, so we use them. Arrange the eggs on a plate, drizzle them with some good olive oil, and add a generous sprinkle of salt and freshly ground black pepper. Garnish them simply with fresh tender herbs—chives, oregano, parsley, or dill—or with chopped preserved lemon or bacon, or as you like (see page 15).—*makes as many as you like*

*Facing page, clockwise from top left: Soft-Boiled Eggs in an eggcup with "soldiers" (page 11); Soft-Boiled Eggs in a bowl with toast and butter (page 11); Deviled Eggs; "Buttered" Eggs*

salmon roe & finely chopped fresh chives

asparagus tip & minced preserved lemon rind

chopped fresh chives & parsley

tiny croutons, shards of bacon, parsley

harissa, diced preserved lemon rind, fresh marjoram

smoked salmon, black pepper, fresh dill

ham, sliced scallions, black pepper

chopped bacon & fresh chives

# THIS IS THE WAY WE TOP OUR BUTTERED EGGS . . .

smoked salmon & fresh chive tip

anchovy-stuffed olive, chives, a drop of olive oil

anchovy, red chile flakes, a drop of olive oil

sliced cherry tomato, olive oil, pepper, fresh basil

asparagus tip & chopped ham

crumbled bacon & sliced scallion greens

bacon shard, chutney, fresh chives

sliced ham, chopped fresh chives, black pepper

## POACHED EGGS ☞ makes 2

When we are serving poached eggs for a crowd (that is, for more than a manageable group of two), we make it easy on ourselves and poach the eggs ahead. It's a restaurant trick and a simple one to do at home. Poach the eggs for 2–3 minutes, then transfer them directly to a bowl of ice water to quickly stop the cooking. They will keep in the cold water in the fridge for up to 12 hours. When you are ready to serve them, slip the eggs into barely simmering water until they are warmed through, 1–2 minutes.

Salt
2 large eggs
Freshly ground black pepper
2 teaspoons softened butter, optional
1–2 slices buttered toast, optional

Bring a medium saucepan of water to a boil over medium-high heat. Reduce the heat to maintain a gentle simmer. Add 1 tablespoon salt.

Meanwhile, crack an egg into a small cup or saucer. Hold the cup in the simmering water and slip in the egg (1). Repeat with the remaining egg. Gently slip a spatula under the eggs, giving them a gentle nudge to keep them from resting on the bottom of the pan.

Poach the eggs until the whites turn opaque but the yolks remain soft, 2–3 minutes. Transfer the eggs with a slotted spoon or spatula to paper towels to drain (2). Trim off any ragged egg whites to tidy up the egg into a neat shape, if you like (3).

Season the eggs with salt and pepper. We like to serve our poached eggs set on warm buttered toast with a little butter on top.

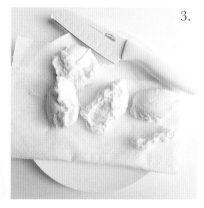

*Facing page, clockwise from top left: Poached Eggs on Buttered Toast; Poached Eggs in Broth-Cooked Noodles (page 18); Poached Eggs on Spinach with Lemon Zest (page 18); Poached Eggs on Leftovers (page 19)*

## POACHED EGGS IN BROTH-COOKED NOODLES ☞ makes 2

Obvious but true: the better the flavor of something, the better it will taste. A good-tasting broth (like the ones on pages 84–87) will make this ramen-inspired recipe a bowl of deliciousness. But sometimes it is inconvenient to make broth from scratch, so we sacrifice a little flavor for ease. If all you have on hand to make this dish is store-bought broth, go ahead and use it.

6 cups chicken, beef, or
   vegetable broth
6 ounces vermicelli
Salt
2 poached eggs (page 16)
Chopped trimmed scallions
Chopped fresh chives
Freshly ground black pepper

Bring the broth to a boil in a medium pot over medium-high heat. Reduce the heat to medium. Add the noodles and cook, stirring often, until they are just tender and swollen, about 4 minutes. Season with salt.

Divide the noodles and broth between two warm soup bowls. Set a poached egg in each bowl and scatter scallions and chives on top. Season with salt and pepper.

## POACHED EGGS ON SPINACH WITH LEMON ZEST

Sometimes we whip up a Lemon-Butter Sauce (page 358) to spoon over this dish to add a layer of luxurious richness.

Put 4–6 ounces washed, tender young spinach leaves in a heatproof colander or steamer basket and set over a pot of gently boiling water over medium heat. (Don't let the bottom of the colander or steamer basket touch the water.) Cover and steam the spinach, turning the leaves a few times as they wilt, until tender, about 5 minutes. Transfer the spinach to a warm bowl or dish and gently toss with 2–3 tablespoons soft butter. Set 1–2 poached eggs (page 16) on top. Add a dab or more of butter, if you like. Season with salt and freshly ground black pepper. Garnish with a flourish of finely grated lemon zest and Lemon-Butter Sauce.—*serves 1*

## POACHED EGGS ON LEFTOVERS

We don't "do" Chinese takeout very often, but when we do, we like to order extra fried rice, lo mein, or chow mein so we can reheat the leftovers the next day for a quick breakfast, lunch, or dinner. (Paella, risotto, and spaghetti make good leftovers, too.) We're kind of crazy for eggs—practically everything tastes better with an egg on it. Leftovers like these, embellished with a poached egg or two, really do.

Reheat 2–3 cups (depending on your appetite) fried rice, lo mein, chow mein, paella, risotto, or spaghetti until it is piping hot. Transfer the leftovers to a bowl or plate. Top with a poached egg or two (page 16). Season with salt and freshly ground black pepper, if you like.—*serves 1*

## CRUMB-COVERED POACHED EGGS ☞ makes 8

When you cut into these eggs, the crunchy crust gives way to the tender egg inside, and the crumbs mingle and soak up the velvety yolk. Both rustic and sophisticated, it's a great guest dish. Everything is done ahead, then the eggs get their final finish in the oven just before serving.

FOR THE SEASONED CRUMBS
8 strips bacon, chopped
3 tablespoons butter
1½ cups panko
2 good pinches of cayenne
Salt and freshly ground
   black pepper

FOR THE EGGS
1 tablespoon salt
8 eggs for poaching
½ cup Wondra flour, or
   all-purpose flour
3 eggs, for coating the
   poached eggs

For the seasoned crumbs, put the bacon in a medium skillet and cook over medium heat, stirring often, until browned and crisp, about 5 minutes. Transfer the bacon with a slotted spoon to paper towels to drain. Melt the butter in the skillet with the bacon fat over medium heat, then add the panko. Toast, stirring constantly, until golden brown, about 5 minutes.

Transfer the crumbs to a medium bowl. Chop the cooked bacon very finely. Add it to the crumbs and toss well. Season with cayenne, salt, and pepper. There should be about 1¾ cups. Set aside.

For the eggs, bring water in a medium saucepan to a boil over medium-high heat. Reduce the heat to maintain a gentle simmer. Add the salt. Fill a medium bowl with ice water and set aside.

Poach 4 eggs at a time. Crack 1 egg into a small cup or saucer. Hold the cup in the simmering water and slip the egg in. Repeat with 3 more eggs. Slip a spatula under the eggs, giving them a

*continued*

*Crumb-Covered Poached Eggs (continued)*

gentle nudge, to keep them from resting on the bottom of the pan. Poach the eggs until the whites turn opaque but the yolks remain soft, 2–3 minutes. Lift the eggs from the pan with a slotted spoon or spatula into the bowl of ice water to quickly stop the cooking. Meanwhile, poach the remaining 4 eggs.

When the eggs are cold, set them on paper towels to drain. Trim off any ragged egg whites to tidy up the egg into a neat shape. Gently pat the 8 eggs all over with paper towels so they are dry for coating.

Put the flour in a medium bowl. Beat the remaining 3 eggs with 1 tablespoon water in another medium bowl. Arrange 3 bowls as follows: flour–eggs–crumbs. Working with 1 poached egg at a time, gently dredge in flour; next gently roll in beaten eggs, covering it completely; then dredge in the crumbs. Set the crumb-coated egg on a parchment paper–lined baking sheet. Repeat with the remaining 7 eggs, spacing the eggs evenly in one layer. The eggs can stay like this, at room temperature, for up to 2 hours.

Preheat the oven to 350°F. Bake the prepared eggs until they are deep golden brown and warmed through, 10–15 minutes.

PANCETTA & PARMIGIANO CRUMBS: Follow the directions for seasoned crumbs (page 19), omitting the bacon. Melt 4 tablespoons butter in a medium skillet over medium heat. Add ½ cup finely diced pancetta and cook until lightly browned, about 15 minutes. Continue with the recipe, adding ¼ cup finely grated Parmigiano-Reggiano with salt and freshly ground black pepper.

TARRAGON & PARSLEY CRUMBS: Follow the directions for seasoned crumbs (page 19), omitting the bacon. Melt 8 tablespoons butter in a medium skillet over medium heat, and continue with the recipe, adding 1 tablespoon minced fresh tarragon leaves and 3 tablespoons minced fresh parsley leaves with salt and freshly ground black pepper.

CHORIZO CRUMBS: Follow the directions for seasoned crumbs (page 19), omitting the bacon. Melt 4 tablespoons butter in the skillet over medium heat, and continue with the recipe, adding ¼ cup finely minced Spanish chorizo with salt and freshly ground black pepper.

HOW TO FRY AN EGG ☞ makes as many as you like

AFTER ALL, IT'S JUST EGGS. And fried eggs are probably the easiest to cook of all the egg recipes. Heat up a skillet with a little butter, olive oil, or maybe some rendered bacon fat, crack in the egg, and before you know it, the soft yolk is surrounded by a firm, opaque white, and the egg is ready to eat. Sometimes we add a little refinement to the technique and either cover the eggs with a lid halfway through cooking, or we baste our eggs with the frying fat to fix that thin, jiggly layer of uncooked white and still have the yolk shining up at us.

Here's a little trick we do when we want our fried eggs to look picture-perfect (and really, only then). Crack the egg into a small sieve over the sink or a bowl to drain out the thin, watery whites from the thick whites. Then tip the egg into the hot skillet. The cooked white will have a cleaner, round edge, and the yolk will sit more in the center.

Nonstick pans are so slippery that you can fry an egg in them without adding any fat. Use moderate heat (below 500°F) to avoid any health concerns. Stainless steel or seasoned cast iron work well too, you'll just need to add a little fat (which adds flavor) to keep the egg from sticking.

When frying more than one egg at a time, crack them into the skillet one at a time, as far apart from each other as possible. A small skillet holds 2 eggs; a medium skillet holds 4 eggs; a large skillet holds 6 eggs.

SUNNY-SIDE UP: Melt 1 tablespoon butter or other fat in a medium skillet over medium heat, swirling it around to coat the bottom. Crack an egg into the skillet. Fry the egg without moving it until the white just becomes opaque, about 1½ minutes. Cover the skillet and continue frying the egg until the white toward the center is no longer jiggly and the yolk is soft, 1–2 minutes. Uncover the skillet and fry the egg longer if you like a firmer yolk. Slip a thin spatula under the egg and transfer it to a plate. Season with salt and freshly ground black pepper.

OVER-EASY: Follow the directions above for frying an egg sunny-side up, but don't cover the skillet. When the egg is almost finished cooking, about 3 minutes, slip a thin spatula under the egg and carefully turn it over. Fry the egg for less than a minute, then transfer it yolk-side up to a plate. Season with salt and freshly ground black pepper.

BASTED IN OLIVE OIL OR BUTTER: Heat 3 tablespoons olive oil or butter in a medium skillet over medium-high heat until quite warm. Crack eggs into the skillet and reduce the heat if it begins to smoke. Fry the eggs and basting them with the olive oil, until the whites are opaque and crisp and lacy around the edges, the yolks remain soft. Transfer the eggs to a plate and season with salt and freshly ground black pepper. Spoon a little oil on top.

*Facing page, clockwise from top left: Sunny-Side Up Fried Egg in Butter; Over-Easy Fried Egg in Butter; Basted Fried Egg in Olive Oil; Over-Easy Egg*

## CANAL HOUSE CROQUE MADAME

Leave it to us *mesdames* to go messing around with the classic French grilled ham and cheese. We go "topless" and make it an open-face sandwich.

Preheat the broiler. Cut off and discard the crust of 1 slice of brioche, challah, or other tender white bread. Toast both sides of the bread until golden brown, spread with 1 tablespoon butter, and transfer it to a small nonstick baking sheet. Cover the toast with about ¼ cup grated Gruyère cheese. Cover the cheese with a slice of ham. Spread 2–3 tablespoons warm Mornay Sauce (below) on top, and cover with 2–3 tablespoons grated Gruyère. Broil the sandwich until the cheese is melted and lightly browned on top. Transfer the sandwich to a plate and set a fried egg sunny-side up (page 22) on top. Season with salt and freshly ground black pepper.—*makes 1*

## MORNAY SAUCE

This classic French cheese sauce, a béchamel enriched and thickened with Gruyère, can be thinned with a little milk and stirred into hot macaroni or spooned over warm cauliflower, broccoli, or asparagus.

Melt 2 tablespoons butter in a heavy medium saucepan over medium-low heat. Whisk in 2 tablespoons flour and cook for 1½ minutes, stirring constantly to prevent it from taking on any color whatsoever. Whisk in 1 cup hot milk and cook, whisking constantly, until smooth and thick, about 2 minutes. Add 4 ounces cubed Gruyère (about 1 cup), stirring until the cheese is melted and the sauce is smooth. Season with finely grated nutmeg and salt to taste. Remove pan from heat. Lay a sheet of plastic wrap directly on the surface of the sauce to prevent a skin from forming.—*makes 1⅓ cups*

## CRISPY FRIED EGG IN TOMATO SAUCE

We "toast" our bread in olive oil to give it a deeper flavor and extra crunch, a doubly good foil for the bright, saucy tomatoes.

Heat 2–3 tablespoons olive oil in a medium skillet over medium heat. Add 1 slice of bread and fry until deep golden brown, about 2 minutes per side. Transfer the bread to a paper towel and sprinkle with a little salt. Put ½ cup warm Fresh Tomato & Basil Sauce (page 159) in a wide bowl or dish and set the fried bread on top. Fry 1–2 eggs in olive oil (page 22) and set them on the bread, spooning some of the hot oil over the eggs and tomato sauce. Garnish with a small handful of chopped parsley. Season with salt and freshly ground black pepper.—*makes 1*

*Facing page: top, Croque Madame; bottom, Crispy Fried Egg in Tomato Sauce*

## EGGS EN COCOTTE ☞ makes 4

This delicate egg and cream dish, baked in a custard cup or ramekin, cooks gently and evenly when set in a hot water bath. We make this dish for breakfast, brunch, lunch, or a light dinner with a salad and good bread. There is a lovely simplicity to its flavor with lots of room for embellishing.

4 tablespoons butter, softened
8 asparagus spears, top thirds only, blanched and chopped
¼ cup diced ham
Small handful chopped chives
Salt and freshly ground black pepper
4 eggs
¾ cup heavy cream

Preheat the oven to 400°F. Butter four custard cups or 6-ounce ramekins with 2 tablespoons of the butter (1).

Divide the asparagus and ham between the buttered ramekins, covering the bottom of each. Add half of the chives (2), reserving the rest for garnish. Season with salt and pepper. Crack 1 egg into each cup. Pour the cream equally over each egg. The cream should pretty much cover the eggs. Season with a little salt and pepper. Top each with a knob of the remaining 2 tablespoons butter (3).

Set the cups into a deep baking dish or roasting pan filled half-way with simmering water. Carefully transfer the pan to the oven. Bake the eggs until the cream is bubbling, the tops have browned, and the eggs are barely set and still jiggle, about 10 minutes. They should tremble when you shake the cups. (The eggs will continue to cook after they're removed from the water bath.)

Lift the cups from the water bath with a spatula (or a canning jar lifter works well). Garnish the eggs with the remaining chives (4) and serve with slices of hot buttered toast, if you like.

LOBSTER, LEMON ZEST & TARRAGON: Substitute ½ cup chopped lobster meat for the asparagus and ham. Substitute 2 sprigs chopped fresh tarragon leaves for the chives. Add some finely grated lemon zest to the filling in each cup.

SHRIMP, HARISSA & SCALLIONS: Substitute ½ cup peeled, small raw shrimp for the asparagus and ham. Add ½ teaspoon harissa paste to each cup. Substitute 1 handful chopped trimmed scallions for the chives.

CHICKEN, SHIITAKES & PEAS: Substitute ¼ cup diced poached chicken, 4 chopped shiitake mushroom caps, and 2 tablespoons blanched or defrosted frozen peas for the asparagus and ham.

1.

2.

4.

3.

## SCRAMBLED EGGS ☞ serves 1

If we tried to guess how many eggs we have scrambled in our collective lifetime, 200,000 is more than likely. By now, making them is second nature. And we both like our scrambled eggs served about the same way—buttery, with big, soft curds, seasoned with salt and pepper. (On occasion, ketchup makes an appearance.) But recently, we discovered a subtle difference in preferences. CH adds a splash of cream or whole milk to her eggs before scrambling them. MH adds nothing but a pinch of salt. Habits and tastes set long ago. Is one way more correct than the other? Does adding cream make them fluffier, moister, more better? We don't think so. It makes them rounder and creamier tasting. Without the cream, they're eggier. It's simply a matter of preference. If you want tender scrambled eggs, the important thing to remember is to undercook them slightly before tipping them out of the skillet onto the plate. They will continue to cook. By the time the eggs reach your plate, they will be just right.

3 eggs
1–2 tablespoons butter
Splash of heavy cream (about 1 tablespoon), optional
Salt and freshly ground black pepper

Crack the eggs into a medium bowl. Add the cream, if using, and a pinch of salt. Using a whisk or fork, vigorously beat the eggs until well combined (1).

Melt the butter in a medium nonstick skillet over medium heat (2). Pour the eggs into the bubbling butter. After a few seconds, pull the set eggs into the center of the skillet using a spatula. The uncooked eggs will rush out to the edges. Wait until the uncooked eggs begin to set again, then pull them into the center, making big soft curds (3). Continue doing this until all the eggs are very softly set or a little bit undercooked, about 2 minutes total. Quickly remove the skillet from the heat. Transfer the eggs to a plate and season with salt and pepper (4).

1.

2.

3.

4.

## CHEESE OMELET ▷ makes 1

A perfect French omelet is oval-shaped with tapered ends; a smooth sponge; tender, delicate, and slightly custardy. It should not have any color from the cooking. But that omelet is not our preferred style. We like ours with a little more character: tender and delicate, of course, but less spongy, its shape more relaxed, with a bit of golden brown color for flavor. We think of our omelets as having terrific personalities, each one a little different from the last, whether it's a plain omelet or one filled with cheese, chutney, or something else savory or sweet. A country omelet, if you like. It's more forgiving to make but equally delicious.

2 eggs
1 tablespoon heavy cream
Salt
1 tablespoon butter
½ cup grated or crumbled cheese (like Gruyère, Cheddar, Monterey Jack or Parmigiano-Reggiano)
Freshly ground black pepper

Crack the eggs into a medium bowl. Add the cream and a pinch of salt. Melt the butter in a medium nonstick skillet over medium-low heat, swirling the pan to evenly coat the bottom and sides. Using a whisk or fork, beat the eggs and cream until well combined.

When the butter is foaming, pour the eggs into the skillet. Quickly swirl the eggs around so they evenly coat the bottom of the skillet. Tilting the skillet, use a spatula to pull the lightly set eggs halfway toward the center of the pan, allowing the raw eggs to flow back to coat the bottom of the skillet. Repeat on the opposite side.

Reduce the heat to low. Let the omelet cook, undisturbed, until the eggs have set on the bottom, yet are still loose on top, about 1 minute.

Scatter the cheese over the eggs. Season with salt and pepper. Continue cooking the omelet until the cheese begins to melt and the eggs are just soft on top and a pale shade of brown on the bottom, about 2 minutes.

Using the spatula, fold the omelet into thirds (as you would a business letter), toward the center. Tip the omelet out of the skillet, folding it onto itself, onto a plate. If the omelet is misshapen, as ours often is, and you want a neat, oval shape, use your fingers to tuck in any stray edges.

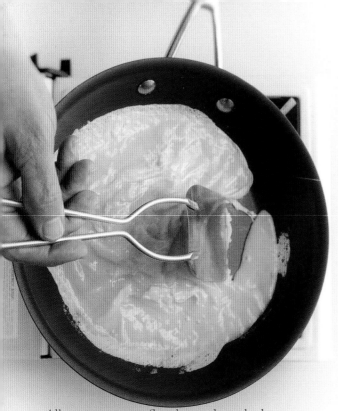

Allow raw eggs to flow beneath cooked eggs.

Add the cheese or filling evenly over the omelet.

Apple & Sausage

Bacon Chutney

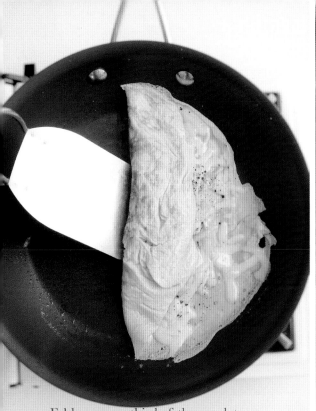

Fold over one third of the omelet.

Tip and fold the omelet onto a plate.

Avocado & Green Chile

Cream Cheese & Caraway

## APPLE & SAUSAGE OMELET FILLING ☞ enough to make 6 omelets

Look for quality bulk sausage meat that hasn't been formed into sausage links. But if it isn't available, use sausages and cut off the casings with scissors.

3 tablespoons butter
½ pound bulk pork sausage meat or sausages, casings removed
1 apple, cored, peeled, and cut into large dice
Salt and freshly ground black pepper
Small handful chopped scallions

Melt the butter in a medium skillet over medium heat. Add the sausage and cook, stirring and breaking the meat up with a spatula or the back of a spoon. Cook until the sausage is no longer pink, about 3 minutes. Add the apples to the skillet and season with salt and pepper. Cook, stirring occasionally, until the sausage is cooked through and the apples are tender, about 5 minutes. Stir in the chopped scallions. Season with salt and pepper.

Follow the directions for making an omelet (page 30) and in place of the cheese, scatter ½ cup warm Apple & Sausage Omelet Filling and ⅓–½ cup grated Muenster cheese over the eggs.

## BACON CHUTNEY OMELET

Bacon goes with just about any flavor. For this omelet, we like to use mango chutney like Major Grey's or tomato chutney. The sweet-tart flavors are just right with the salty, smoky bacon.

Follow the directions for making an omelet (page 30) and in place of the cheese, scatter ½ cup grated Monterey Jack cheese, 3 slices crisp bacon torn into pieces, and 2 tablespoons chutney over the eggs. Garnish the omelet with lots of chopped fresh chives. Season with freshly ground black pepper.—*makes 1*

## AVOCADO & GREEN CHILE OMELET

Anaheim chiles, the type commonly used for canned green chiles, are relatively mild, just the way we like them, as we are sissies when it comes to spicy-hot food. Add or substitute a chopped fresh jalapeño if you want a kick to your omelet.

Tear 1 canned, peeled whole green chile into quarters lengthwise. Dice ¼ peeled, pitted ripe Hass avocado. Chop 1 trimmed scallion. Follow the directions for making an omelet (page 30) and in place of the cheese, scatter ⅓ cup grated Monterey Jack cheese, the prepared green chiles, avocados, and scallions over the eggs. Garnish the omelet with a dollop of sour cream. Season with salt and freshly ground black pepper.—*makes 1*

## CREAM CHEESE & CARAWAY OMELET

Gently toasting the caraway seeds in a warm skillet deepens their flavor and brings them to life.

Follow the directions for making an omelet (page 30) and in place of the cheese, scatter ½ cup softened cream cheese over the eggs. Scatter ¼ teaspoon toasted caraway seeds over the cream cheese, and season with salt and freshly ground black pepper.—*makes 1*

## BUTTERED TOAST & D'AFFINOIS OMELET

There are a couple of splurge omelets we make using luxury ingredients: translucent slices of smoked salmon, trout roe that bursts sea-saltiness with every bite, or shaved black truffles. But this omelet, wrapped around a rich French double-cream soft cheese atop buttery toast is a luxury we can always afford. A ripe Brie can be substituted for the Fromager d'Affinois.

Preheat the oven to 200°F. Toast a slice of brioche, challah, or white bread. Trim off the crusts and cut it into a 2 × 4-inch rectangle. Butter the toast and place a 2 × 4-inch slice of Fromager d'Affinois on top. Transfer the cheese toast to a heatproof tray and heat in the oven until barely warm. You just want to take the chill off the cheese and warm up the toast. Meanwhile, follow the directions for making an omelet (page 30) and in place of the cheese, set the cheese toast, cheese-side up, in the center of the eggs. Season the omelet with salt and freshly ground black pepper and garnish with parsley leaves, if you like.—*makes 1*

*Overleaf: Buttered Toast & d'Affinois Omelet*

## FRITTATA WITH POTATO & SAUSAGE ☞ serves 4–6

Every cook is well served knowing how to make the versatile frittata, a crustless quichelike Italian egg dish. Filled with any number of vegetable, cheese, and/or sausage or cured meat combinations, it is delicious eaten piping hot, at room temperature, even cold.

2 medium russet potatoes, peeled and thickly sliced crosswise
Salt
2 tablespoons olive oil
2 Italian sausages, casings removed
2 pinches of crushed red pepper flakes
Freshly ground black pepper
6 eggs
½ cup grated Parmigiano-Reggiano
Small fresh oregano leaves, chopped fresh parsley, or chives, for garnish

Preheat the oven to 400°F. Put the potatoes into a medium pan, add enough cold water to cover them by about 1 inch, and season with a generous pinch of salt. Bring to a gentle boil over medium-high heat. Reduce the heat to medium-low and simmer until the potatoes are parboiled (cooked about halfway through), about 5 minutes. The potatoes should be just tender yet still a bit firm in the center. Drain the potatoes and pat dry with paper towels.

Heat the oil in a medium, nonstick, ovenproof skillet over medium heat. Add the meat and cook, breaking it up with the back of a spoon, until lightly browned all over, 6–8 minutes. Using a slotted spoon, transfer the meat to a small bowl.

Return the skillet with the oil and browned bits of meat to the stove over low heat. Arrange some of the potato slices in the bottom of the skillet in a single layer and scatter some of the meat on top. Season with a pinch of crushed red pepper flakes and salt and pepper. Continue layering, seasoning as you go.

Whisk the eggs in a medium bowl with 1 tablespoon water and salt and pepper, until well combined. Pour the eggs over the potatoes and meat. Gently shake the skillet so the eggs run between the layers to the bottom. Increase the heat to medium and cook until the eggs begin to set around the edge and the center is still runny, about 5 minutes.

Scatter the grated cheese over the eggs. Transfer the skillet to the oven and bake until the frittata is set, 5–10 minutes.

Remove the frittata from the oven. Serve cut into wedges. For a prettier presentation, loosen the frittata from the skillet and carefully invert it onto a cutting board. Cut into 4–6 wedges. Serve warm or at room temperature, garnished with fresh herbs.

## CHORIZO & PIQUILLO PEPPER FRITTATA

Follow the directions for making a frittata (page 38), substituting 6–8 ounces sliced Spanish chorizo for the Italian sausage and omitting the crushed red pepper flakes and grated cheese. In step 2, sauté the chorizo in the skillet until lightly browned, 2–3 minutes. Drain 12 piquillo peppers and pat dry with paper towels. Add the peppers when layering the frittata in step 3. Garnish with chopped fresh parsley, if you like.—*serves 4–6*

## ASPARAGUS & SCALLION FRITTATA

Follow the directions for making a frittata (page 38), substituting 1 pound peeled, trimmed asparagus for the potatoes and parboiling them for 2 minutes. Substitute 4 tablespoons butter for the olive oil and 1 bunch chopped, trimmed scallions for the sausage. Sauté the scallions in the butter until soft, about 5 minutes. Lay the asparagus on top in a single layer. Add the crushed red pepper flakes.—*serves 4–6*

## FENNEL & PANCETTA FRITTATA

Follow the directions for making a frittata (page 38), substituting 2–3 trimmed fennel bulbs for the potatoes. Thickly slice the fennel lengthwise and parboil it for 4–5 minutes. Substitute ¼ pound chopped pancetta for the sausage, sautéing it for 4–5 minutes.—*serves 4–6*

## ONION & GRUYÈRE QUICHE ☞ makes one 12-inch tart

Plenty of obstacles give us pause and prevent us from making what we want to eat when we want to eat it, things like washing and drying lettuce or stirring together a vinaigrette for a salad can be "too much trouble". Making pastry dough and rolling it out into a crust for a pie or tart? That has definitely given us pause when we are pressed for time. We could and have, of course, used store-bought pie crusts. But they are never as tender and flavorful as our own. A good crust shouldn't get in the way of making something as classic and delicious as a delicate, savory quiche. When making pastry crust, we've gotten in the habit of making extra disks of dough and storing them in the freezer. The dough defrosts by the time the oven is preheated. And when we're on our game (and there's enough room), we stash well-wrapped, rolled-out crusts in the freezer, ready to fill. A little discipline helps a lot.

*continued*

*Facing page, clockwise from top left: Chorizo & Piquillo Pepper Frittata;*
*fat asparagus; Onion & Gruyère Quiche*

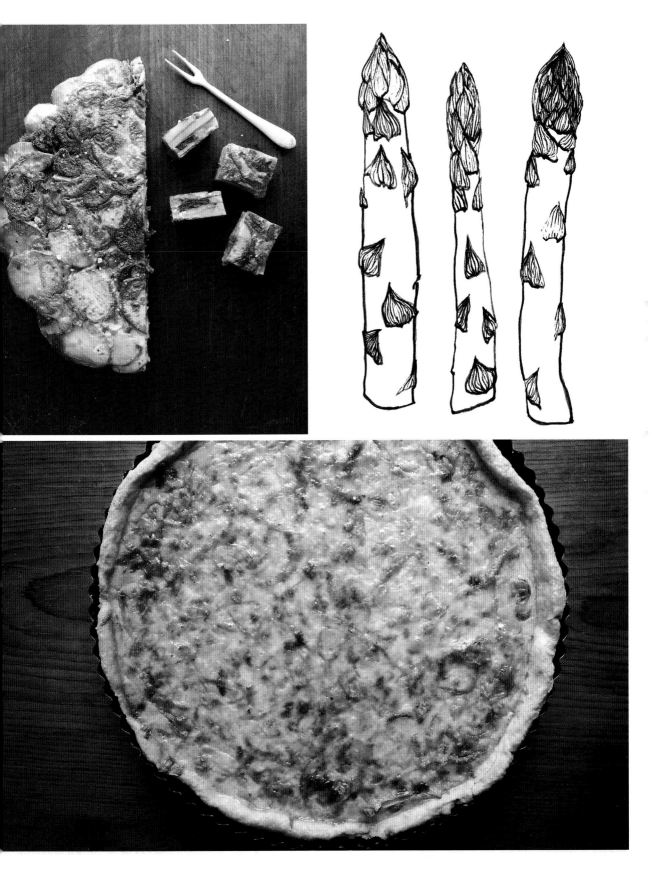

*Onion & Gruyère Quiche (continued)*

FOR THE CRUST
2 cups flour
Large pinch of salt
8 tablespoons cold butter,
     cut into small pieces
3 tablespoons cold vegetable
     shortening, cut into small
     pieces
1 egg, lightly beaten

FOR THE FILLING
8 tablespoons butter
2 medium onions, peeled,
     halved, and sliced
1 garlic clove, sliced
Salt and freshly ground
     black pepper
1 tablespoon Dijon mustard
1 cup grated Gruyère cheese

FOR THE CUSTARD
3 eggs
1 cup half-and-half
½ cup heavy cream
Grated nutmeg
½ teaspoon salt
Freshly ground black pepper

For the crust, whisk together the flour and salt in a medium bowl. Work the butter and shortening into the flour using a pastry blender or 2 knives until it resembles coarse cornmeal. Gradually sprinkle in up to 6 tablespoons ice water, while stirring with a fork, until it just begins to hold together. Using your hands, press the dough firmly into a rough ball, then transfer to a lightly floured work surface. Knead the dough in several quick turns to form a smooth dough. Shape the dough into a ball and flatten it slightly to make a disk. Wrap the dough in plastic wrap and refrigerate for at least 1 hour or overnight.

Allow the dough to soften slightly at room temperature before rolling it out on a lightly floured surface into a 14-inch round, about ¼ inch thick. Roll the dough loosely around the rolling pin, then unfurl it into a 12-inch tart pan with a removable bottom. Fit overhanging dough down along the sides to make the quiche edges a little thicker and sturdier. Run the rolling pin over the top of the pan to remove any overhanging dough. Prick the bottom lightly with a fork. Cover with plastic wrap and refrigerate for at least 1 hour or overnight.

Preheat the oven to 375°F with a rack set in the middle of the oven. Line the crust with aluminum foil that hangs over the edges by at least 2 inches, then fill with pie weights or dried beans. Bake until the crust is set and the edges are just beginning to color, about 20 minutes. Remove the foil and weights. Brush the crust bottom and sides with the egg and continue baking until the crust is pale golden, about 5 minutes. Transfer the tart pan to a baking sheet. Set aside.

For the filling, melt the butter in a large skillet over medium-high heat. Add the onions and sauté, stirring often, until they begin to soften, about 5 minutes. Add the garlic and season with salt and pepper. Continue sautéing the onions, stirring often, until soft and golden, 15–20 minutes. Stir in the mustard. Scatter ½ cup of the grated cheese on the bottom of the prepared crust. Cover the cheese with the onions in an even layer.

*continued*

For the custard, preheat the oven to 375°F. Beat the eggs in a medium bowl with a whisk until well combined. Gently whisk in the half-and-half and cream. Season with nutmeg and salt and pepper. Pour the custard over the cheese and onions in the crust, filling it no more than three-quarters full. Scatter the remaining ½ cup cheese over the custard. Transfer to the oven and bake until the quiche is puffed and golden brown and just set in the center, about 30 minutes. Serve the quiche warm or at room temperature, cut into wedges.

## HAM & SPINACH QUICHE

Put 1 pound washed, tender young spinach leaves in a colander or steamer basket and set it over a pot of gently boiling water over medium heat. (Don't let the bottom of the colander or steamer basket touch the water.) Cover and steam the spinach, turning the leaves a few times as they wilt, until tender, about 5 minutes. Set aside and allow to drain. Melt 4 tablespoons butter in a medium skillet over medium-high heat. Add 1 chopped, peeled onion and cook until soft, about 15 minutes. Season with finely grated nutmeg, salt, and freshly ground black pepper. Stir in the spinach. Remove from the heat. Follow the directions for making quiche (pages 40–43), substituting the prepared spinach for the cooked onion filling. Scatter 2 cups diced ham over the spinach and substitute 1 cup grated Gouda cheese for the Gruyère.—*serves 6–8*

## CHÈVRE & LEEK QUICHE

Coarsely chop 8 cleaned, trimmed medium leeks, white and pale green parts only. Follow the directions for making quiche (pages 40–43), substituting the leeks for the onions, omitting the mustard, and substituting 1 cup crumbled fresh goat cheese for the Gruyère.—*serves 6–8*

## WILD MUSHROOM & EMMENTAL QUICHE

Follow the directions for making quiche (pages 40–43), substituting 2 pounds cleaned, trimmed, thickly sliced chanterelles or other wild mushrooms for the onions, 2 pinches crushed red pepper flakes for the nutmeg, omitting the mustard, and substituting 1 cup grated Emmental cheese for the Gruyère.—*serves 6–8*

1. PREPARE THE SOUFFLÉ DISH ⊙ Rub the inside of a deep soufflé dish with softened butter, then dust it completely with finely grated Parmigiano-Reggiano.

2. COOK THE FLOUR IN BUTTER ⊙ Melt the butter in a heavy saucepan over medium heat. Don't let it brown. Stir in sifted flour with a wooden spoon to make a smooth roux. Cook, stirring to prevent it from taking on any color whatsoever, for about 2 minutes.

3. ADD THE SPICES ⊙ Season the roux—in a cheese soufflé we use nutmeg, cayenne, salt, and freshly ground black pepper. White pepper is classic, but we prefer the flavor of black pepper.

4. ADD THE MILK ⊙ Gradually pour the milk into the seasoned roux, whisking constantly to prevent lumps. Cook, whisking all the while, until smooth and thick.

5. ADD EGG YOLKS ⊙ Remove the pan from the heat. Add one egg yolk at a time, whisking well after each addition. Set the soufflé batter aside.

6. ADD SALT TO THE EGG WHITES ⊙ Put room-temperature egg whites into a clean, dry, mixing bowl. Add a pinch of salt, which helps stabilize the whites.

JFFLÉS AS LIGHT AS AIR

3.

4.

7.

8.

11.

12.

7. BEAT THE EGG WHITES ⊙ Using the whisk attachment of an electric mixer, beat the egg whites on medium speed until foamy. Gradually increase the speed to high and continue beating until the whites hold smooth, stiff peaks.

8. CHECK THE BEATEN WHITES ⊙ Stop beating the whites from time to time to check their progress. Use the whisk to pull out some of the whites. When they hold a smooth, stiff peak, they are ready. Whites beaten too long will be dry and clumpy, preventing the soufflé from rising properly.

9. ADD WHITES TO THE BATTER ⊙ Using a rubber spatula, stir a spoonful of whites into the soufflé batter to loosen and lighten it up. In two batches, gently fold the remaining whites into the batter.

10. FOLD CHEESE INTO THE BATTER ⊙ Gently fold the coarsely grated cheese into the batter.

11. BEFORE BAKING ⊙ Carefully spoon the batter into the prepared soufflé dish, filling it to 1 inch from the rim.

12. SOUFFLÉ JUST OUT OF THE OVEN ⊙ *Et voilà!* The soufflé, puffed and golden, straight from the oven.

## CHEESE SOUFFLÉ ☞ serves 2–4

A soufflé, savory or sweet, may be "old-fashioned" or seem too intimidating to make. It's not. Crack a few eggs! Invite everyone to the table. It's a glorious dish, and the big ta-da factor never gets old.

4 tablespoons butter, at room temperature
¼ cup finely grated Parmigiano-Reggiano
¼ cup all-purpose flour, sifted
2–3 pinches of grated nutmeg
1 pinch of cayenne
Salt and freshly ground black pepper
1 cup whole milk
4 large egg yolks
6 large egg whites, at room temperature
3 ounces (¾–1 cup) coarsely grated or crumbled cheese, such as Gruyère, Cheddar, or Roquefort

Preheat the oven to 400°F with a rack set in the lower third of the oven. Use 1 tablespoon of the butter to butter the inside of a 7–8-cup soufflé dish, then dust it with the Parmigiano-Reggiano, tapping out any excess. Set the prepared dish aside.

Melt the remaining 3 tablespoons of the butter in a heavy medium saucepan over medium heat. Stir in the flour with a wooden spoon and cook, stirring constantly to prevent the paste from browning or taking on any color whatsoever, for 1–2 minutes. Season with nutmeg, cayenne, and salt and pepper to taste. Gradually whisk in the milk, beating until smooth. Cook the roux, whisking constantly, until thick, 4–5 minutes. Remove the pan from the heat. Whisk in the egg yolks one at a time, whisking well after each addition. Set the soufflé batter aside.

Beat the egg whites and a pinch of salt in a large mixing bowl with an electric mixer fitted with the whisk attachment on medium speed until the whites are foamy. Gradually increase the speed to high, beating the whites until they just hold smooth, stiff peaks. Beating time will vary depending on your mixer.

Using a rubber spatula, stir a heaping spoonful of whites into the soufflé batter to lighten it, then gently fold in the remaining whites until just combined. Avoid overmixing the batter; it's fine if it is streaked with whites. Fold the grated or crumbled cheese into the batter until just combined. Gently spoon the batter into the prepared soufflé dish, filling it to 1 inch below the dish rim.

Place the soufflé in the oven. Reduce the heat to 375°F. Bake for 25 minutes, resisting all temptation to open the oven door and peek inside. Continue to bake the soufflé until it is puffed, deep golden brown, and the top appears set, 5–15 minutes. Remove it from the oven. Use two forks to gently pull apart big mounds of the soufflé into 2–4 servings, then spoon the soufflé onto plates.

## CHOCOLATE SOUFFLÉ ☞ serves 2–4

1 tablespoon butter, at room temperature

6 tablespoons granulated sugar

6 ounces bittersweet chocolate, finely chopped, or use chocolate chips

2 tablespoons whole milk or heavy cream

2 tablespoons brewed espresso or strong coffee

3 large egg yolks

1 teaspoon vanilla extract

1 pinch of salt

4 large egg whites, at room temperature

¼ teaspoon cream of tartar

Powdered sugar, for garnish

Preheat the oven to 400°F with a rack set in the lower third of the oven. Butter the inside of a 7–8-cup soufflé dish with the butter, then dust it with 3 tablespoons of the granulated sugar, tapping out any excess. Set the prepared dish aside.

Melt the chocolate, milk, and espresso together in a large heatproof bowl set in a skillet of gently simmering water over medium heat. Stir until smooth. Set aside to cool slightly. Whisk in the egg yolks one at a time, then add the vanilla and salt, whisking until smooth. Set aside.

Beat the egg whites and cream of tartar in a large mixing bowl with an electric mixer fitted with the whisk attachment on medium speed until foamy. Increase the speed to high and gradually add the remaining 3 tablespoons of granulated sugar, beating until soft, glossy peaks form. Beating time will vary depending on your mixer.

Using a rubber spatula, stir a heaping spoonful of whites into the chocolate soufflé batter to lighten it, then gently fold in the remaining whites, in thirds, until just combined. Avoid overmixing the batter; it's fine if it is streaked with whites. Gently spoon the batter into the prepared soufflé dish, filling it to no more than 1 inch below the dish rim.

Place the soufflé in the oven. Reduce the heat to 375°F. Bake for 30 minutes, resisting all temptation to open the oven door and peek inside. Continue to bake the soufflé until it is puffed and the top has set and begun to crack. The soufflé is done when a wooden skewer inserted into the center comes out slightly coated or clean, 5–10 minutes. Serve the soufflé immediately, sifting powdered sugar on top while it is puffy (it will deflate within 10 minutes). Use two forks to gently pull apart big mounds of the soufflé into 2–4 servings, then spoon the soufflé onto plates.

# Good Beginnings

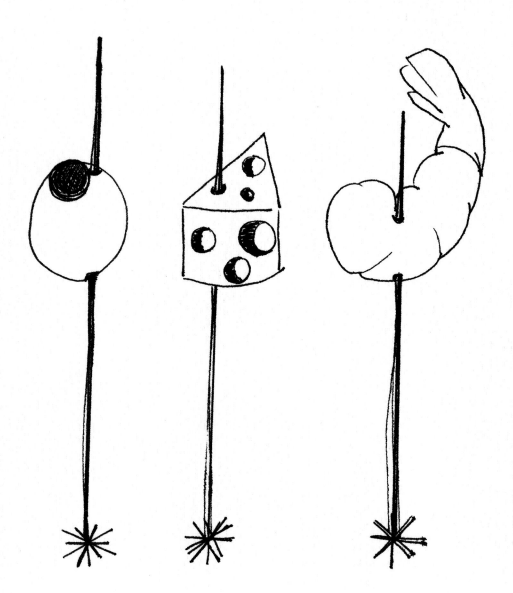

# The Perfect Bite

*Be not inhospitable to strangers, lest they be angels in disguise.* —Hebrews 13:2
a favorite quotation of George Whitman, founder of Shakespeare and Company, Paris,
known for his kindness and hospitality to struggling artists

COCKTAIL PARTY FOOD AND AN HORS D'OEUVRE before dinner are two completely different animals. Food at a cocktail party can and should be miniature versions of bigger ideas, like fried chicken with watermelon pickle. These morsels should help subdue and soak up the alcohol. An hors d'oeuvre is a small bite to be eaten with an aperitif before you sit down to dinner. It should encourage the appetite rather than sate it. After all, you are about to eat a full-course meal.

There are many names for party food: *canapé* (a French word for sofa, a small piece of bread or pastry with a savory topping); *hors d'oeuvre*, a small savory dish served before or at the beginning of a meal; finger food, easily picked-up food, bite-sized snacks. In this case, size matters; an hors d'oeuvre of two messy bites has been the ruin of many a silk tie.

While attending a neighborhood meeting in the chairwoman's living room, we watched a gentleman next to us compulsively nibble his way through a large silver bowl of cashews. The discussion went on forever, and when it was finally over, the hostess announced cocktails and told the guests to help themselves to the nuts, gesturing toward a now empty silver bowl. Our hostess looked first at the bowl, then at us. Our sofamate, the real culprit, had cleverly slipped away. Nuts are like that, they disappear easily.

Our pockets aren't quite deep enough to finance big bowls of cashews, so we opt to fry almonds in their skins, sometimes seasoning them with garam masala or other spices. And when we are short on time but hungry for company and can't resist inviting friends for drinks, we just put out a big bowl of potato chips. (Dip a potato chip in chocolate and it may be the perfect bite—crunchy, salty, and sweet.) It's okay to keep it simple: a bowl of meaty olives or a platter of thinly sliced salami served right on the deli counter paper.

We make little toasts and/or simply pull out a box of saltines and top them with savory things to whet appetites. We whip up flavored butters like Blue Cheese & Black Pepper or Anchovy & Lemon. They have a long fridge life so they are ready to smear on crackers at a moment's notice and serve with a glass of wine.

When we have more time, we twist puff pastry into elegant, crisp parmigiano-flavored cheese straws, or bake buttery Melba toasts to top with sardines and lemon zest, or pale green lima bean mash. On a trip to a Norwegian island in the North Sea, we learned how to cure salmon into gravlax. So when we can, we cure our own and serve it on dense rye slathered with a mustard butter, inspired by traditional Scandinavian mustard sauce.

The idea is to create a bite with perfectly balanced flavor. That is most likely why the appetizer part of a restaurant menu versus the main course is so appealing. When servings are smaller, it is easier to get their proportions correct. Once in Burgundy we stopped at a two-star *auberge* for lunch. We were led to a sunny terrace where they poured us glasses of champagne. The only hors d'oeuvre was a bowl of just-picked cherry tomatoes with flaked salt crystals clinging to their wet skins. First a sip of the cold bubbles, then a bite of the sun-warmed, salted, sweet tomatoes— still a vivid memory years later. To understand the complexity and beauty of something so simple, you have to know a great deal. We are still learning.

# Olives

◉ the perfect juicy-salty bite before dinner ◉

We like to serve olives with a pre-dinner apéritif. Here is a sampling of our favorites.

1. CASTELVETRANO: Italy; naturally vivid green. Mild, buttery sweet; fruity; meaty texture.

2. NIÇOISE: France; grown in the Mediterranean region near Nice, the pebble-size Cailletier olives are handpicked and cured in a fresh brine. Picked ripe, color ranges from pale brownish black to purplish black. A lot of flavor—rich, faintly earthy, savory—for such a small olive.

3. KALAMATA: Greece; dark purple; firm juicy texture. Briny, rich, red wine–sharp flavor.

4. GREEN BELDI: Morocco; firm texture; mild flavor. Snack on or serve in an icy-cold martini.

5. BLACK BELDI: Morocco; oil-cured, dense, meaty; intense, concentrated flavor. A few go a long way.

6. BLACK CERIGNOLA: Italy; large beauties; smooth skin; firm, mild, meaty flavor. Fruit of the gods.

7. LUCQUES: France; Languedoc; beautiful green; tight skin, firm meaty flesh; mild buttery, nutty flavor. Very easy to snack on.

8. ALFONSO: Peru; brined and stained deep purple from macerating in red wine. Large, plump, soft, meaty, and downright juicy. Bright, delicately salty flavor.

9. GAETA: Italy; oval shape; pretty range of purples. Brine-cured, plump, meaty, salty, and sharp.

10. THASSOS: Greece; Thassos; harvested when fully ripe, black, shriveled and wrinkled like a raisin. Dry-cured. Meaty, dark, rich, complex, fruity flavor. Serve as is or drizzled with olive oil.

11. "RIPE" BLACK GREEK: Greece; picked unripe (green), cured and treated to turn the smooth skin shiny black. Mild, generic flavor. For those nostalgic for the taste of ripe black canned olives.

1. Castelvetrano
2. Niçoise
3. Kalamata
5. Black Beldi
6. Black Cerignola
7. Lucques
8. Alfonso
9. Gaeta
10. Thassos
11. "Ripe" black Greek

## FRIED ALMONDS

Like fresh corn tortilla chips, these nuts freshly fried in olive oil are in a completely different league from store-bought roasted almonds. For spicy nuts, after frying, toss them with 1 teaspoon ground cumin, or 1 teaspoon pimentón (hot or sweet), or 1 teaspoon garam masala along with the salt.

Heat ¼ cup olive oil in a medium skillet over medium heat until hot but not smoking. Add 1 cup whole raw almonds and fry, stirring frequently to brown the nuts evenly, until they are toasted a few shades darker brown on both sides, about 5 minutes. Transfer the nuts with a slotted spoon to paper towels to drain. Toss with coarse salt while still hot. They can be made up to 1 week ahead. When they have cooled completely, store them in an airtight container.—*makes 1 cup*

## CHEESE TOASTS ☞ make as many as you want

These open-face toasts can be made with any cheese (except processed cheese, god forbid!)—Gruyère, Taleggio, and Cheddar are a few we typically use. Choose any good-quality bread. We make these for breakfast, lunch, or a light supper, but cut into cracker-size pieces, they are just the kind of crunchy, melty, savory bite we want with a cocktail.

Softened butter, preferably salted
Good-quality bread, white, brown, or pumpernickel, sliced
Grated or sliced cheese, about 2 ounces per toast
Crushed red pepper flakes, ground cayenne, or freshly ground black pepper

Preheat the oven to 450°F with a rack set in the upper third of the oven. Butter the bread. Place the bread on a baking sheet and bake until just lightly toasted.

Cover the toast with cheese. Toast in the oven until the cheese is melted and golden brown around the edges. Sprinkle with crushed red pepper flakes to taste. Leave whole, or cut into quarters or thirds, if you like, and serve immediately.

GARLICKY CHEESE TOAST: Follow the above recipe, omitting the butter. Lightly toast the bread. Rub one side of the toast with a peeled garlic clove (to suit your taste), drizzle with some extra-virgin olive oil, and sprinkle with a little salt. Proceed with the recipe.

*Facing page: top, Fried Almonds; bottom, Cheese Toasts*

## PIMIENTO CHEESE ☛ makes 2 cups

Our refrigerator can be full of stuff yet with nothing in it to eat. In our dreamworld life, we'd have it stocked with all sorts of delicious things already made ahead, so that when hunger struck or friends dropped by and we needed an impromptu hors d'oeuvre, we'd just reach in and pull out something to snack on. This classic Southern spread would be one of our staples. Traditionally, it is spread between two slices of soft white bread, but we like it on saltines, Club Crackers, or celery stalks. And it keeps about a week in the fridge. Note to selves: make dreamworld a reality.

8 ounces extra-sharp
  Cheddar cheese, grated
½ cup mayonnaise
⅓ cup cream cheese
One 4-ounce jar pimientos,
  drained and chopped
1 teaspoon grated yellow
  onion
½ teaspoon salt
¼ teaspoon freshly ground
  black pepper
1 pinch of ground cayenne

Put the Cheddar, mayonnaise, cream cheese, pimientos, onions, salt, pepper, and cayenne in a medium bowl and mix with a wooden spoon or rubber spatula until it is well blended and the Cheddar becomes creamy. Refrigerate for about 1 hour before serving.

## TWIRLED-UP GOAT CHEESE

We appreciate the subtle earthiness of an artisanal chèvre and always eat it unadorned out of respect. But we stash supermarket chèvre in our fridges and feel free to dress up its mild, pleasantly tart flavor with fixin's of our choice. We are also mighty partial to a good old Saltine cracker—delicate, crisp, and salty.

Sometimes we spice up a 5-ounce pyramid of chèvre with freshly cracked black pepper, really good extra-virgin olive oil (sometimes lemon-flavored), and minced fresh chives. Or we'll mash some chèvre onto a small plate, give it a good drizzle of really good extra-virgin olive oil, and generously sprinkle ground, toasted fennel seeds on top.—*makes a generous ½ cup*

*Pimiento Cheese*

## CHEESE STRAWS ⌁ makes about 2 dozen

These elegant crispy straws are a perfect bite with cocktails. You can jazz them up by seasoning the cheese with black pepper, ground cayenne, or pimentón to your taste. We use frozen store-bought puff pastry, pull it out of the freezer, and by the time the oven is preheated, the pastry has defrosted and is ready for rolling in the grated cheese. One of the beauties of flaky puff pastry is its buttery taste. If using store-bought puff pastry, and that sweet, rich flavor matters to you, be sure that butter (not vegetable oils or cream) is listed in the ingredients. We keep all-butter Dufour Pastry Kitchens puff pastry in our freezer.

1 cup finely grated Parmigiano-Reggiano
1–2 sheets frozen puff pastry, defrosted but not unfolded

Preheat the oven to 375°F with a rack set in the middle of the oven. Dust a clean work surface with about ¼ cup of the grated cheese. Put 1 unfolded sheet of puff pastry on top of the cheese and dust it with another ¼ cup of cheese. Roll the pastry out with a rolling pin, gently pressing the cheese into the dough (1). Roll the pastry into a rectangle about ⅛ inch thick, dusting it with more cheese, if necessary.

Using a sharp knife or a pastry cutter, cut the pastry into long ¼–½-inch-wide strips (2). Twist each strip several times into a corkscrew shape and lay them on a parchment paper–lined baking sheet about ¼ inch apart (3). Repeat the rolling out and cutting and twisting process with the remaining sheet of puff pastry and cheese.

Bake the cheese straws until they are puffed and golden, about 10 minutes. Let them cool to room temperature before peeling them off the paper (4). Cheese straws can be made ahead, cooled completely, and stored in an airtight container for up to 1 week.

1.

2.

3.

4.

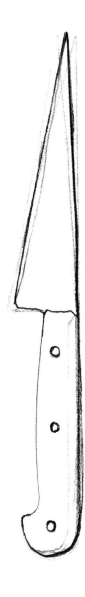

# Charcuterie

⊙ savory, chewy flavor ⊙

Rather than serving heavy hors d'ouevres before dinner, we prefer to whet a guest's appetite, not kill it. We typically serve a few deviled eggs, a dish of olives, a pile of peppery radishes, and best of all, the salty, chewy goodness of various cured and smoked meats. They are full of flavor and texture, so a little goes a long way.

When shopping, we take our time to survey the delicatessen display counter. We have our favorites, but always want to discover new ones, so we ask for a taste before making our decision. Maybe we'll go for sweet soppressata (we'll have to peel back the paper-thin casing before slicing it into thick rounds), or perhaps we'll get silky sheets of *prosciutto di Parma* to drape over fresh figs, or slices of mortadella, as wide as dinner plates, that we'll need to fold over to serve.

When it comes to slicing, we have to admit, we are a little particular. Each cured meat requires a certain thickness. So we let the counter person know our preference when we place our order. "Not too thin, please, we don't want any tearing when we pull the slices apart." When the slices are beautifully laid out like shingles on the butcher paper, the layers separated by sheets of waxed paper, we ask that the package be gently folded and not rolled up tightly. That way, when it is time to serve, we simply open the package and lay the whole sheet of sliced meat on a board, paper and all—a beautiful display.

Take it from us: Cut yourself a break; spend time with your guests; keep things simple. No one will starve before dinner is served.

Pork Queen Salami

Genoa Salami

Saucisson Sec

Sweet Soppressata

Soppressata

Prosciutto di Parma

## SHUCKING & SLURPING OYSTERS

1. START SHUCKING ⊙ You'll need a kitchen towel to hold the oyster in place (and a rubber glove to protect your hand if you are fearful of hurting yourself) and an oyster knife, which has a stubby blade with a pointed tip, to open the oyster. (An ice pick or thin-headed screwdriver will work, too.)

Rinse the shells under cold water to remove grit. Oysters are easier to open when they are very cold. Keep them packed in ice (not cold water).

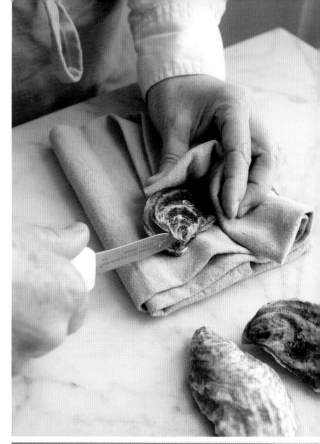

2. POP ⊙ Place the oyster, flatter side up, on a towel on a sturdy work surface. Hold the wider end of the oyster securely in place with the towel. Stick the tip of the knife in the pointed hinge end. The shell (or shuck) is both tough and crumbly. Apply gentle force to wedge the knife between the top and bottom shells; if the shell crumbles, the knife will slide in easily. Gently rock the knife up and down, prying the knife tip in. Twist the knife to pop open the oyster.

3. SLIDE AND RELEASE ⊙ Keep the oyster flat to prevent the liquor from tipping out. Slide the knife around inside the top shell, cutting the muscle that keeps the shell closed. Discard the top shell. Slide the knife under the oyster to cut the muscle and release the oyster from the bottom shell.

4. CONDIMENTS ⊙ Serve oysters plain, with lemon wedges, hot sauce, or mignonette sauce: ¼ cup red wine vinegar; 1 small, finely diced shallot; and freshly ground black pepper. —*makes ¼ cup*

5. SERVE ⊙ Arrange the shucked oysters on crushed ice to keep them icy-cold.

6. SLURP ⊙ Lift an oyster to your mouth, tip your head back, and slurp the oyster and its liquor straight down your gullet (pearl earrings optional).

## QUICK-CURE SALMON

Use pristine, wild salmon for this dish. The filet should be free of any pin bones, but double-check by running your fingers across the flesh. If you feel a sharp bump, grab onto it with a pair of tweezers or pliers. Give the soft white bone a tug, then pull. It will slip out fairly easily.

Place ½ pound center-cut, sushi-grade, wild salmon filet on a work surface. Using a very sharp, long-blade knife, cut the salmon at an angle, crosswise against the grain, into very thin slices. Save any scraps of raw salmon for another use and discard the skin. Arrange the salmon slices in a single thin layer on a chilled serving platter. Squeeze the juice of ½–1 lemon over the salmon and sprinkle with coarse sea salt (preferably Maldon). Scatter some Pickled Carrots, Pickled Red Onions, and Pickled Cucumbers (below) over the salmon, spooning a little of the pickling liquid over the fish as well. Garnish the salmon with small wedges of lemon and tiny sprigs of fresh dill leaves. Serve with thinly sliced, dense black bread, toasts, or crackers, buttered with salted butter or Mustard Butter (page 72), if you like.—*serves 4–8*

## QUICK PICKLES

Simple, bright, and colorful pickles like these are a traditional foil for the rich flavors and supple textures of smoked and cured fish. We prepare ours using Japanese rice wine vinegar, because we like the way its perfect balance of sweetness and acidity complement the fish. When making the cucumber or red onion pickles, only make what you need for the meal; the extra slices will go limp after too long a soak.

PICKLED CUCUMBERS: Use the little, narrow Persian or "gourmet" cucumbers for these. If you can't find them, an English seedless one will do. Put thin slices of cucumber in a bowl. Cover with Japanese rice wine vinegar and let them soak for at least 15 minutes and up to 1 hour.

PICKLED RED ONIONS: Soak thin slices of peeled red onion in a bowl of Japanese rice wine vinegar for at least 15 minutes and up to 1 hour.

PICKLED CARROTS: Blanch round slices of peeled carrot in boiling salted water for about 30 seconds; drain and put into a bowl. Cover the carrots with Japanese rice wine vinegar, add a few whole cloves, black peppercorns, and a bay leaf, and cool to room temperature. Cover and refrigerate for at least 1 day and up to 2 weeks.

GRAVLAX ↩ makes about 20 slices or enough for 8–10 servings

We typically make this at Christmas, curing two whole sides of salmon to last us through the entire holiday season. That's a lot of salmon! But it's a style of cured salmon we like too much to eat only once a year, so we've starting curing more manageable portions to have in any season (see photos pages 70–71).

2 pounds center-cut, sushi-grade, wild salmon filet
2 tablespoons coarse salt
1 tablespoon sugar
1 tablespoon coarsely ground white pepper
1 bunch fresh dill, leaves finely chopped
2 tablespoons aquavit or Cognac

Place the salmon on a sheet of plastic wrap, flesh-side up. Mix together the salt, sugar, pepper, and dill in a bowl, then rub all over the salmon flesh. Sprinkle the aquavit or Cognac over the fish. Slide the fish into a resealable plastic bag. Press out the air and seal it shut.

Place the bag with the fish flat in a pan, skin-side up. Place a pan of similar size on top of the fish. Weight the pan with heavy cans to press down on the fish. This will press out any liquid as the fish cures and will give the gravlax a firm, silky texture. Refrigerate the weighted salmon.

After 3 to 5 days, the salmon will be cured. Remove the salmon from the plastic bag and wipe off any salt and herbs. Using a very sharp, long-blade knife, cut the salmon at an angle, cross-wise against the grain, into very thin slices. Arrange the slices, overlapping, on a large plate, if you like. Serve with slices of buttered black bread or crackers, and lemon wedges. Or butter the slices of bread with Mustard Butter (page 72) and/or serve with Mustard-Dill Sauce (page 72). Refrigerate well-wrapped gravlax for up to one week.

Sugar and salt mixture, dill, white pepper, Cognac

Dry-cure mixed together

Sealing the salmon in an airtight plastic bag to cure

Weighting the curing salmon

Rubbing the dry-cure on the raw salmon

Drizzling Cognac

Slicing the gravlax

## IN PRAISE OF SMOKED SALMON

We usually keep a package of cold-smoked salmon in the refrigerator. It's one of our staples, ready to use anytime. We crown deviled eggs with it, drape silky slices on warm buttered toasts, tuck it into hot corn tortillas with soft ripe avocado, serve it with scrambled eggs, whirl it into a butter spread with preserved lemon, serve it with fat asparagus, lemon juice, and chopped chives. We leave smoking to the pros. With so many available, the best way to choose is simply to taste your way through, though we avoid those with an artificial-looking pink or orange hue, and ultimately settle on smoked salmon with a good pedigree, and with a silky texture, well balanced between the salt and smoke. Spending the extra money on good smoked salmon is a little luxury that is worth every cent.

## MUSTARD BUTTER

Spread this on sliced dark rye or on crackers like Ryvita and serve with smoked or cured salmon, like Quick-Cure Salmon (page 66) or Gravlax (page 69). Like any butter, it spreads best at room temperature.

Mix together 10 ounces (2½ sticks) softened butter, 4–5 tablespoons honey mustard, 2–3 tablespoons finely chopped fresh chives, and 2–3 tablespoons finely chopped fresh dill in a medium bowl until well combined. This will keep, covered, in the refrigerator for up to 1 week.—*makes about 1¼ cups*

## MUSTARD-DILL SAUCE

The classic Swedish accompaniment to Gravlax (page 69).

Put ¼ cup Dijon mustard, 2 tablespoons chopped fresh dill, 2 tablespoons sugar, and ½ teaspoon white wine vinegar into a small bowl and whisk in ¼ cup vegetable oil until smooth.—*makes ½ cup*

## MELBA TOASTS

Preheat the oven to 400°F. Cut the crusts off sliced brioche or white bread, squaring off each slice (1). Cut the slices in half into rectangles or triangles. Lay the slices out on a parchment paper–lined baking pan. Brush both sides of the bread with melted butter (2). Cover the bread with a sheet of parchment paper, then set another baking pan directly on top. This prevents the bread from curling as it bakes (3). Bake until golden brown on the bottom, about 8 minutes. Turn the toasts over, cover, and bake until the other side is golden, 2–3 minutes (4).

*Making Melba Toasts*

## AVOCADO TOASTS ☞ makes 4

Everybody loves avocados. Depending on what part of the country you live in, you may find cultivars such as Fuerte or Gwen, but the pebble-skinned Hass avocado is the most common variety. We have friends in California who grow them in their backyard (lucky dogs!), and send us a box when they are harvesting them (then we're the lucky dogs!). Avocados ripen after they are picked, from the inside out. We buy hard-as-rock, deep green Hass avocados and set them on the counter out of direct sunlight. Within a few days, the color of the skin deepens and their flesh begins to yield under gentle pressure. When perfectly ripe, their skins have turned midnight green, they are softer (just barely firm), and the flesh is rich and creamy. To slow down the ripening process, we put the avocados in the fridge.

4 slices good bread

Really good extra-virgin
  olive oil

2 ripe Hass avocados, halved,
  pitted, and peeled

1–2 lemons, preferably Meyer,
  halved

Aleppo pepper or other
  crushed red pepper flakes

Flaky sea salt, such as Maldon

Toast the bread, then drizzle one side with the olive oil while still warm. On each piece of toast put ½ an avocado and mash it with a knife or fork, spreading the flesh to the edges of the toast. Drizzle olive oil on top. Squeeze some lemon juice over the toasts, sprinkle with a pinch or two of Aleppo pepper, and season with salt. Cut into halves or quarters. Serve with lemon halves, if you like.

## PAN CON TOMATE

For this rustic Spanish treat, raw garlic and tomato are grated directly on the toast.

Toast 4 slices crusty bread. Rub each toast on one side with 1 peeled garlic clove; rubbing more firmly will impart more flavor. Cut 2 ripe tomatoes in half crosswise. Rub each toast with the cut side of a tomato, rubbing it to spread the pulp and flesh on the toast's rough surface to the edges; discard the tomato skins. Drizzle the toasts with really good extra-virgin olive oil and sprinkle with flaky sea salt. Garnish the toasts with anchovies, if you like.—*makes 4*

TOASTS & CRACKERS are the perfect cocktail crunch as you sip an apéritif. We also slather these mashes and butters on grilled steaks, lamb chops, roast chicken, and baked potatoes.

## CURED MEAT & CORNICHON

Lightly rub 1 toast with 1 peeled garlic clove. Add a few drops extra-virgin olive oil. Top with 1 small piece sliced, cured meat (salumi or charcuterie) and 1 sliced cornichon.—*makes 1*

## GREEN & BLACK OLIVE TAPENADE

We use green Castelvetrano, Cerignola, Lucques, or picholine olives for a milder, more buttery-tasting paste; and briny black olives, like Kalamata, Alfonso, or Niçoise to make a more assertive spread.

Finely chop 1 cup green or black pitted olives and put them in a bowl. Stir in 4–6 minced anchovy filets, 1 tablespoon chopped drained capers, 1 minced peeled garlic clove, 6–8 sprigs chopped fresh parsley leaves, 1–2 pinches of crushed red pepper flakes or ground cayenne, and 3–4 tablespoons extra-virgin olive oil.—*makes about 1 cup or enough to spread on about 2 dozen toasts or crackers*

## FIERY ANCHOVY & LEMON SUPREME

Use the side of a knife to mash together 1 anchovy filet and 1 pinch of crushed red pepper flakes. Spread on 1 Melba Toast (page 72), toast, or a cracker. Top with 1 small lemon supreme (see Lemon-Anchovy Vinaigrette, page 128) or segment. Garnish with 1 sliver lemon zest, if you like.—*makes 1*

## ROASTED RED PEPPER, CAPERS & CURRANTS

Put a few drops extra-virgin olive oil on a little toast. Top with 1 small piece roasted red pepper, a few drained capers, and some currants or golden raisins. Add a few drops extra-virgin olive oil. Garnish with chopped fresh parsley, if you like.—*makes 1*

## BLUE CHEESE & WATERCRESS MASH

Finely chop ½ bunch watercress leaves and ½ bunch fresh chives or dill. Add the herbs to a bowl along with 2 ounces room temperature blue cheese and 1 tablespoon softened butter. Mash to a paste. Season with pepper. Spread on Melba Toasts (page 72), toasts, or crackers. Garnish with watercress, chives, or dill, if you like.—*makes about ½ cup or enough to spread on about 8 toasts or crackers*

## SARDINE & LEMON

Put 1 piece tinned sardine filet on 1 Melba Toast (page 72), toast, or a cracker. Add a few drops fresh lemon juice and garnish with 2 slivers lemon zest, if you like.—*makes 1*

## LIMA BEAN & LEMON MASH

Frozen limas work as well as fresh for this recipe. Put 1 cup cooked lima beans, 1 chopped, peeled garlic clove, finely grated zest of $\frac{1}{2}$ lemon, 1 small squeeze fresh lemon juice, and 2–4 tablespoons extra-virgin olive oil in the bowl of a food processor and purée until smooth. Season to taste with salt and pepper. Spread on Melba Toasts (page 72), toasts, or crackers. Garnish with chopped fresh chives, if you like.—*makes about 1 cup or enough to spread on about 16 toasts or crackers*

## TUNA & LEMONY MAYONNAISE

Spread 1 Melba Toast (page 72), toast, or a cracker with a dab of mayonnaise. Add a few drops fresh lemon juice and some finely grated lemon zest. Top with 1 piece drained, olive-oil packed tuna. Garnish with celery leaves and chopped chives, if you like.—*makes 1*

## BLUE CHEESE & BLACK PEPPER BUTTER

Use a fork to mash together 8 tablespoons room temperature butter, 2 ounces blue cheese and a good grinding of black pepper in a bowl. Or use a food processor for a smoother butter. Spread on saltines or other crackers, or on little toasts.—*makes about $\frac{3}{4}$ cup or enough to spread on about 12 crackers or toasts*

## SMOKED SALMON BUTTER

Use a fork to mash together 8 tablespoons room-temperature butter, 2 ounces chopped smoked salmon, 2 pinches of ground cayenne, and finely grated zest of $\frac{1}{2}$ lemon and some of its juice in a bowl. Or use a food processor for a smoother butter. Garnish with chopped fresh chives, if you like.—*makes about $\frac{3}{4}$ cup or enough to spread on about 12 crackers or toasts*

## ANCHOVY & LEMON BUTTER

Put 8 tablespoons room-temperature butter into a bowl. Add 6 oil-packed anchovy filets, 2 pinches of ground cayenne, and finely grated zest of 1 lemon. Use a fork to blend it together into a coarse mash or blend it together in a food processor for a smoother butter.—*makes about $\frac{1}{2}$ cup or enough to spread on about 12 crackers or toasts*

## BACON SCALLION BUTTER

Put 8 tablespoons room-temperature butter into a bowl. Add 8 ounces bacon, cooked and finely chopped, 2–3 finely chopped trimmed scallions, finely grated zest of $\frac{1}{2}$ lemon, and 2–3 pinches of ground cayenne. Use a fork to blend it together into a coarse mash. Garnish with thinly sliced scallion greens or fresh chives, if you like.—*makes about $\frac{1}{2}$ cup or enough to spread on about 12 crackers or toasts*

Cured meat & cornichon

Green & black olive tapenade

Blue cheese & watercress mash

Sardine & lemon

Blue cheese & black pepper butter

Smoked salmon butter

Fiery anchovy & lemon supreme

Roasted red pepper, capers & currants

Lima bean & lemon mash

Tuna & lemony mayonnaise

Anchovy & lemon butter

Bacon scallion butter

Beautiful Soup, so rich and green,
Waiting in a hot tureen!
Who for such dainties would not stoop?
Soup of the evening, beautiful Soup!
Soup of the evening, beautiful Soup!

—— Lewis Carroll, *Alice's Adventures in Wonderland*

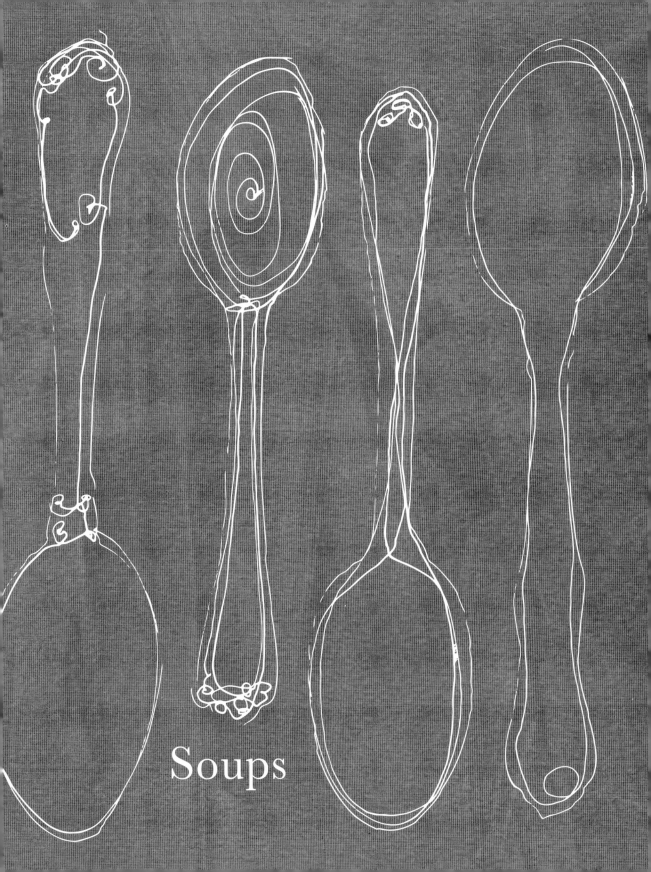

Soups

# A Big Pot of Soup

*There is nothing like soup. It is by its nature eccentric: no two are ever alike, unless of course you get your soup in a can.*—Laurie Colwin

NOBODY CAN BECOME A SOMEBODY WITHOUT MASTERING HIS OR HER CRAFT. And it's often the humble tasks—the day-to-day practice of a simple skill—that build the foundation for excellence. We love to make stocks and broths. Stocks are made with meaty bones that give them a sticky, lip-smacking quality. Delicate broths are lighter versions of stock, but also made with meat, fish, vegetables, or a combination of them. Both are the basis of all good soups, so we make them with care and patience. We'll buy pounds and pounds of chicken wings to make a vat of stock that will bubble away all day. But we'll also throw onion trimmings, and the back, wing tips, and innards from a chicken cut up for dinner into a small pot of water to simmer for only an hour. The resulting reduced elixir will be added to pan juices for a sauce or to leftover vegetables that will be whirled into a puréed soup.

We used to add a beaten egg white raft to clarify our stock. This classic French technique sometimes involves ground chicken and a classic *mirepoix* (diced carrots, celery, and onions). The principle is that the proteins in the egg whites and the meat will coagulate and rise to the surface of the simmering stock, forming a raft that all the rising particles will cling to and be caught in, ensuring a sparkling clear stock. But it involved a great deal of fussiness that discouraged us. So we now simply allow the proteins from the meat in the stock to rise to the surface and form a frothy film that many recipes say to skim away. This film is our raft as the stock gently simmers, depositing particles that potentially could make the stock cloudy. It turns out to work perfectly for our uses. It is always good to know the rules first, then you know how to break them.

Our freezers, both in our houses and at the studio, are chockablock with containers of stocks in various sizes at the ready whenever we need them.

It seems just as easy to make a big pot of soup as a small one. So we've started a new Canal House tradition: weeknight soup suppers at our studio. "Stop by after work", we say to friends. "We'll just make a big pot of soup with loaves of garlic bread and pour a good red plonk—a Sangiovese." We are generous with the invitations, the more the merrier. If everyone shows up, we'll just use smaller bowls and make more bread.

When Thursday comes, the table is set simply—a brown paper "tablecloth", dish-towel napkins, old hotel silverware, mismatched glasses for wine and water. We put everything down the center: wine bottles, long loaves of warm garlic bread, tureens of soup, and bowls of green salsa. Everyone can help themselves.

When we entertain, we care first about the food and wine. One of our favorite soups is Hearty Squash & Bean Minestrone with Green Sauce. It is studded with chunks of butternut squash and creamy white navy beans. Smoked ham hocks pull all the vegetable flavors together and impart a satisfying richness. We add pasta to our minestrone, but we're fussy about it. We like small shapes, shells or tubes that can cup a bean in each spoonful of soup, which gets even better flavor from our peppery arugula salsa verde.

The bread is a crusty baguette for us. Chewy, not the cottony Italian loaves. And since we both prefer a light touch with garlic, we infuse the melted butter with crushed garlic rather than minced, which can burn in the oven while the bread gets toasted.

People happily ladle soup and pasta into their bowls and swirl in great verdant dollops of green sauce. They tear off hunks of bread and dunk them into the soup. It's a peasant meal, satisfying after a day's labor. Soon our friends are out the door and off—after all, it's a work night. "That was fun and easy", we say to each other. Another Canal House tradition to share and savor.

STOCK IS THE FOUNDATION OF ALL GOOD SOUPS. Good, wholesome food nourishes us, so we make stocks and broths with ingredients that are full of *prana*—energy and life. We always return to our favorites—Old-Fashioned Chicken Stock, Rich Chicken Stock (enriched with a ham hock and white wine), cleansing Ginger Chicken Stock, and Beef Broth (pages 84–87). They are not only for making soups and stews. We sip hot mugfuls in the morning and afternoon to build up our stamina.

## OLD-FASHIONED CHICKEN STOCK ☞ makes about 12 cups

We used to fuss over our stocks, skimming the foam that rises to the surface as the stock simmers. But now we leave the foam alone—it acts as a "raft", catching particles that circulate and rise to the surface. They eventually drop to the bottom of the pot and get strained out at the end. To keep the stock from getting cloudy, resist the urge to stir while it cooks, and don't boil it hard. A gurgling simmer will ensure a clear stock.

1 tablespoon extra-virgin
    olive oil
6–8 pounds chicken wings
2 celery stalks, quartered
2 carrots, peeled and
    quartered
1 yellow onion, unpeeled
    and quartered
½ bunch parsley
4 sprigs fresh thyme
3 bay leaves
10 black peppercorns
Salt

Put the oil and chicken wings into a heavy large pot. Cover the pot and cook the wings over medium heat, stirring often to prevent them from browning, until they lose their raw appearance and have released some of their fat and juices, about 20 minutes.

Add the celery, carrots, onions, parsley, thyme, bay leaves, and peppercorns to the pot. Add enough cold water (about 6 quarts) to cover everything well. Bring to a boil over medium-high heat. Reduce the heat to medium-low and simmer (gently bubbling), uncovered, for about 4 hours. Resist the urge to stir the stock as it simmers; it will make the stock cloudy. Simmer the stock until reduced by about half.

Strain the stock through a colander into a bowl, then again through a fine-mesh sieve into a bowl, discarding the solids. Season with salt to taste. We like to keep the layer of fat that floats to the surface. It will make the stock more flavorful. (If you are making the stock ahead, allow it to cool to room temperature, then cover and refrigerate or freeze it.)

*Facing page, clockwise from top left: ingredients for Old-Fashioned Chicken Stock; ingredients for Rich Chicken Stock (page 86); ingredients for Beef Broth (page 87); ingredients for Ginger Chicken Stock (page 86)*

## RICH CHICKEN STOCK ☞ makes about 12 cups

6–8 pounds chicken wings
1–2 meaty smoked ham hocks
2 celery stalks, quartered
2 carrots, peeled and
 quartered
1 yellow onion, unpeeled
 and quartered
1 bottle dry white wine
½ bunch parsley
3 bay leaves
10 black peppercorns
Salt

Put the chicken wings, ham hock, celery, carrots, onions, wine, parsley, bay leaves, and peppercorns into a heavy large pot. Add 6 quarts (24 cups) cold water. Bring to a boil over medium-high heat. Reduce the heat to medium-low and simmer (gently bubbling) for about 4 hours. Resist the urge to stir the stock as it simmers; it will make the stock cloudy. Simmer the stock until reduced by about half.

Remove the ham hock and reserve. Strain the stock first through a colander into a bowl, then through a fine-mesh sieve into a bowl, discarding the solids. Return the stock to the pot. Season with salt to taste. Don't skim off the fat; it will add richness to the stock. (If you are making the stock ahead, allow it to cool to room temperature, then cover and refrigerate or freeze it.)

Remove and discard the skin, bones, and any gristle from the ham hock. Tear or slice the ham into pieces and add it to hot soup, if you like, just before serving. There is enough meat for about 4 servings.

## GINGER CHICKEN STOCK ☞ makes about 8 cups

Ginger adds a little heat to this aromatic, rich stock. We remove the chicken breast halfway through cooking to keep it tender and juicy.

2 celery stalks, quartered
1 yellow onion, unpeeled
 and quartered
1 hand fresh ginger (about
 8 ounces), unpeeled and
 sliced into big pieces
2 garlic cloves, peeled
10 black peppercorns

Put the celery, onions, ginger, garlic, and peppercorns into a heavy large pot. Add the chicken pieces, placing the breasts on top so they will be easier to remove from the pot partway through cooking. Add 6 quarts (24 cups) cold water to the pot and bring just to a boil over medium-high heat. Reduce the heat to medium-low. Resist the urge to stir the stock as it simmers, it will make it cloudy. After about 30 minutes, remove the chicken breasts and set them aside. Continue to gently simmer the stock for 1½ hours.

*continued*

1 chicken, cut into 7 pieces
   (2 breasts, 2 thighs and legs,
   2 wings, back)
Salt

Remove the remaining chicken pieces from the stock and set them aside. Strain the stock through a colander into a bowl, then again through a fine-mesh sieve into a bowl, discarding the solids. Return the stock to the pot. Boil the stock over high heat until reduced to about 8 cups. Season with salt to taste. We like to keep the layer of fat that floats to the surface. It adds more flavor to the stock. (If you are making the stock ahead, allow it to cool to room temperature, then cover and refrigerate or freeze it.)

Pull off and discard the skin, bones, and any gristle from the reserved chicken. Tear or slice the chicken into pieces and add it to hot soup just before serving, if you like. There is enough chicken for about 6 servings.

## BEEF BROTH ☞ makes about 10 cups

3–4 pounds beef short ribs
   (about 9 pieces)
2 carrots, peeled and quartered
2 celery stalks, quartered
1 yellow onion, unpeeled
   and quartered
2 garlic cloves, peeled
3 bay leaves
10 black peppercorns
Salt

Put the short ribs, carrots, celery, onions, garlic, bay leaves, and peppercorns into a heavy large pot. Add 5 quarts (20 cups) cold water or enough water to cover the meat by about 3 inches. Bring to a boil over medium-high heat. Reduce the heat to medium-low and simmer (gently bubbling) until the meat is tender, 5–6 hours. Resist the urge to stir the stock as it simmers; it will make the stock cloudy. Simmer the stock until reduced by a little over half.

Remove and reserve the short ribs. Strain the stock through a colander into a bowl, then again through a fine-mesh sieve into a bowl, discarding the solids. Season with salt to taste. Don't skim off the fat; it will add a delicious richness to the stock. (If you are making the stock ahead, allow it to cool to room temperature, then cover and refrigerate or freeze it.)

Pull off and discard the fat, bones, and any gristle from the reserved beef. Tear or slice the meat into pieces and add it to hot soup just before serving, if you like. There is enough meat for 4–6 servings.

## BEEFY BROTH & SHIITAKE MUSHROOM SOUP ☞ serves 4–6

6–8 cups Beef Broth (page 87)
24 shiitake mushrooms,
   stemmed, caps sliced
2 garlic cloves, thinly sliced
Short rib meat from Beef Broth
Salt
1 bunch fresh chives, chopped

Bring the broth to a simmer in a medium pot over medium heat. Add the mushroom caps and garlic, cover the pot, and simmer until the mushrooms are tender, about 10 minutes.

Add the short rib meat to the pot and simmer until just heated through, about 2 minutes. Season the soup with salt to taste. Serve in warm soup bowls garnished with chives.

## RICH STOCK WITH SPRING VEGETABLES ☞ serves 6–8

Green or spring garlic, pulled from the earth before the garlic cloves grow into mature bulbs, appears in the market in early spring. Usually sold in bunches, they look like robust, sturdy scallions. The green stalk and immature bulb add a mild garlic flavor to this soup.

3–4 young green garlic stalks
   and bulbs, or 2 leeks, white
   and light green parts only
1–2 bunches scallions, trimmed
2 bunches asparagus, trimmed
4 tablespoons butter
2 tablespoons extra-virgin
   olive oil
10 cups Rich Chicken Stock
   (page 86)
Ham hock meat from Rich
   Chicken Stock, finely diced
1½ cups tiny pasta
2 cups shelled or frozen peas
Salt and freshly ground
   black pepper
½ bunch parsley, leaves
   chopped

Cut the green garlic stalks and immature bulbs crosswise into thin rounds. If using leeks, cut them crosswise into thin rounds and wash them to remove any grit. Cut the scallions crosswise into thin rounds, separating the white and dark green parts. Peel the asparagus stalks. Cut the stalks crosswise into thin rounds, leaving the tips whole. Set the vegetables aside separately.

Melt the butter and olive oil together in a heavy large pot over medium heat. Add the green garlic and white scallion parts and cook, stirring occasionally, until soft but not browned, about 10 minutes. Add the stock and ham and bring to a simmer. Stir in the pasta and cook until tender, about 10 minutes. Add the asparagus, peas, and green scallion parts, and cook until tender, 4–5 minutes. Season with salt and pepper to taste. Before serving, add the chopped parsley.

*Overleaf, left page, clockwise from top: Beefy Broth & Shiitake Mushroom Soup; Chicken Noodle Soup; Rich Stock with Spring Vegetables; right page: Ginger Chicken Soup with Asian Greens*

## CHICKEN NOODLE SOUP ᕲ serves 6–8

Make this classic soup ahead, but wait to add the noodles until just before serving.

3 tablespoons butter
1 tablespoon extra-virgin
    olive oil
1 yellow onion, peeled
    and chopped
2 carrots, peeled and sliced
1 celery stalk, diced
1 bay leaf
2–3 wide strips lemon peel
Salt and freshly ground
    black pepper
8 cups Old-Fashioned
    Chicken Stock (page 84)
2 boneless chicken breast halves
6 ounces wide egg noodles
½ bunch parsley, leaves
    chopped

Melt the butter with the oil in a heavy large pot over medium heat. Add the onions and cook, stirring often to keep them from browning, until softened, 5–10 minutes. Add the carrots, celery, bay leaf, lemon peel, and salt and pepper to taste. Cook until the vegetables just soften, about 5 minutes.

Add the stock to the pot and bring to a simmer. Add the chicken and poach until just cooked through, about 8 minutes. Reduce the heat to low. Transfer the chicken to a plate and when cool enough to handle, remove and discard the skin and tear it into bite-size pieces.

Cook the noodles in a medium pot of salted water over high heat, stirring often, until tender. Drain the noodles and add them to the pot of soup along with the chicken. Adjust the seasonings. Discard the lemon peel and bay leaf. Garnish the soup with parsley.

## GINGER CHICKEN SOUP WITH ASIAN GREENS ᕲ serves 4–6

We like to use baby bok choy, Chinese broccoli, mustard greens, or spinach for this aromatic soup.

8 cups Ginger Chicken Stock
    (page 86)
1 pound Asian greens, leaves
    separated and sliced
Chicken meat from Ginger
    Chicken Stock, chopped
½ pound silken tofu, drained
    and cut into cubes
Salt
4 scallions, trimmed and sliced

Bring the stock to a boil in a medium pot over medium heat. Add the greens, cover the pot, and remove it from the heat. Set aside to let the greens wilt and become just tender, about 5 minutes depending on the greens. Add the chicken.

Add the tofu to the hot soup. Season with salt to taste. Garnish the soup with the scallions.

## EXOTIC BROTH WITH ANGEL HAIR PASTA

A neighbor dropped off a quart of rich, exotically-flavored chicken broth. Think cinnamon, lemongrass, ginger, then imagine the heavenly aroma. We added no more than a tangle of aptly named angel hair pasta and some cilantro. It filled us up and soothed our restless spirits.

## CHICKEN VEGETABLE & PASTA SOUP

We made a brothy stew of roast chicken, braised onions, garlic, carrots, and parsnips for dinner. There were enough leftovers the next day to make a delicious chicken vegetable soup, augmented with a handful of string beans and orecchiette, for lunch. That is our kind of recycling.

## BEANS IN BROTH

A good bowl of soup can be as easy as warming up tender canned beans, like cannellini or navy beans, in a flavorful stock (pages 84–87) and adding a handful of chopped fresh herbs. Simple.

## CHICKEN TOMATO BROTH WITH RAVIOLINI

We had hot dogs and sauerkraut for breakfast. That didn't sit well with either of us. But by afternoon we were hungry. So, we added a few crushed canned tomatoes to some homemade chicken stock (pages 84–87) and simmered little cheese raviolini in the tomato-enriched broth until tender. This lunch made us feel all better.

## VEGETABLE RICE SOUP

The contents of our vegetable drawer—1 onion, 1 garlic clove, 1 carrot, 1 parsnip, 1 handful of green beans, and 3 collard leaves—plus 2 scoops of cooked sticky rice and 4 cups of really good homemade chicken stock (pages 84–87) added up to two big bowls of delicious, fortifying vegetable soup. Try it; you'll be ready to take on the world.

## RICE NOODLE & MUSHROOM SOUP

Friends gave us a bag of wide scallion rice noodles from NYC's Chinatown. So we heated up some Ginger Chicken Stock (page 86), added sliced hen-of-the-woods mushrooms, and a large handful of chopped scallions. Then we slid in the noodles. If Milford were big enough to have its own Chinatown, we'd slurp bowls of noodle soup like this every day.

*Overleaf, left page, clockwise from top left: Exotic Broth with Angel Hair Pasta; Chicken Vegetable & Pasta Soup; Beans in Broth; Chicken Tomato Broth with Raviolini; Vegetable Rice Soup; Rice Noodle & Mushroom Soup*

## TOMATO RICE SOUP

With a frozen block of Old-Fashioned Chicken Stock (page 84), one 28-ounce can of San Marzano plum tomatoes, and some short-grain rice from our pantry, we made tomato-rice soup. We always feel lucky when, with the fewest ingredients, we make something nourishing and delicious.

## POTATO ESCAROLE SOUP

A vegetarian-ish soup: Simmer slices of peeled russet potatoes in good homemade stock (pages 84–87) or even corned beef broth (page 280), if you happen to have any on hand. Add some escarole leaves and a pinch or two of crushed red pepper flakes. Well, okay, so this is *our* version of vegetarian. A little meat adds a whole lot of flavor.

## GINGER CHICKEN RICE SOUP

Using up the last of a big pot of Ginger Chicken Stock (page 86) that we made earlier in the week, we added cooked Arborio rice and scallions warmed in butter. Amazing how flavorful and satisfying a dish this simple can be.

## UDON NOODLE SOUP

We simmered 2 pieces of beef shank in some homemade chicken stock (pages 84–87) along with 1 peeled parsnip, 1 peeled carrot, 1 peeled shallot, some parsley stems, and 3 star anise. The resulting broth was lip-smackingly sticky and rich with flavor. To the strained hot broth, we added some sliced, peeled carrots and a tangle of udon, the Japanese wheat noodles. Slurp!

## A SIMPLE COCIDO

With cooked chickpeas and Rich Chicken Stock (page 86) on hand, we nourish ourselves with warm bowls of this: poached chicken, shredded ham hock, chopped blanched kale, cooked rice, and garbanzo beans simmered in rich broth, garnished with chopped fresh parsley.

## RICH BROTH WITH TURKEY-SCALLION MEATBALLS

One of us was fit as a fiddle; one of us was under the weather. But both of us were grateful to have big bowls of homemade chicken stock (pages 84–87) with diced fennel and little Turkey-Scallion Meatballs (page 312). This delicate elixir served both as prevention and cure.

*Overleaf, right page, clockwise from top left: Tomato Rice Soup; Potato Escarole Soup; Ginger Chicken Rice Soup; Udon Noodle Soup; A Simple Cocido; Rich Broth with Turkey Meatballs*

1. SWEATING THE ONIONS ⊙ Sweated onions are never brown. They are cooked slowly in fat (our soups use salted butter) over moderate heat, taking care that the onions don't caramelize, until they turn translucent. (Caramelization adds flavor but it also adds a brown color.) Sometimes covering the pot allows the onions to release more of their flavorful liquid. We use this technique all the time when making puréed vegetable soups to maintain their bright vegetal colors.

2. TO PURÉE OR NOT ⊙ Although we agree on most things, one of us likes brothy, chunky soups—something you can chew—while the other prefers puréed soups. We allow the soup to cool slightly, then we work in batches, using a food processor or blender, to purée the soup until it is smooth. Sometimes it pays off to blend an extra minute to ensure a very silky soup, a refined potage.

3. PURÉED SOUP ⊙ These soups cry out for embellishment. We favor heavy cream, whipped or not, sour cream, snipped chives or minced scallions, or a drizzle of melted butter or olive oil to add more flavor.

1.

LICIOUS PURÉED SOUPS

2.

3.

## CARROT SOUP ✺ serves 4–6

Puréeing hot soup in an electric blender can cause the lid to blow off (scary and dangerous)! The steam from the hot soup builds up when whirling it smooth. Cooling the soup a bit first and working in small batches helps prevent this. Or remove the stopper in the center of the blender lid, and cover the hole with a kitchen towel—this allows the steam to escape—then purée away.

4 tablespoons butter

1 yellow onion, peeled and chopped

Salt and freshly ground black pepper

2 pounds carrots, peeled and sliced

1 large russet potato, peeled and diced

Wide strips of peel from ½ lemon

2 bay leaves

6 cups chicken stock, preferably Old-Fashioned Chicken Stock (page 84)

Melt the butter in a heavy large pot over medium heat. Add the onions and cook, stirring occasionally, until soft but not browned, about 10 minutes. Season with salt and pepper. Add the carrots, potatoes, lemon peel, bay leaves, and 5 cups of the chicken stock. Cover the pot and cook until the vegetables are very soft, 30–45 minutes.

Discard the bay leaves. Working in small batches, purée the soup in a blender or food processor until very smooth. Add some of the remaining 1 cup stock if the soup is too thick. Season with salt and pepper. Serve hot or cold, garnished with a dollop of sour cream and finely chopped scallions or fresh chives, if you like.

FOR A CHUNKY SOUP: Discard the bay leaves and lemon peel. In the pot, lightly crush some of the carrots and potatoes using the back of a large spoon or a potato masher. Add more stock if the soup is too thick. Adjust the seasonings. Serve the soup hot, garnished with finely grated lemon zest or diced preserved lemon rind, and lots of chopped fresh chives, parsley, dill, or scallion greens, if you like.

LEMONY CARROT SOUP: Follow the directions for making Carrot Soup and add 2–3 teaspoons fresh lemon juice, ¼–½ freshly grated whole nutmeg, and a pinch of cinnamon to the pot just before puréeing the soup.—*serves 4–6*

CARROT CUMIN SOUP: Follow the directions for making Carrot Soup and add 1 tablespoon cumin seeds to the pot along with the onions. Serve the soup puréed, garnished with a dollop of plain yogurt seasoned with salt and freshly ground black pepper and finely chopped preserved lemon, if you like.—*serves 4–6*

THERE ARE ENDLESS VARIATIONS on the puréed soup theme. We follow the same basic steps for making Carrot Soup (page 98) when we make all of these Canal House favorites.

## CARROT GINGER SOUP

Follow the directions for making Carrot Soup (page 98), using 5–6 cups Ginger Chicken Stock (page 86). For extra ginger flavor, add a piece of peeled fresh ginger to the pot along with the stock. Discard the ginger and bay leaves before puréeing the soup. Garnish each serving with thinly sliced scallion greens and finely grated lemon zest, if you like.—*serves 4–6*

## PARSNIP & CARAWAY SOUP

Melt 4 tablespoons butter in a heavy large pot over medium heat. Add 1 chopped, peeled yellow onion and 2 teaspoons caraway seeds, and cook until soft, about 10 minutes. Season with salt and freshly ground black pepper. Add 2 pounds sliced, trimmed, peeled parsnips; 1 diced, peeled russet potato; 1 sliced, trimmed, peeled carrot; 2 bay leaves; and 5–6 cups Old-Fashioned Chicken Stock (page 84). Cover the pot and cook until the vegetables are very soft, 30–45 minutes. Discard the bay leaves. Purée the soup with 1 cup heavy cream. Garnish the soup with sliced scallions, diced peeled apple or ripe pear, or chopped fresh chives, if you like.—*serves 4–6*

## VICHYSSOISE

Trim off and discard the roots and dark green leaves of 4 leeks. Cut the leeks in half lengthwise, wash them under cold running water, and coarsely chop them. Melt 4 tablespoons butter in a heavy large pot over medium heat. Add the leeks and cook until soft, 10–15 minutes. Season with salt and freshly ground black pepper. Add 3 diced, peeled russet potatoes; a pinch of ground nutmeg; and 5–6 cups Old-Fashioned Chicken Stock (page 84). Cover the pot and cook until the vegetables are very soft, 30–45 minutes. Purée the soup with 1 cup heavy cream. Serve the soup cold, garnishing each bowl with a dollop of softly whipped cream and chopped fresh chives, if you like.—*serves 4–6*

## ROASTED BEET SOUP

Melt 4 tablespoons butter in a heavy large pot over medium heat. Add 1 chopped, peeled yellow onion and cook until soft, about 10 minutes. Season with salt and freshly ground black pepper. Add 1 diced, peeled russet potato; 1 sliced, trimmed, peeled carrot; 2 bay leaves; and 5–6 cups Old-Fashioned Chicken Stock (page 84). Cover the pot and cook until the vegetables are very soft, 30–45 minutes. Add 4–6 diced peeled, roasted beets (page 372) to the pot a few minutes before the vegetables are finished cooking. Discard the bay leaves.

*continued*

*Overleaf, left page, clockwise from top left: Parsnip & Caraway Soup; Vichyssoise; Minty Pea Soup; Roasted Beet Soup; right page, top: Silky Corn Soup; bottom: Cauliflower Soup with Gorgonzola & Cracked Black Pepper*

Purée the soup. Season with 2–3 teaspoons fresh lemon juice or 2 tablespoons balsamic vinegar. Serve soup garnished with a dollop of sour cream or plain yogurt and lots of chopped fresh chives or finely chopped scallions, if you like.—*serves 4–6*

## MINTY PEA SOUP

Melt 3 tablespoons butter in a heavy large pot over medium heat. Add 1 chopped, peeled yellow onion and cook until soft, about 10 minutes. Season with salt and freshly ground black pepper. Add 4 cups Old-Fashioned Chicken Stock (page 84) and bring to a simmer. Add 6 cups shelled English peas (from about 6 pounds of pods) or thawed frozen peas, and cook until tender, about 5 minutes for fresh peas, about 2 minutes for frozen. Remove the pot from the heat. Add ¼ cup each fresh parsley and fresh mint leaves to the pot. Purée the soup, thinning it with a little water if too thick. Serve the soup hot or cold, garnished with ½–1 cup finely diced ham and lots of chopped fresh chives.—*serves 4–6*

## CAULIFLOWER SOUP WITH GORGONZOLA & CRACKED BLACK PEPPER

Melt 4 tablespoons butter in a heavy large pot over medium heat. Add 1 chopped, peeled yellow onion and cook until soft, about 10 minutes. Season with salt and freshly ground black pepper. Add 1 head coarsely chopped, trimmed cauliflower; 2 diced, peeled russet potatoes; 1 sliced, trimmed, peeled carrot; 2 bay leaves; and 5–6 cups Old-Fashioned Chicken Stock (page 84). Cover the pot and cook until the vegetables are very soft, 30–45 minutes. Discard the bay leaves. Serve the soup puréed, and place a thin slice of Gorgonzola piccante on top of each serving with a good grinding of black pepper.—*serves 4–6*

## SILKY CORN SOUP

Cut the kernels off 10 ears shucked corn into a heavy large pot, scraping the cobs to release all the milky juice. Break each cob in two or three pieces. Put all the cobs into the pot along with 1 diced, peeled russet potato; 2 bunches chopped, trimmed scallions; and 6 cups whole milk. Season with ¼ teaspoon crushed red pepper flakes, and salt and freshly ground pepper to taste. Bring to a simmer over medium heat. Reduce heat to low. Cover the pot and gently simmer until the potatoes are soft, about 30 minutes. Using tongs, remove and discard the cobs from the pot. Working in small batches, purée the soup in a blender or food processor until very smooth. For a silky smooth soup, strain it through a fine-mesh sieve into a bowl, discarding any solids. Adjust the seasonings. Serve the soup hot or cold, garnished with a drizzle of heavy cream and edible flower blossoms, if you like.—*serves 4–6*

## FISH STOCK ☞ makes about 12 cups

Use white fish carcasses with heads and tails attached for this stock. Cod, snapper, bass are all good. Oily fish like salmon and bluefish give the stock an unpleasant, strong flavor. Fishmongers have bones; order them ahead, they're usually happy to give them away. And ask them to cut any large fish frames into pieces so they will fit into your pot. Shrimp shells are good to use, too. Peel shrimp, keep the shells in a bag in the freezer, adding to them each time you have more, until you are ready to make fish stock. Make a big pot of fish stock and store it in small containers in the freezer. You'll be stocked (sorry). Or make a saucepan of fish stock quickly and use it to make any fish soup, a seafood risotto, or a brothy fish dish more flavorful.

3–5 pounds fish bones and heads from lean, white-flesh fish, such as cod, snapper, or bass
1 tablespoon vegetable or olive oil
1 celery stalk, coarsely chopped
1 carrot, peeled and coarsely chopped
1 yellow onion, unpeeled and quartered
4 sprigs fresh thyme
2 bay leaves
6 black peppercorns
1 cup white wine
4 sprigs parsley
Salt

Rinse the fish bones and heads thoroughly under cold running water. (Remove and discard any fish gills, which can make the stock bitter.) Put the fish bones and heads, the oil, celery, carrots, onions, thyme, bay leaves, and peppercorns into a heavy large pot. Cover the pot and cook over medium heat, stirring occasionally to prevent anything from browning, until the vegetables begin to soften, about 10 minutes.

Add the wine and parsley to the pot along with 4 quarts (16 cups) cold water. Bring just to a simmer over medium-high heat. Reduce the heat to medium and simmer (gently bubbling), uncovered, for about 3 hours. You don't need to skim the foam that rises to the surface, the particles will eventually drop to the bottom of the pot and get strained out at the end. Resist the urge to stir the stock as it simmers; it will make the stock cloudy.

Strain the stock through a cheese cloth–lined colander into a bowl, discarding the solids. Season with salt to taste. (If you are making the stock ahead, allow it to cool to room temperature, then cover and refrigerate or freeze it.)

*Facing page, clockwise from top left: ingredients for Fish Stock; Clam Chowder (page 106); Smoked Fish Chowder (page 107); Cod Chowder (page 106)*

## CLAM CHOWDER ☞ serves 4

3 tablespoons butter
2 celery stalks, finely diced
1 small yellow onion,
    peeled and chopped
1 garlic clove, minced
1 tablespoon flour
2 cups whole milk
One 8-ounce bottle
    clam juice
One 10-ounce can whole
    baby clams
2 small all-purpose white or
    Yukon gold potatoes, peeled
    and cut into small cubes
1 bay leaf
Leaves from 1 sprig fresh
    thyme
Salt and freshly ground
    black pepper

Melt the butter in a medium pot over medium-low heat. Add the celery, onions, and garlic, and cook, stirring occasionally, until soft, 15–20 minutes. Add the flour, stirring constantly to prevent it from browning, and cook for 1–2 minutes. Gradually whisk in the milk and clam juice.

Add the clams and their juice, potatoes, bay leaf, and thyme. Season with salt and pepper to taste. Simmer the soup over medium to medium-low heat, stirring often, until the potatoes are tender and the soup has thickened, about 30 minutes. Remove the bay leaf before serving.

## COD CHOWDER ☞ serves 6–8

Sometimes we spice up this traditional New England soup with a few Spanish embellishments. Take care not to add too much salt; the crisp salt pork will provide that. If you use a flavorful enough fish stock, this soup can be served as a clear, brothy chowder. Just omit the half-and-half and replace it with fish stock.

10 ounces salt pork, diced
1 large yellow onion, peeled,
    halved, and sliced

Put the salt pork in a heavy large pot and cook over medium heat, stirring occasionally so the pieces get brown and crisp all over, about 15 minutes. Using a slotted spatula or spoon, transfer the

*continued*

1 pinch of saffron threads

2 bay leaves

Freshly ground black pepper

6–8 small all-purpose white or
Yukon gold potatoes, peeled
and cut into large cubes

8 cups Fish Stock (page 104)

1½ pounds cod filet, cut
into 6–8 pieces

2 cups half-and-half, optional

Pimentón, optional

salt pork to paper towels to drain. Pour off and discard all but about 2 tablespoons of the rendered fat in the pot.

Add the onions, saffron, bay leaves, and a few grinds of pepper to the pot. Cover the pot and cook, stirring from time to time, until the onions have softened but not browned, about 20 minutes. Add the potatoes and fish stock. Bring to a simmer, reduce the heat to keep the stock from boiling, and cook until the potatoes are soft, 15–20 minutes.

Add the cod and half-and-half, if using, to the pot and simmer until the fish is opaque and just cooked through, about 10 minutes. (To keep the fish in large pieces, don't stir too much.) Taste the soup and adjust the seasonings. Remove and discard the bay leaves. Ladle the chowder into bowls. Divide the salt pork between the bowls and sprinkle each with a pinch of pimentón, if you like.

## SMOKED FISH CHOWDER ☞ serves 6

4 tablespoons butter

3 leeks, white and pale green
parts only, trimmed, thickly
sliced crosswise, and washed

3 russet potatoes, peeled and
thickly sliced

8 cups whole milk

1 pound smoked whitefish

Lots of chopped fresh chives
or scallions for garnish

Melt the butter in a heavy large pot over medium heat. Add the leeks and cook, stirring often to prevent them from browning, until softened, 10–15 minutes. Add the potatoes and pour in 6 cups of the milk. Bring to a simmer (do not let the milk boil or it will curdle). Reduce the heat to maintain a gentle simmer, and cook until the potatoes are tender, about 30 minutes.

Meanwhile, carefully remove the skin and bones from the fish without breaking the pieces up too much. Place the fish in a medium pot, add the remaining 2 cups milk, and heat over medium-low heat until warm.

Carefully add the fish and milk to the pot with the potatoes. Serve the chowder warm, garnished with lots of chopped fresh chives.

## LOBSTER STEW ☞ serves 4

If you are squeamish about killing lobsters (who wouldn't be?), you can ask your fishmonger to steam and crack the lobsters for you. Let them know you want the lobsters a bit undercooked (or steamed just long enough to release the meat easily from the shell) and that you want to keep the juices (to add more flavor to the stew). To make life even easier, you can also pick up fish stock, though it probably won't match the flavor of the one you took the time and care to make yourself. Either way, this stew is luxuriously delicious.

Salt
Two 1½-pound lobsters
4 tablespoons butter, plus
    more for garnish
1 yellow onion, peeled and
    finely chopped
1 celery stalk, diced
2 sprigs fresh tarragon
Freshly ground black pepper
2 russet potatoes, peeled
    and diced
1 cup white wine
1 cup Fish Stock (page 104)
1 cup heavy cream
Chopped chives for garnish

Bring a large pot of water to a boil over high heat and season it with 2 tablespoons of salt. Plunge the tip of a large sharp knife into the head of each lobster just behind the eyes. Drop the lobsters head first into the boiling water and cook for about 8 minutes. Transfer the lobsters to a large bowl and set aside until they are cool enough to handle.

Working over the bowl to catch any juices, crack the lobster shells with a pair of lobster crackers, pliers, or a hammer, or cut them open with sturdy kitchen scissors. Remove the meat from the lobster, reserving the large pieces of shell and any juices. Cut the lobster meat into large bite-size pieces, leaving the claw meat whole, and set aside.

Melt the butter in a heavy large pot over medium-low heat. Add the onions, celery, and tarragon. Season with salt and pepper to taste. Add the reserved lobster shells along with any juices and cook, stirring occasionally, for 10 minutes. Add the potatoes, wine, and fish stock. Cover the pot and gently simmer until the vegetables are just soft, about 15 minutes. Remove and discard the tarragon and lobster shells.

Add the cream and the reserved lobster meat to the pot and simmer until the lobster is just heated through, about 5 minutes. Adjust the seasonings. Ladle the stew into bowls and garnish each serving with a knob of butter and some chives.

*Facing page, clockwise from top left: cutting through the underside of the abdomen with scissors; cracking the claws with a hammer (a kitchen towel absorbs any splatter); pulling claw meat from the shell; Lobster Stew*

## JIM'S MUSSEL SCALLION SOUP ☞ serves 8

Jim Hamilton, MH's father and our former Canal House neighbor, was a great cook. He was always curious, always tearing out recipes from various newspapers and food magazines. He would try out the recipes (they were often the catalyst for a dinner party), respectfully following them as printed. If he liked the dish well enough to make again, he usually tinkered with it, adapting it to suit his taste. Many had a short cycle in his long life. The best ones became part of his repertoire, and into his fat ring-binder they went, handwritten or typed out. Some he even rated, marking the page with stars using his felt-tip pen. This flavorful, mussel-rich soup got four stars. Over the years, we shared many bowls of this favorite soup with Jim, and though the recipe has now become part of our repertoire, to us it will always be Jim's.

2 yellow onions, peeled and
   coarsely chopped
2 teaspoons fennel seeds
1 sprig fresh thyme
2 bay leaves
1 teaspoon crushed
   red pepper flakes
1 bottle white wine
6 pounds mussels, rinsed
   and debearded
4 tablespoons butter
4 bunches scallions, trimmed,
   white and green parts
   chopped separately
One 28-ounce can whole,
   peeled plum tomatoes
2 cups heavy cream

Put the onions, fennel seeds, thyme, bay leaves, crushed red pepper flakes, and wine into a large pot. Cover the pot and cook over medium-high heat for 10 minutes. Add the mussels, cover the pot, and steam them, shaking the pot from time to time, until the shells have opened, 5–10 minutes.

Strain the mussels through a colander set over a large bowl. Pick the mussels from the shells and put them into a separate bowl. Discard the shells and any unopened mussels. Set the broth aside. (Avoid disturbing the broth as it rests, so any grit in it can settle to the bottom of the bowl.)

Melt the butter in a heavy medium pot over medium-low heat. Add the white parts of the scallions and cook until soft, about 5 minutes. Add the tomatoes and any juices from the can into the pot, crushing them with your hand as you put them in. Simmer the tomatoes for about 10 minutes.

Carefully pour the mussel broth (leaving any grit in the bottom of the bowl) into the pot. Add the cream and simmer for 10 minutes. Reduce the heat to medium-low. Add the mussels and the scallion greens and simmer until the mussels are heated through.

## MINESTRONE ☞ serves 6

Like most versions of this familiar soup, we change ours with the seasons. It plays off what's available from our gardens or at the market. But generally speaking, we make our soup with fewer vegetables than more, and like it a little brothier than dense and stewy. We use small pasta like ditalini (little thimbles) that are no bigger than the cut of the vegetables.

¼ cup extra-virgin olive oil, plus more for drizzling
1 medium yellow onion, peeled and chopped
2 garlic cloves, finely chopped
2 tablespoons tomato paste
8 cups Old-Fashioned Chicken Stock (page 84)
1 pound fresh beans, such as romano, string, or wax, trimmed and cut into 1-inch pieces
1 pound baby zucchini, sliced into thick rounds
Salt and freshly ground black pepper
1 cup ditalini or other short tubular pasta
1 cup Green Sauce

Heat the olive oil in a large pot over medium heat. Add the onions and cook, stirring often, until soft and translucent, about 5 minutes. Add the garlic, then stir in the tomato paste and cook for about 1 minute.

Add the chicken stock, beans, and zucchini. Simmer the soup until the vegetables are tender, about 45 minutes. Season to taste with salt and pepper.

Bring a small pot of salted water to a boil over high heat. Add the pasta and cook, stirring occasionally, until just cooked through, 8–10 minutes. Drain the pasta, add it to the soup, and simmer for about 15 minutes.

Serve the soup, adding a spoonful or two of green sauce and a drizzle of olive oil to each bowl.

## GREEN SAUCE

Using mature arugula leaves instead of the baby variety will make for a more peppery sauce. Mix grated zest of 1 lemon; 1 minced, peeled garlic clove; 3 cups arugula leaves, finely chopped; ¼ cup coarse fresh bread crumbs; 1 tablespoon finely chopped capers; and 1 tablespoon red wine vinegar in a small bowl. Stir in ¾ cup extra-virgin olive oil, then ¼ cup finely grated Parmigiano-Reggiano. Pour a little oil on the surface to keep the sauce from discoloring.—*makes about 2 cups*

## HEARTY SQUASH & BEAN MINESTRONE ☞ serves 12

To prevent the pasta from getting too soft, we cook it separately and toss it with olive oil and chopped parsley, then spoon it into each bowl of soup.

2 smoked ham hocks
1 pound dried navy or
  cannellini beans
¼ cup plus 2 tablespoons
  extra-virgin olive oil, plus
  more for drizzling
1 yellow onion, peeled and
  finely chopped
2 leeks, white and pale green
  parts only, washed and
  finely chopped
2 small celery ribs with
  leaves, chopped
2 garlic cloves, finely chopped
Salt and freshly ground
  black pepper
1 butternut squash, seeded,
  peeled, and cut into
  ½-inch pieces
1 pound Romano or string
  beans, cut into 1-inch pieces
8 cups Old-Fashioned
  Chicken stock (page 84)
1 pound small pasta, such
  as pipette or tiny shells
1 bunch parsley, leaves
  chopped
1 cup Green Sauce (page 112)
  or Pesto (page 176)

Remove the meat from the ham hocks, cut into large pieces, and set the meat aside. Put the navy beans and ham bones into a large pot. Add enough cold water to cover by 2 inches. Bring to a boil over high heat, reduce the heat, and simmer for 2 minutes. Remove the pot from the heat, cover, and set aside to soak for 1 hour.

Heat ¼ cup of the oil in another heavy large pot over medium-low heat. Add the ham hock meat, onions, leeks, celery, and garlic. Season with salt and pepper. Cook, stirring occasionally, until the vegetables have softened, about 20 minutes.

Add the squash, Romano beans, navy beans and their soaking liquid, stock, and ham bones to the pot. Bring to a simmer over medium heat. Reduce the heat to low, cover the pot, and gently simmer until the navy beans are tender, 1½–2 hours.

When the soup is almost finished cooking, cook the pasta in a large pot of boiling salted water, stirring occasionally, until just tender. Drain and transfer to a large bowl. Drizzle with the remaining 2 tablespoons of olive oil, add half the chopped parsley, and toss well.

Discard the ham bones from the pot of soup.

Spoon the soup into bowls, adding some pasta, a spoonful or two of green sauce or pesto, and a drizzle of olive oil to each bowl.

## FRENCH ONION SOUP  ✥  serves 6–8

This is quite a miraculous soup, the miracle of the onion. It tastes like it has simmered on the stove for days, but you can make a big pot in a couple of hours. If you're like us, always fooling around with some low-carb diet, you can skip the toast and just add grated Gruyère. The cheese won't brown but it will melt deliciously into the hot soup.

FOR THE SOUP
3 tablespoons extra-virgin olive oil
3–4 large yellow onions (about 3 pounds), peeled, halved and thinly sliced
2 garlic cloves, sliced
2 bay leaves
Salt and freshly ground black pepper
2 tablespoons flour
1 large tablespoon Dijon mustard
1 bottle white or red wine
4–6 cups Old-Fashioned Chicken stock (page 84)

FOR THE CHEESE TOASTS
Butter, at room temperature
6–24 baguette slices
8 ounces Gruyère, thinly sliced

For the soup, heat the olive oil in a heavy large pot over medium heat. Add the onions, garlic, and bay leaves, and cook, stirring often with a wooden spoon, until the onions are soft and brown, about 20 minutes. Season with salt and pepper to taste. Stir in the flour and cook for a few minutes to remove the raw flour taste. Stir in the mustard. Add the wine and stir to mix everything together.

Increase the heat to medium-high and cook until the soup comes to a simmer, about 10 minutes. Add 4 cups of the stock and, when the soup comes to a boil, reduce the heat to medium-low. Gently simmer the soup until it has developed a rich flavor and has thickened slightly, 45–60 minutes. Thin the soup with more stock if needed. Adjust the seasonings. Remove and discard the bay leaves.

For the cheese toasts, preheat the broiler with a rack set in the top third of the oven. Butter both sides of the bread and arrange them on a baking sheet in a single layer. Toast them on both sides under the broiler until lightly browned. Top the toasted bread with the Gruyère and return them to the broiler until the cheese is bubbly and golden.

Meanwhile, ladle the soup into bowls. Float some of the cheese toasts on top of each, if using.

*Facing page, clockwise from top: Hearty Squash & Bean Minestrone (page 113); French Onion Soup; pasta for Hearty Squash & Bean Minestrone*

Salads

# Salad Days

*She digs in her garden / With a shovel and a spoon, / She weeds her lazy lettuce / By the light of the moon. / [. . .] / Her lawn looks like a meadow, / And if she mows the place / She leaves the clover standing / And the Queen Anne's lace.*—Edna St. Vincent Millay

WHEN THE EARTH WARMS UP BUT THE AIR IS STILL COOL, we scatter tiny lettuce seeds in our gardens. We harvest the tender leaves, along with the sorrel and wild arugula that come back every year. Add to that the lettuces of every variety that we gather from our local farm stands and markets (not to mention the bunches brought by friends), and it satisfies our spring-jones for a good salad.

The leaves we love offer the trinity of vitality, texture, and flavor. We take care to choose a dressing that complements rather than overwhelms them. For example, we serve thick, creamy dressings like Green Goddess on hardy, tight-headed lettuces that can hold the weight, and thinner dressings and vinaigrettes on sturdy and delicate leaves alike.

When it comes to making a basic vinaigrette, these are our building blocks: We like an oil-to-acid ratio of 4:1, and use lemon juice, vinegar (sometimes rice, seldom balsamic), even soy sauce for acid. (We want the acid to just lift up the vinaigrette from being oily. We don't want pushback from it!) Experiment to create your own house vinaigrette. Just remember that it is worth the splurge for top-quality extra-virgin olive oil because it carries the other flavors.

Also remember that really good dressing can be almost effortless: We make what we've come to call our Canal House Classic Vinaigrette right in the bottom of a well-loved wooden bowl. First, we grate a clove of garlic into a pungent paste, using salt and pepper for seasoning and grit. Next goes a dollop of Dijon mustard and a splash of red wine vinegar. Then we drizzle in our very best olive oil, whisking until the dressing emulsifies. A taste tells us if it needs more oil or vinegar.

We both agree that chives are our favorite herb. From early spring well into fall, we go back and forth from our kitchens into our gardens to snip chives from pots that we have planted near our back doors. Each year, while the sage straggles back to life and the thyme takes its time shedding dead leaves to make new ones, clumps of chives—harbingers of warm weather—come back fuller and more vigorous than the previous year. By June, lavender-pink blossoms appear on their scapes and seem to float in the air above the slender, tubular leaves. We always keep a bouquet in a tall glass on the shelf over the studio sink. This seasonal vinaigrette couldn't be simpler: just really good olive oil, a splash of white wine vinegar, a tiny crescent of garlic, and (of course) a ton of chives. We pull apart the blossoms into lavender confetti and toss them in salads, a touch that's as decorative as it is flavor-enhancing. Once we get a taste for chives, we have to remind ourselves to use other herbs.

Chives *(Allium schoenoprasum)* belong to the lily family. Cousin of onions, leeks, and scallions, it is the smallest of the *Allium* genus. The entire plant is edible, from bulb to flower. We love its delicate flavor: green, lightly sharp, with just the right amount of onion. You can buy chives year-round, but their flavor (and aroma) is much more pungent when they're freshly cut in season. We use kitchen shears to strategically snip at the base to make room for new growth, taking care not to hack away or give them a bad haircut. Blooming is prolonged by picking off (deadheading) the spent blossoms.

A few years ago, we cooked a big-deal meal, pulling out all the stops, for an illustrious food writer. At the end of the evening, the knowing guest of honor thanked us, noting, "That salad was simply delicious." We took it as the highest compliment.

## WASHING AND STORING SALAD GREENS

We find that the hardest part about making a salad is getting the energy up to wash and dry the lettuce. So we get a jump on it and prep our greens when we bring them home from the market (see pages 122–123). That way, the hard part is over and we only have to make a dressing to toss the leaves in.

For head lettuces, separate the leaves, discarding any bruised or tough outer leaves. Fill a large bowl with cold water (1). Plunge the greens into the water, then lift the leaves out, leaving any dirt to settle on the bottom of the bowl (2). Refresh the water and continue washing until there is no more dirt on the leaves or in the bottom of the bowl. Shake off any water from the leaves and lay them out on a clean dish towel or a length of paper towels (3). Roll the leaves up in the towels (4) and store in an open big plastic bag (5) in the refrigerator. Greens can be prepped several days ahead.

## OUR FAVORITE SALAD GREENS

THE BITTERS: *Radicchio di Treviso*, radicchio, escarole, puntarelle, Belgian endive, and dandelion greens are some of the bitter greens that we use. We especially love escarole for its sturdiness and crunch. It is kind of perverse what we do to it. Like Morticia from the Addams family, who used to cut off the heads of the roses, leaving a vase full of spiky stems, we prefer the crisp, flavorful, slightly bitter ribs of escarole to the pretty green leafy part—so we chop off all the dark green, ruffly leaves and feed them to the chickens. Bitter greens make delicious salads on their own, but when mixed with other milder lettuces, they add their zesty flavor and color.

THE TENDERS: Boston, bibb, spinach leaves, and watercress make the loveliest salads of all. The simplest green salad—tender leaves gently tossed in a few spoonfuls of vinaigrette—is at the top of our list. Velvety spinach comes washed and ready to go, but look for larger, sturdier leaves, rather than limp baby spinach. They have more flavor. We aren't fans of Spring Mix either for the very same reason—too wimpy! But we love the peppery flavor that watercress adds to a salad.

THE STURDIES: Romaine, baby romaine, and iceberg are the workhorses of the salad world. Some people turn their noses up at these ubiquitous leaves, but their satisfying crunchiness highly recommends them. We discard romaine's outer leaves and cut off the tough dark green tops. The tender inner leaves have flavor and crunch, and their shape holds thicker dressings nicely. Iceberg cut into big wedges is a classic favorite when dressed with Creamy Blue Cheese Dressing (page 133) or Green Goddess Dressing (page 133).

THE HERBS: Adding tender leaf herbs like fresh tarragon, parsley, oregano, basil, or mint leaves (to name a few) to salad greens makes every bite surprising. We always sprinkle lively-tasting chopped chives into greens.

the bitters

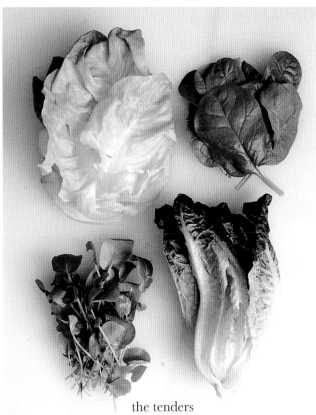

the tenders

the sturdies

the herbs

2.

4.

5.

# Oils & Vinegars

⊙ These two don't mix? Why, they're the best of friends! ⊙

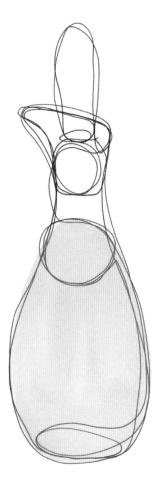

We rely on our local markets to buy the best extra-virgin olive oil we can afford. Freshness is key. We check the harvest or "best before" date on the label. If properly stored (up to 18 months is fine), a less expensive, freshly pressed, extra-virgin olive oil can taste better than an expensive one with an older date. We experiment until we find brands we like. An affordable extra-virgin olive oil with a rich, balanced flavor is our everyday workhorse for cooking and making salad dressings. We use special reserve or single varietal oils—with distinct peppery or buttery flavors—as "finishing" oils to drizzle on everything—toast, fresh mozzarella, salads. Tucked in our fridge are nut and seed oils—pistachio, walnut, hazelnut, pumpkin seed. Used sparingly, on their own or mixed with olive oil, they add a whole lot of flavor. Keep all oils away from heat, out of direct sunlight, and in airtight containers.

Good red wine vinegar is hard to find. Specialty food shops carry aged balsamic and flavored vinegars, but often there is no top-shelf red wine variety to be found. So, we make our own. Its flavor is sparkling and fresh. We have vinegar mothers (a gift from a friend, though wine- and beer-making suppliers carry them) that float in wine and some water in gallon crocks draped with cheesecloth in the cool darkness of our basements. It's this live starter that transforms wine into vinegar (acetic acid) through alcoholic fermentation and bacterial activity, with an assist from oxygen. There's not much to do besides add more wine every so often. The better the wine, the finer the vinegar, so whatever we're drinking, we share a glass with our fermenting vinegar. Then we wait for the vinegar to mellow as it matures over a few months. Aged red wine vinegar has a tawny reddish color, a clean but sharp aroma, and a subtly intense flavor. Making vinegar reminds us of a love affair. As in all great romances, you must pay attention to its needs, take care of it, and have patience as it ages and transforms into something beautiful.

1. PIT OLIVES ⊙ There are gadgets specifically designed to remove the pits from olives. But since we are usually chopping up the pitted olives, we go low tech and just press down on each olive with the flat side of a knife to release it from the pit.

2. MASH ANCHOVIES ⊙ We love their rich, salty flavor. We mash oil-packed filets with a dinner fork, then mix them into vinaigrettes and dressings.

3. TINY HOT CHILES ⊙ We buy these tiny Italian chiles at an Italian specialty store. We keep a small bowl of them on the counter to crush and sprinkle over salads to spice things up. Wash your hands right away and don't touch your eyes!

4. PRESERVED LEMONS ⊙ We discard the pulpy flesh, then scrape out the pith from preserved lemons, using only the rind to add a salty lemon flavor to our vinaigrettes.

5. PEEL GARLIC ⊙ The quickest way to peel garlic is to press individual cloves with the flat side of a knife. The papery peel will pop right off.

6. GRATE GARLIC ⊙ The microplane has replaced the old hard-to-clean garlic press. It works like a charm, grating peeled garlic into a fine purée.

ADS WITH GREAT FLAVOR

3.

4.

7.

8.

11.

12.

7. MINCE GARLIC ⊙ Old habits die hard, so we still find ourselves mincing garlic with a chef's knife. Adding a pinch of salt provides grit that helps with the mincing. When we want a finer, smoother paste, we add a little more salt and using the side of the blade in a back and forth motion, crush the minced garlic into a purée.

8. RUB GARLIC ⊙ Sometimes when we are making a salad, we want to restrain garlic's pungent power. So instead of adding it to the vinaigrette or dressing, we just rub the inside of the salad bowl with a peeled clove. Amazingly, it adds lots of subtle flavor to the salad.

9. DRESSING IN THE SALAD BOWL ⊙ This good trick, long used by the clever French housewife, is to make the vinaigrette right in the salad bowl.

10. ADD THE LETTUCE ON TOP ⊙ Pile all the prepared lettuce greens into the bowl on top of the vinaigrette. If you like, cross your salad fork and spoon over the vinaigrette, and add the lettuce.

11. TAKE IT TO THE TABLE ⊙ Take the salad to the table and it is ready to toss when you are ready to serve it.

12. TOSS AND SERVE ⊙ We like to eat our salad after the main course, preferably with a piece of bread and cheese.

## CANAL HOUSE CLASSIC VINAIGRETTE ☞ makes about ½ cup

Make this once with measuring spoons and cups; the next time, just eyeball it, adjusting any or all of the ingredients to suit your palate. Then you can call it your own.

1 small garlic clove,
   finely grated
2 teaspoons Dijon mustard
Salt and freshly ground
   black pepper
2 tablespoons wine vinegar or
   fresh lemon juice
½ cup extra-virgin olive oil

Using the back of a wooden spoon, mash together the garlic, mustard, and a pinch of salt and a grinding of pepper in a salad bowl. Stir in the vinegar. Gradually whisk in the oil until the vinaigrette is emulsified. Adjust the seasonings.

## LEMON-ANCHOVY VINAIGRETTE ☞ makes about ⅔ cup

A lighter, brighter option for all Caesar salad lovers. This vinaigrette involves *supreming* the lemon, a French technique (they always know how to refine things) that removes the peel and the pith, then cuts the juicy fruit out from the membranes. This method works well with all citrus fruits.

2 lemons
4 anchovy filets packed
   in oil, drained and
   finely chopped
½ cup extra-virgin olive oil
¼ teaspoon crushed red
   pepper flakes
Salt and freshly ground
   black pepper

Using a sharp knife, cut off and discard all the peel and white pith from the lemons. Working over a medium bowl, cut lemons along sides of membranes to release the segments into the bowl. Squeeze the juice from the membranes into the bowl, and discard the membranes.

Stir in the anchovies, oil, and crushed red pepper flakes, breaking up the lemon segments against the side of the bowl with a spoon. Season with salt and pepper to taste.

## ANOTHER ANCHOVY VINAIGRETTE

Put 6 minced anchovy filets; 1 peeled, minced, or grated garlic clove; a small pinch of salt; and a good grinding of pepper in a bowl and mash together in the bottom of the bowl with a spoon. Add 1 tablespoon vinegar or lemon juice. Stir in ¼ cup olive oil. Adjust the seasonings.—*makes about ⅓ cup*

## SIMPLEST ASIAN VINAIGRETTE ✍ makes about ½ cup

The delicate flavor of rice vinegar along with the other Asian ingredients in this vinaigrette is ideal on tender greens like mizuna or mâche.

½ small garlic clove,
   finely grated
1 tablespoon reduced-sodium
   soy sauce
2 teaspoons unseasoned
   rice vinegar
½ cup extra-virgin olive oil
½ teaspoon toasted
   sesame oil
Salt and freshly ground
   black pepper

Whisk the garlic, soy sauce, and vinegar together in a salad bowl. Gradually whisk in the olive oil, then the sesame oil. The vinaigrette will thicken slightly. Season with salt and pepper to taste.

## FRESH CHIVE VINAIGRETTE ✍ makes about ½ cup

Herbs in this vinaigrette beg for herbs in the salad, too. We toss this dressing with tender salad leaves, like bibb lettuce, and lots of the tender green herbs, like mint, chervil, and parsley.

1 small garlic clove,
   finely grated
Salt
1 tablespoon wine vinegar
   or fresh lemon juice
4 tablespoons extra-virgin
   olive oil
2 tablespoons chopped
   fresh chives
Freshly ground black pepper

Using the back of a wooden spoon, mash the garlic and a pinch of salt together in a salad bowl. Stir in the vinegar, then the oil and chives. Season with salt and pepper to taste.

*Overleaf, left page, clockwise from top left: Canal House Classic Vinaigrette (page 128); Lemon-Anchovy Vinaigrette (page 128); Green Goddess (page 133); Simplest Asian Vinaigrette (page 129); right page: making Lemon-Anchovy Vinaigrette*

## SPICY OLIVE VINAIGRETTE ☞ makes about ¾ cup

Brine-cured olives, like black Kalamata or Alfonso, or green manzanilla or picholine, add a brightness to this assertive vinaigrette. But if we are in a hurry (or feeling lazy), we just use jarred tapenade. We use it to dress cannellini, string beans, sliced tomatoes, asparagus, hard-boiled eggs, and toast. Yes, a long list of delicious things that keeps growing.

½ cup finely chopped, pitted, briny black olives
1 garlic clove, finely chopped
1–2 pinches of crushed red pepper flakes
2 tablespoons wine vinegar
½ cup extra-virgin olive oil
Salt and freshly ground black pepper

Stir together the olives, garlic, crushed red pepper flakes, and vinegar in a bowl. Stir in the oil. Season with salt and pepper. This dressing keeps in the refrigerator, covered, for up to 1 week.

## HARISSA VINAIGRETTE ☞ makes about ⅔ cup

Harissa, the Tunisian chile-spice paste, adds a warm, but not too hot, flavor to this vinaigrette. We like to spoon this dressing over grilled vegetables, fish, and chicken—its mild heat is a good match with smoky flavors.

1 garlic clove, grated
1–2 pinches of fennel seeds, crushed
1–2 pinches of cumin seeds, crushed
Salt and freshly ground black pepper
2 tablespoons harissa paste
Juice of 1 lemon
6 tablespoons extra-virgin olive oil

Put the garlic, fennel, cumin, and a good pinch of salt and some pepper into a small bowl. Stir in the harissa and lemon juice. Stir in the oil. Adjust the seasonings.

## GREEN GODDESS DRESSING ☞ makes about ¾ cup

Spoon this creamy dressing onto tight-headed or sturdy lettuces, like Little Gem, romaine, escarole, and iceberg. They can stand up to the dressing's weight. We only use flat-leaf parsley. Period. And especially when it matters, like it does for this dressing. It has an herbal green flavor that curly parsley lacks.

½ bunch watercress, tough stems discarded, coarsely chopped (about 2 cups)

4 anchovy filets packed in oil, drained

½ cup mayonnaise

2 tablespoons sour cream

½ cup (lightly packed) fresh parsley leaves

2 tablespoons chopped fresh chives

2 tablespoons chopped fresh tarragon leaves

1 tablespoon white wine vinegar

Salt and freshly ground black pepper

Put the watercress, anchovies, mayonnaise, sour cream, parsley, chives, tarragon, and vinegar into a blender and purée until smooth. Season with salt and pepper to taste.

## CREAMY BLUE CHEESE DRESSING

We spoon this dressing onto wedges of iceberg lettuce and crunchy hearts of romaine. Use it as a dip for celery, or go retro and serve it with potato chips. There is always French Roquefort, but since there are such great American blues right now, try one of them.

Put ½ cup sour cream, ½ cup mayonnaise, ½ cup buttermilk, 2 finely chopped trimmed scallions, and 1 finely grated small garlic clove into a medium bowl and stir until well combined. Fold in ½ cup crumbled blue cheese. Season with a little salt, if the dressing needs it, and a good grinding of black pepper.—*makes about 2 cups*

## AVOCADOS WITH LEMON & OLIVE OIL

We have generous California friends with an avocado grove in their backyard. And sometimes Hass avocados show up by surprise at our door. These West Coast beauties are rich enough to eat plain, but we like to gild the lily. We split an avocado, remove the pit, drizzle good extra-virgin olive oil into the halves, a couple squeezes of lemon juice, two pinches of crushed red pepper flakes, and salt. Not so much a recipe as a reminder: so simple, so perfect.—*serves 2*

## TOMATOES WITH MAYONNAISE

We peel and slice handsome heirloom Big Red tomatoes over a plate to catch all their sweet juices. A spoonful of Fresh Chive Vinaigrette (page 129), a sprinkle of salt and freshly ground black pepper, and a plop of good mayonnaise is all it needs after that. Sometimes we add avocados and basil, but like earrings and a necklace on a beautiful woman, it's nice but not necessary.—*make as much as you like*

## RÖSTI WITH A GREEN SALAD ON TOP

Rösti is a Swiss potato pancake. A big russet potato on the kitchen counter was our inspiration. Grate 1 large, peeled, russet potato (about 1 pound), on the large holes of a box grater into a bowl. Add 4 chopped scallions, and season with salt and pepper. Melt 2 tablespoons butter in a nonstick skillet over medium-high heat. Add the potatoes, pressing them into a flat cake. Fry until golden, about 10 minutes. Cover the skillet with a large plate and flip the skillet and the plate over so that the rösti is cooked-side up on the plate. Add 2 tablespoons butter to the skillet and slide the rösti back into the skillet. Fry until golden, about 10 minutes. While the potato cake finishes browning, toss bibb lettuce, radicchio, and parsley leaves in Another Anchovy Vinaigrette (page 128). Divide the rösti between dinner plates and pile the salad on top. Add a flourish of silky smoked salmon for garnish.—*serves 2–4*

## SALADE NIÇOISE OUR WAY

As the end of summer looms, we eat from the garden every day until the frost comes. One of our favorite meals is a *salade niçoise* of sorts, with smoked Atlantic salmon replacing tuna. The rest is *de rigueur:* marble-size potatoes, heirloom tomatoes, fat green beans, tiny radishes, and crunchy butter lettuce. *Bon appétit!*

## SUCCOTASH SALAD

A favorite late summer lunch is warm succotash salad. We toss together in a large bowl blanched chopped zucchini and blanched green beans, bicolor corn (boiled and cut off the cob), chopped fresh parsley, salt and pepper, and Fresh Chive Vinaigrette (page 129).—*make as much as you like*

*Overleaf, left page, clockwise from top left: Avocados with Lemon & Olive Oil; Tomatoes with Mayonnaise; Rösti with a Green Salad on Top; Salade Niçoise Our Way; Succotash Salad; Feta, Fennel & Tomato Salad*

## FETA, FENNEL & TOMATO SALAD

Warm ¼ cup of good extra-virgin olive oil in a big skillet over medium heat. Add 2 thickly sliced peeled tomatoes, and salt and pepper. When the tomatoes begin to soften and warm (less than a minute), slide them onto a serving platter. Add a handful of sliced cherry tomatoes and chopped mint and parsley. Then sauté quartered fennel similarly, but longer, until it is tender and golden brown. Dress the fennel in Lemon-Anchovy Vinaigrette (page 128). Add a slab of French feta to pair up the fennel and tomatoes. Serve with good bread to sop up the delicious juices.—*serves 2–4*

## CHOPPED CELERY SALAD

Chop the inner stalks and leaves from 1 head of celery and put them in a bowl. Add 4–8 chopped anchovy filets, finely grated zest of 1 lemon, 1 tablespoon capers, and ¼ cup extra-virgin olive oil, and toss well. Season with salt and cracked black pepper and with enough juice from 1 lemon to suit your taste. Refrigerate until well chilled. Toss with arugula and bibb lettuce leaves.—*serves 2–4*

## SUMMER PASTA SALAD (WITH MORE SALAD THAN PASTA)

In midsummer, sometimes we just stare at the vegetables and they tell us what to do. Here's how they told us to make a summer pasta salad: Sauté a sliced red onion and a minced clove of garlic in good extra-virgin olive oil in a large skillet over medium heat for about 5 minutes. Add a big handful of blanched, trimmed string beans and a big, chopped, peeled ripe tomato (we scoop out the seeds, but you don't have to). Season with salt and pepper. Cook until everything is just hot, about 5 minutes. Add about 2 cups of cooked pasta (we used campanelle). Toss everything together and add a little Canal House Classic Vinaigrette (page 128). Transfer to a platter and add some torn, fresh basil leaves.—*serves 2–4*

## CORN & ZUCCHINI WITH CUMIN CHÈVRE

Cook 4–6 ears of shucked corn in a large pot of boiling salted water for 3 minutes. Remove the corn from the water with tongs and set aside to cool on a cutting board. When the water returns to a boil, add 2 zucchini sliced into thick rounds and cook until just tender, about 2 minutes. Drain the zucchini and arrange on a plate in a single layer. Season with salt and freshly ground black pepper and drizzle with a little extra-virgin olive oil. Use a knife to slice the corn kernels from the ears of corn into a mixing bowl. Add spoonfuls of Harissa Vinaigrette (page 132) to the corn. Stir together 1 teaspoon ground cumin, 1 tablespoon extra-virgin olive oil and ⅓ cup chèvre. Slather the chèvre onto the zucchini rounds, then add some torn basil leaves. Spoon the corn onto a platter, arrange the zucchini on the corn, then drizzle everything with more extra-virgin olive oil.—*serves 4*

*Overleaf, right page, clockwise from top left: Chopped Celery Salad; Summer Pasta Salad (with More Salad than Pasta); Corn & Zucchini with Cumin Chèvre*

## PECORINO & BLACK PEPPER DRESSING

Pecorino Romano, Italian sheep milk cheese, has a salty flavor that replaces vinegar or lemon juice in this creamy Caesar-like dressing. We spoon it on sturdy lettuce leaves like escarole or romaine, or toss it with shaved stalks of fat raw asparagus. Don't be tempted to substitute Parmigiano-Reggiano for the pecorino—it will not dissolve in the hot water.

Finely grate 2 ounces Pecorino Romano on a microplane or the fine holes of a box grater into a medium bowl, about 1 cup. Add 1 grated small garlic clove. Whisk in ⅓ cup boiling water. Add 3 minced anchovy filets and a good grinding of black pepper. Gradually whisk in ¼ cup really good extra-virgin olive oil. Adjust the seasonings.—*makes ¾ cup; serves 4–6*

## CHICORY LEAVES WITH ORANGES VINAIGRETTE ☞ serves 4–6

In late winter, deliciously bitter Italian red chicories—elongated *radicchio di Treviso* and flowerlike *tardivo*—arrive in the markets when red-fleshed blood oranges and other sweet varieties are available. Elegant Belgian endive and round *radicchio di Chioggia* are more common and, like navel oranges, available year-round (see pages 140–141).

FOR THE VINAIGRETTE
1 blood orange
1 Cara Cara or navel orange
¼ cup extra-virgin olive oil
1 pinch of crushed red
  pepper flakes
Salt and freshly ground
  black pepper

FOR THE SALAD
1 *radicchio di Treviso*, leaves
  separated
1 Belgian endive, leaves
  separated
Extra-virgin olive oil
1 small bunch fresh chives,
  chopped

For the vinaigrette, start with one orange and slice the ends off. Stand the orange on the cut end and slice off the rind and white pith, exposing the flesh (1). Working over a bowl to catch any juice, slice between each fruit segment, cutting it away from the membrane, and let the segments or supremes and juice fall into the bowl. Repeat with the second orange (2). Squeeze any juice from the pulp into the bowl (3). Add the olive oil. Add the crushed red pepper flakes to the bowl and season with salt and pepper (4).

For the salad, arrange the radicchio and endive on a serving platter and spoon the vinaigrette and orange supremes over the leaves. Drizzle the salad with a little olive oil. Scatter the chives on top.

*Pecorino & Black Pepper Dressing on escarole*

1.

3.

# Hard & Soft Cheeses

⊙ *Cheese is milk's leap toward immortality.*—Clifton Fadiman ⊙

We always serve cheese in the French fashion after the main course, usually with the salad. We believe it aids in digestion, and along with a little *vin rouge,* is good for our health!

CAVE-AGED GRUYÈRE: (Switzerland, Gruyères) Cow's milk, hard cheese. Dense, slightly granular texture; nutty and fruity flavor. Melts beautifully. Our go-to cheese for quiches, soufflés, omelets, gratins, and French onion soup. Add to ham sandwiches, escarole or chef's salads, or serve with apples.

AGED GOUDA: (Holland, Gouda) Cow's milk, hard cheese. Deep yellow, granular texture, very fruity flavor. Delicious served on its own, and with dried cherries, or cherry or fig preserves.

COMTÉ: (France, Franche-Comté) Cow's milk, hard cheese. A magnificent yellow cheese with a supple, slightly granular texture and a sweet, nutlike flavor. We use this versatile cheese the same way we do its cousin, Gruyère. Its subtleties shine on its own.

MANCHEGO: (Spain, Castilla-La Mancha) Sheep's milk, hard cheese. Firm, creamy, and dotted with irregular "eyes". Reminiscent of nuts and burnt caramel with a complex "lamby" flavor. Traditionally served with slices of quince paste (*membrillo*). Delicious with apple jelly.

PARMIGIANO-REGGIANO: (Italy, Parma) Cow's milk, hard cheese. A brittle, crumbly, and granular texture; intense flavors from pineapple to caramelized onions. Grate it on pasta, into risottos, vegetables, soups, over leafy salads, fried or scrambled eggs, or asparagus. Serve shards with pears, apples, or dates.

CLOTH-BOUND CHEDDAR: (England, Somerset) Cow's milk, hard cheese. Firm texture with rich, complex flavors, like tasting a fine wine. This gem excels with tender-leaf lettuce salads, apples, sliced cold ham, mustard, or fruit chutney.

MOUNTAIN GORGONZOLA: (Italy, Lombardy) Cow's milk, blue cheese. Slightly firm, mild tang. Serve with honey and walnuts, a salad of tender and bitter lettuces, ripe apricots, peaches, or figs.

STILTON: (England, Derbyshire, Leicestershire, Nottinghamshire) Cow's milk, blue cheese. Dry, tough rind, creamy straw-yellow color with blue veins throughout. Though traditionally served with port, it pairs better with a late-harvest wine like Sauternes.

BLEU D'AUVERGNE: (France, Auvergne) Cow's milk, blue cheese. Firm, orangish, crusty rind; firm creamy interior; a clean, sharp flavor of butter and herbs. Serve this cheese with sliced ripe pears, walnuts or pecans, or crumbled in a green salad with beets.

TALEGGIO: (Italy, Lombardy) Cow's milk, semisoft cheese. When ripe, this cheese has a reddish rind with a soft almost oozing interior and a wonderfully strong flavor. Good with charcuterie.

CAMEMBERT: (France, Normandy) Cow's milk, soft white rind cheese. Fine-textured thin white rind with a supple, voluptuous consistency from edge to center; yeasty, meatlike flavor. One thing we never do is bake a Camembert—*mais, non!* We like to serve this cheese with a leafy green salad and good crusty bread. It pairs well with apples, pears, and nuts.

FROMAGE D'AFFINOIS: (France) Cow's milk, soft white rind double-cream cheese. A rind and interior much like Brie, this cheese is all about its soft, creamy texture. Ultrafiltration speeds up the whole process, so it is always "ripe" with a buttery flavor without the tang of an artisanal cheese. We can't help ourselves—it has good gooeyness.

MOZZARELLA DI BUFALA: (Italy, Campania, Lazio, Apulia, Molise) Water buffalo's milk, fresh cheese. A very soft texture, porcelain white in color, sweet and slightly nutty. Serve it sliced, drizzled with extra-virgin olive oil, with sliced ripe tomatoes and torn basil leaves.

FRESH RICOTTA: (Italy; United States) Cow's milk, fresh cheese. Soft, moist curds just pressed together; a sweet, fresh taste. Used in Italian cooking and we serve it after a salad with honey and almonds, or with Amarone-stewed cherries.

LE CHEVROT: (France, Poitou) Goat's milk, soft white rind cheese. A thick-textured, wrinkly, bloomy, pale golden rind; creamy and lusciously ripe just under the rind, delicately herbaceous, smooth, and velvety in the center. Eat it just as it is or serve with wild honey.

BOUCHERON: (France, Loire) Goat's milk, soft white rind cheese. Rich texture and flavor beneath the rind changing to a smooth, white, sharp-flavored interior. Like most cheeses, this pairs well with grapes and fresh figs.

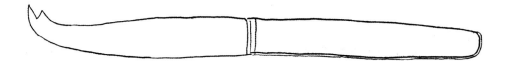

Cave-Aged Gruyère

Aged Gouda

Comté

Manchego

Parmigiano-Reggiano

Cloth-Bound Cheddar

Mountain Gorgonzola

Bleu d'Auvergne

Stilton

Taleggio

Le Chevrot

Fresh Ricotta

Camembert

Boucheron

Mozzarella di Bufala

Fromage d'Affinois

## LOBSTER SALAD

Lobster salad is the queen of our summer table. We dream about it for the rest of the year. We also prepare it with Green Olive or Lemon-Anchovy Mayonnaise (see below).

Toss plump chunks of cold lobster (see pages 108–109 for how to remove meat from lobster shells) with a dab of mayonnaise, extra-virgin olive oil, fresh lemon juice, a little chopped celery, fresh tarragon leaves, and minced fresh chives. Dress haricots verts and potatoes in extra-virgin olive oil and salt and freshly ground black pepper.—*one lobster serves 2–4*

## GREEN OLIVE MAYONNAISE

Keep this lovely mayonnaise on hand to serve with grilled salmon or cold roast chicken. We mix it with canned tuna to liven up an everyday tuna sandwich. And sometimes we use it instead of plain mayonnaise in our Old-Fashioned Layered Potato Salad (page 148).

Put 1 cup chopped, pitted green olives; 1 cup finely chopped fresh parsley; 2–3 finely chopped, trimmed scallions; 1 minced anchovy filet; and 1 cup mayonnaise in a medium bowl and stir well. Stir in the zest of 1 lemon, then add just enough lemon juice to taste, stirring until smooth. Season with salt and freshly ground black pepper. The mayonnaise keeps in the refrigerator, covered, for up to 1 week.—*makes about 2 cups*

## LEMON-ANCHOVY MAYONNAISE

Put 2 cups mayonnaise and 8 minced anchovy filets in a medium bowl and stir well. Stir in the zest of 1 lemon, then add lemon juice to taste, stirring until smooth. Season with 1–2 pinches cayenne. The mayonnaise keeps in the refrigerator, covered, for up to 1 week.—*makes about 2 cups*

## WALDORF CHICKEN SALAD

The original Waldorf salad, created in 1893 at the Waldorf Hotel in New York City, did not have chunks of chicken, but we think it's a perfectly acceptable face-lift for an old classic.

Mix together 1 pound cooked chicken torn in small pieces; 2 diced celery ribs; 1 crisp cored and diced apple; ½ cup chopped, toasted pecans; ½ cup dried currants; and 1 tablespoon capers in a large bowl. Add ½ cup mayonnaise and the juice of 1 lemon and fold together with a rubber spatula. Season with salt and freshly ground black pepper. Before serving, garnish with chopped fresh chives.—*serves 4*

*Lobster Salad*

## LEMON-MAYO POTATO SALAD ⊱ serves 6

Assembling the salad while the potatoes are still warm allows them to absorb the flavors of all the fixin's.

2–3 pounds potatoes,
   any variety
Salt
1 cup mayonnaise, or more
2–3 tablespoons sour cream
Zest of 1 lemon
Juice of 1 lemon
¼ cup extra-virgin olive oil
Freshly ground black pepper
3–4 scallions, trimmed and
   finely chopped
4 bacon strips, cooked and
   crumbled

Peel the potatoes if you use a thick-skinned variety or prefer peeled potatoes in this dish. Put the potatoes in a large pot of generously salted cold water. Bring to a boil over medium-high heat and cook until they are tender, about 20 minutes. Drain and set aside until they are cool enough to handle but still warm.

Slice the potatoes and arrange them on a serving platter. Mix together the mayonnaise, sour cream, and lemon zest in a small bowl. Sprinkle the lemon juice, then drizzle the olive oil over the potatoes. Season with salt and pepper. Spread the mayonnaise mixture over the potatoes. Scatter the scallions and bacon on top.

## OLD-FASHIONED LAYERED POTATO SALAD

To keep the flavors of this classic potato salad from becoming confused, we assemble it in layers. It still tastes familiar and delicious.

To assemble the salad, layer sliced warm potatoes, salt and freshly ground black pepper, a nice drizzle of extra-virgin olive oil, some mayonnaise, finely chopped celery, sliced hard-boiled eggs, chopped scallions or minced red onions, and a little crispy bacon in a large shallow bowl or a platter. Repeat the layers. Make it deliciously decadent.—*make as much as you want*

*Lemon-Mayo Potato Salad*

# Italian Gems

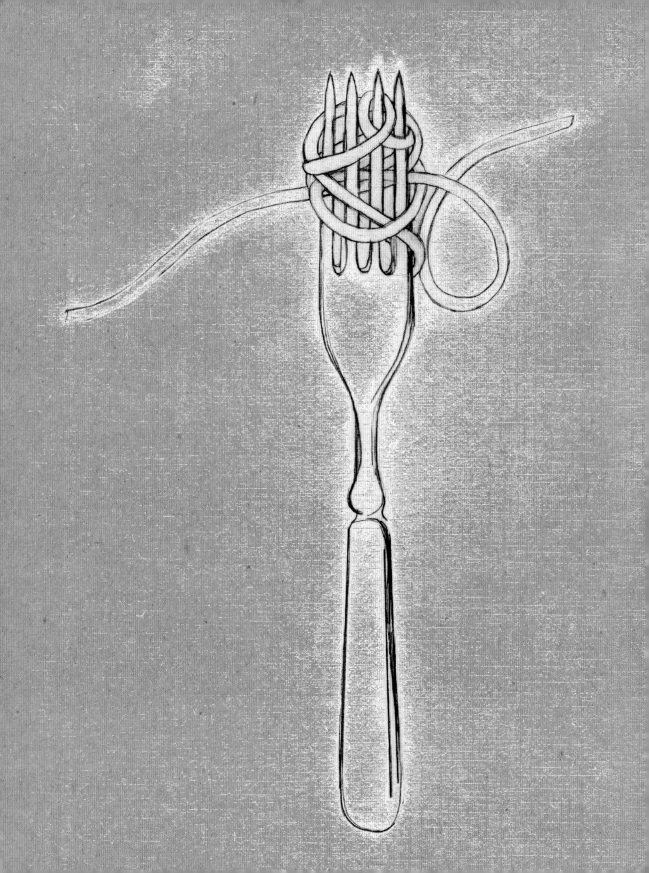

# Cooking Lessons

*The food of Italy appeals to us, seduces us, makes itself indispensable to us, by its sheer sensory confidence—by simply being there, accessible, satisfying, always.*—Colman Andrews

Iт was the 1960s and 1970s when we first began cooking. Young people were curious about the world, and cooking was one of the most interesting ways to learn about it, short of hopping on a plane. There has always been lots of delicious Italian food in restaurants, little corner delis, shops, and in home kitchens. Italians in San Francisco tended to come from Genoa in Liguria and Lucca in Tuscany. In fact, one of us had an Irish-American aunt who married a Genovese, Uncle Fred, who made pesto and delicate ravioli that he rolled out, filled, and shaped on the kitchen table. Everyone was crazy about Italian food.

Many of us first "met" Marcella Hazan through her cookbook *The Classic Italian Cook Book: The Art of Italian Cooking and the Italian Art of Eating,* published in 1973. There weren't many Italian cookbooks around then, so it was snapped up the minute it was in bookstores. Reading through it, you felt as if you had met a great friend and teacher. Cooks used it like a bible, diving in to learn the building blocks of Italian cuisine: learning her besciamella, delicately flavored with grated nutmeg; and Bolognese sauce from the Emilia Romagna, with pork, veal, and beef cooked down into a meltingly subtle sauce. She wrote down all those unwritten recipes that had been passed down solely through word of mouth from mother to daughter. That was her gift to us.

Much of the Italian-American food of the 1970s was a cartoonish reaction to the plenty of America: spaghetti and big meatballs, meat-packed lasagne, thick pizzas heavy with toppings. This food was unknown in Italy (and even today). Then we began traveling, saving our money to buy cheap charter plane tickets and Eurail passes and trained it up and down the boot of Italy. These trips introduced us to the simple elegance of authentic Italian cuisine and, through food, we learned the history, culture, and character of a country. We saw that Italy really had no national cuisine but rather many regional ones— saffron-infused risottos from the Po Valley where rice grew, hand-rolled stuffed pastas from the Emilia-Romagna, delicate crisp fried seafood, *fritto misto*, from the waters of Venice's lagoon. Trekking through Emilia-Romagna, we discovered (for better or worse) balsamic vinegar in Modena and rolled into Parma, birthplace of prosciutto di Parma and Parmigiano-Reggiano.

We actually met Marcella in New York in the 1980s. We cooked a lunch for her at an editorial meeting of *Metropolitan Home* magazine. Thank god we had the good sense not to cook something Italian! Instead we made her a fish stew, a chowder of New England cod, little shrimp, and clams in a rich broth made from all the fish bones. We wanted to cook something American, something regional. We stood in the tiny service kitchen next to where the lunch was held and, through the partially opened door, listened to her speak to the table full of editors. She said, "You have to have the flavor of the finished dish in your mind before you begin cooking so that you will know where you are going and how to get there." We never forgot those important words. She must have seen us standing at the door and graciously asked to meet the cooks who made the fish stew to come out to meet her. Shyly, we took off our aprons and walked out to accept her gracious thank-you. We learned a lesson there, too.

1. SAN MARZANO TOMATOES ⊙
These superior plum tomatoes are
prized for their sweet flavor, low
acidity, firm meaty pulp, deep red
color, and thin skin. Italian San
Marzano tomatoes are grown in the
rich volcanic soil of the Sarno River
valley near Mount Vesuvius. Look
for the words *Pomodoro S. Marzano
dell'Agro Sarnese-Nocerino*. The star-
shaped D.O.P. certification symbol, with the words, *Denominazione
di Origine Protteta* (protected designa-
tion of origin), guarantees they are
true San Marzanos.

2. PEELED WHOLE TOMATOES ⊙ We
follow the advise of our grandmothers, who preferred to hand-crush
or chop whole canned tomatoes for
themselves to be sure that they were
getting top quality and not inferior
tomato "trimming". We sometimes
lift whole tomatoes out of their purée
and slow roast them in the oven with
olive oil and salt and pepper.

3. FINELY CHOPPED/DICED TOMATOES ⊙
Finely chopped peeled tomatoes are
cold-packed in their own juice for a
light and fresh taste with texture.

4. CRUSHED TOMATOES ⊙ Peeled
plum tomatoes are crushed to a fine
consistency then packed in a smooth,
thick, cooked tomato purée.

1.

3.

TA AND SAUCES WITH GREAT FLAVOR

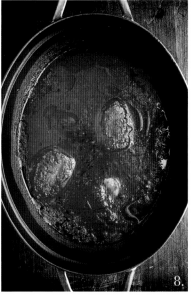

5. TOMATO SAUCE ⊙ Tomato sauce is a smooth cooked purée most often made with other ingredients like garlic, onions, and bell peppers to add flavor. We choose "no salt added", preferring to season the sauce to our own taste.

6. TOMATO PASSATA ⊙ Passata is strained fresh tomato purée. Since it is uncooked, it has a fresher, lighter flavor than tomato sauce. We choose family-owned Mutti products when we can find them. Founded over 150 years ago and based in Italy's Emilia-Romagna region, all Mutti's tomatoes are grown within 100 kilometers of their processing plants.

7. TOMATO PASTE ⊙ Seven kilos of fresh tomatoes make 1 kilo of triple concentrate tomato paste. We prefer convenient tubes over small cans; that way you can squirt out a dollop, recap, and store in the fridge. Available in single, double, and triple concentrate. We use it to add deep flavor and savory umami deliciousness to sauces.

8. CHUNKY HOMEMADE TOMATO SAUCE ⊙ For a simple sauce we simmer a can of peeled whole plum tomatoes; a halved, peeled onion; a clove of garlic; a glug of very good olive oil; and salt and pepper to taste for about 30 minutes. Discard the onions and garlic and crush the tomatoes with the back of a spoon.

TOMATO SAUCE: It's the foundation of many of our beloved Italian dishes. Loose or thick, smooth or chunky, a good tomato sauce should be well balanced, with a rich, round tomato flavor neither too acidic nor too sweet. We keep our tomato sauces simple, simmering them with only onions and garlic. We soften their acidity and round out their flavor with butter or a good olive oil. On occasion, we'll add a pinch or two of sugar to balance acidity. (If it's good enough for the Italians, it's good enough for us.) The sauces below are interchangeable. They're so simple, you're certain to land on one with a consistency just right for you. We use them for pasta pomodoro; saucing polenta, ravioli, or gnocchi (page 231); braising pork, chicken, or turkey (page 237); and sometimes poach eggs in them.

## SIMPLE TOMATO SAUCE I ☞ makes about 8 cups

6 cups passata di pomodoro
    (strained tomatoes) or
    tomato purée
1 medium yellow onion,
    peeled and halved
2–3 garlic cloves, crushed
4–6 tablespoons extra-virgin
    olive oil
Salt and freshly ground
    black pepper

Put the tomatoes into a heavy medium pot, rinsing out the containers with about 4 cups water and adding it to the pot. Add the onions, garlic, and olive oil to the pot, and season to taste with salt and pepper. Gently simmer over medium-low heat for about 1 hour for a thin, loose sauce or 2–3 hours for a richer, thicker consistency. Adjust the seasonings and add more olive oil to round out the flavors, if you like. Discard the onions and garlic before using.

## SIMPLE TOMATO SAUCE II ☞ makes about 3 cups

One 28-ounce can crushed
    tomatoes
1 medium yellow onion,
    peeled and halved
1 garlic clove, crushed
4–6 tablespoons butter
Salt and freshly ground
    black pepper

Put the tomatoes into a medium saucepan. Rinse the can with about 1 cup water to get the remaining tomatoes out and pour this into the pan. Add the onions, garlic, and butter and season with salt and pepper. Simmer over medium-low heat, stirring occasionally, until the sauce thickens a bit, 30–60 minutes. Adjust the seasonings and add more butter for a softer, rounder flavor, if you like. Discard the onions and garlic before using.

## RAW TOMATO SAUCE ✎ makes about 4 cups

Use the juiciest, sweetest summer tomatoes you can find for this light, fresh sauce, and toss it with ½ pound of well-drained hot spaghetti and lots of freshly grated Parmigiano-Reggiano. Or use it to spoon onto Pizza Dough (page 188); over poached, fried, or scrambled eggs; or on grilled fish, chicken, or zucchini; then add a flourish of olive oil and fresh herbs.

1½–2 pounds ripe tomatoes, halved
1–2 garlic cloves, finely grated
½ cup passata di pomodoro, or strained tomatoes
4–6 tablespoons extra-virgin olive oil
1 pinch of crushed red pepper flakes
Salt and freshly ground black pepper

Grate the fleshy sides of the tomatoes on the large holes of a box grater into a big bowl. Discard the skins. Add the garlic, passata, oil, and crushed red pepper flakes, and season to taste with salt and pepper.

## FRESH TOMATO & BASIL SAUCE ✎ makes 2–3 cups

This sauce has more body than the raw tomato sauce above, but is just as dependent on ripe tomatoes in season for its sweet, summery flavor. When the fresh basil hits the hot oil, a rush of basil fragrance fills the air. So much flavor with so few ingredients.

½ cup extra-virgin olive oil
4 garlic cloves, peeled
1 large bunch fresh basil, leaves chopped
6 large ripe tomatoes, cored, halved, squeezed of seeds and juice, and chopped
Salt and freshly ground black pepper

Heat the oil in a medium skillet over medium heat. Add the garlic and cook until it softens and turns a little golden, about 3 minutes. Remove the garlic and discard.

Carefully add all the basil to the hot oil in the skillet. It will immediately give a rush of fragrance. Quickly add the tomatoes and stir until the sauce is just heated through, 2–3 minutes. Season to taste with salt and pepper. Serve sauce over cooked pasta.

*Facing page, clockwise from top left: tomatoes for grating; grating tomatoes; grated raw tomatoes; Raw Tomato Sauce tossed with hot spaghetti*

## RAGÙ BOLOGNESE ☞ makes about 6 cups

Like many long-simmered sauces, this one, perhaps the most delicious of all the Italian meat sauces, is more flavorful and balanced the following day (see illustrations on pages 162–163).

2 tablespoons butter

2 tablespoons extra-virgin olive oil

1 medium yellow onion, peeled and finely chopped

2 small celery ribs, finely diced

1 carrot, peeled and finely diced

2 ounces prosciutto di Parma, finely chopped

¾ pound ground beef chuck

¾ pound ground pork

Salt and freshly ground black pepper

½ whole nutmeg, finely grated

½ cup dry white wine

1 cup whole milk, hot

One 28-ounce can tomato purée

1 cup chicken or beef stock

Heat the butter and oil together in a heavy large pot over medium heat. Add the onions, celery, and carrots (1) and cook, stirring often with a wooden spoon, until the vegetables have softened and the onions are translucent, 5–10 minutes (2). Stir in the prosciutto. Add the ground chuck and pork, season to taste with salt and pepper, and cook, breaking up the clumps of meat with the back of the spoon, until the meat is no longer pink, 5–10 minutes (3). Avoid frying or browning the meat.

Season the meat with nutmeg (4). Add the wine to the pot and cook until evaporated, 10–12 minutes. Reduce the heat to medium-low. Add the milk and cook, stirring occasionally, until absorbed, about 20 minutes (5).

Meanwhile, heat the tomato purée and stock together in a saucepan until hot, then add it to the meat (6). Reduce the heat to low and gently simmer, stirring occasionally, until the meat is tender, 5–7 hours (7). Add water if needed to keep the ragù loose and saucy. Season with salt and pepper.

## FETTUCCINE WITH RAGÙ BOLOGNESE

Bring a large pot of water to a boil over high heat and add 1 tablespoon salt. Add 1 pound dried fettuccine to the pot and cook, stirring often, until just tender, about 10 minutes. Meanwhile, heat 4–6 cups Ragù Bolognese in a wide pan over medium heat until gently bubbling. Drain the pasta, reserving 1 cup of the cooking water. Toss the pasta into the ragù, stirring until thoroughly coated. Stir in some of the reserved cooking water to loosen the sauce, if you like. Serve with grated parmigiano.—*serves 4–8*

## LASAGNE BOLOGNESE ➤ serves 8–12

Don't be hesitant to make sheets of Fresh Pasta (page 178) for this noble layered dish. Or, if that seems like a daunting task, buy sheets of fresh pasta at your market. If you've only had those clunky lasagne made with thick sheets of dried pasta, the tenderness of fresh pasta will be a revelation; you'll need only one bite to understand the difference between ordinary and sublime.

2 tablespoons butter
1 tablespoon salt
4–5 cups warm Ragù Bolognese (page 160)
1¼ cups grated Parmigiano-Reggiano
4 cups warm Besciamella (page 167)
1 pound Fresh Pasta (page 178) sheets, cut into 12-inch lengths

Butter a deep 9 × 13-inch baking dish and set aside. Bring a large pot of water to a boil over high heat and add 1 tablespoon salt. Reduce the heat to maintain a gentle boil. Set the prepared baking dish, ragù, parmigiano, and besciamella on a clean work surface at arm's reach from the stove so you can easily assemble the lasagne.

Cover the bottom of the baking dish with a thin layer of the ragù. Cook 1 sheet of the pasta in the boiling water until tender, 1–2 minutes. Using tongs, lift the pasta out of the water, let most of the water drain off, then lay the sheet out flat over the ragù in the bottom of the dish. Repeat with more pasta to cover the ragù with a layer of pasta, trimming the pasta to fit, and patching, if necessary.

Spread 1½ cups of the ragù evenly over the pasta, then sprinkle with ¼ cup of the parmigiano. Add another layer of pasta, cover it with 1½ cups of the besciamella, then sprinkle with more parmigiano. Repeat the layers again. Add the final layer of pasta, cover it with the remaining ragù, then with the remaining besciamella, and sprinkle the last bit of parmigiano on top.

Preheat the oven to 400°F. Bake the lasagne until it is bubbling around the edges and browned on top, about 15 minutes. Do not overcook. Let lasagne rest for at least 15 minutes before serving.

## RICH MEATY TOMATO SAUCE ✒ makes 7–8 quarts

This recipe, similar to ones known in the Italian-American community as "Sunday gravy", makes a big pot of sauce. Just the thing to have burbling away on the stove for Sunday supper, with plenty left over to stash in convenient-size batches in the fridge or freezer. It can be simmered on top of the stove like any big pot of sauce can, but cooked in the oven, the meats essentially braise in the sauce, releasing all their goodness, and the sauce becomes thicker and deeper in color and flavor. We enrich the sauce when it is finished cooking by shredding or chopping the braised meats and returning them to the sauce. When we want a thinner textured sauce, without any loss of flavor, we don't return the meats to the sauce. Like many sauces of this nature, it is more flavorful served a day or two after it is made.

½ cup extra-virgin olive oil
9–12 ounces tomato paste
2 pinches of crushed red pepper flakes
1 cup red wine
Six 28-ounce cans whole, peeled plum tomatoes, crushed
4–5 pound breast of veal, cut in half
One 3-pound beef chuck roast, cut into 2 pieces
2–3 pounds pork spareribs
2 medium yellow onions, peeled and halved lengthwise
6 garlic cloves, thinly sliced
2 bay leaves
Salt and freshly ground black pepper

Heat the oil in a heavy large ovenproof pot with a lid over medium heat. Add the tomato paste and toast it for about 1 minute. Add the crushed red pepper flakes. Stir in the wine and cook for 2–3 minutes. Add the tomatoes and 4 quarts (16 cups) water, rinsing out each can with a little of the water and adding it to the pot. Add the veal, beef, spareribs, onions, garlic, and bay leaves. Season with salt and pepper. (Divide this between 2 pots if you don't have one large enough for the sauce and/or can't fit the pot in the oven.) Bring to a simmer.

Cover the pot and transfer it to the oven. Cook until the meats are very tender and a layer of fat floats on the surface of the sauce, about 4 hours. (Alternately, simmer the sauce on top of the stove over medium-low heat, stirring occasionally, for about 4 hours.)

For a thinner sauce, remove and discard the meat, onions, and bay leaves. For a thicker sauce, use tongs or a slotted spoon to transfer the meat, onions, and bay leaves to a colander set over a bowl. Remove and discard the onions, bay leaves, bones, cartilage, and fat. Pick through the meat and set aside any that still tastes good and is worth returning to the sauce (the beef will probably be too dry). Shred or finely chop the reserved meat and return it to the sauce. Add any juices from the bowl to the pot. Adjust the seasonings. Serve sauce over cooked pasta.

## BESCIAMELLA ☞ makes about 4 cups

Use this classic Italian white sauce for the Lasagne Bolognese (page 165).

8 tablespoons butter
½ cup flour
4 cups hot milk
½ cup grated Parmigiano-
  Reggiano, optional
¼–½ teaspoon finely
  grated nutmeg
Salt

Melt the butter in a heavy medium saucepan over medium-low heat. Add the flour and cook for 1½–2 minutes, stirring constantly with a wooden spoon to prevent it from taking on any color whatsoever. Gradually add the hot milk in a slow, steady stream, stirring constantly with a whisk to prevent lumps. Increase the heat to medium and cook the sauce, stirring constantly with a wooden spoon, until it has the consistency of very thick cream, 10–15 minutes. Remove the pan from the heat.

Stir in the cheese, if using, and season with nutmeg and salt to taste. Strain the sauce through a sieve if it is lumpy. Lay a sheet of plastic wrap directly on the surface of the besciamella to keep it warm until ready to use and to prevent a skin from forming.

*Overleaf: left, Rich Meaty Tomato Sauce (thinner, less meaty version); right, Rich Meaty Tomato Sauce*

## A SIMPLE, RICH, SUNDAY SUGO ☞ makes a big potful

When it has been nothing but frigid temperatures with snow and sleet, or raining cats and dogs, we make a big pot of our Sunday sugo with tomato-braised pork ribs, short ribs, and sausages. Simple as that, and the sauce lasts us all week.

4 country pork ribs
2 meaty beef short ribs
   on the bone
3 Italian sausages
Salt and freshly ground
   black pepper
½ cup extra-virgin olive oil
2 medium yellow onions,
   peeled and chopped
4 garlic cloves, thinly sliced
1 pinch of crushed red
   pepper flakes
3 tablespoons tomato paste
1 cup red wine
One 28-ounce can crushed
   plum tomatoes
One 24.5-ounce jar passata di
   pomodoro or tomato purée

Preheat the oven to 325°F. Pat the pork ribs, short ribs, and sausages dry with paper towels, then season with salt and pepper. Heat the oil in a heavy large ovenproof pot with a lid over medium-high heat. Cook the meat in batches until browned on all sides, about 10 minutes per batch. When it is browned, transfer the meat to a plate and set aside.

Reduce the heat to medium. Add the onions, garlic, and crushed red pepper flakes to the pot and cook, stirring often, until soft, about 10 minutes. Push the onions and garlic out to the edges of the pot. Increase the heat to medium-high and add the tomato paste to the center of the pot. "Toast" the tomato paste for about 2 minutes. Push the paste out to the edges of the pot. Add the wine, stirring with a wooden spoon to loosen any browned bits stuck to the bottom of the pot. Cook until the wine is reduced by half, about 5 minutes. Add the crushed tomatoes and passata, rinsing out the can and jar with some cold water (about ½ cup is fine) and add it to the pot. Return the meat and any accumulated juices to the pot. When the sauce begins to bubble, cover the pot, and transfer it to the oven.

Cook the sauce until the meats are very tender and a layer of fat floats on the surface, 2–4 hours. Alternately, you can cook the sauce on top of the stove over low heat with the pot partially covered, stirring occasionally, until the meats are tender, 2–4 hours.

Use tongs or a slotted spoon to transfer the meats from the pot to a wide dish or baking sheet. Remove and discard all the bones, cartilage, and extra fat from the meat. Tear the pork and beef into meaty chunks and slice the sausages. Return the meats to the sauce. Adjust the seasonings. Serve over cooked pasta.

## DECONSTRUCTED LASAGNE BOLOGNESE

Sometimes we defrost a batch of Ragù Bolognese (page 160) and a few frozen sheets of Fresh Pasta (page 178) stashed in the back of the freezer to make some Loose Ravioli (page 180). All that is left to do is to whip up some Besciamella (page 167) and grate a little Parmigiano-Reggiano. Then, before we can say "How about a deconstructed lasagne bolognese?" we are sitting down to the best lunch in town (if we do say so ourselves).

## PASTA WITH TUNA, GREEN OLIVES & GREEN BEANS

We keep good jars of tuna packed in olive oil in our pantry. The best ones are albacore, ventresca (Italian tuna belly), ventrèche (the same, but French), and bonito (a dark-fleshed tuna variety from Spain). They are full of flavor and just perfect for tossing into a tangle of pappardelle with Spanish anchovy-stuffed olives (another Canal House pantry staple), green beans, extra-virgin olive oil, salt, and freshly ground black pepper. Keep it simple!

## ESCAROLE, PROSCIUTTO & BURRATA PIZZA

We don't feel one bit guilty on cold mornings when we crank up the oven temperature to 500°F for the day's lunch—it takes the chill out of the air faster than our temperamental studio thermostat. We make Pizza Dough (page 188) and by noon we are feasting on one of our favorite pizzas—Braised Escarole (page 367), prosciutto, burrata, crushed red pepper flakes, and good olive oil. If we don't have burrata, we use fresh mozzarella instead.

*Overleaf, left page, clockwise from top: Deconstructed Lasagne Bolognese; Escarole, Prosciutto & Burrata Pizza; Pasta with Tuna, Green Olives & Green Beans; right page, clockwise from top left: Burrata & Toast; Pasta with Raw Tomato Sauce; Peaches & Tomatoes*

## BURRATA & TOAST

Often, our work takes us away from our studio, our homes, our families for way too long. Like Mr. Toad on his wild ride in *The Wind in the Willows*, we are often off driving all over the countryside shooting for one project or another. It's usually fun, and certainly interesting, but every time we return, we're happy just to be back and to ease into our daily routine. Who can remember what's stashed in the studio's fridge, let alone if it's still good? On our way into work, we'll make a quick stop at the market and pick up something easy to make for lunch, like this. Garlic-rubbed toast and luscious burrata, both drizzled with really good Italian extra-virgin olive oil and sprinkled with Maldon salt and coarsely ground black pepper, is a simple and perfect welcome home for us.

## PASTA WITH RAW TOMATO SAUCE

When summer tomatoes are ripe and so plentiful we practically have to kick them out of the way, we cut them in half horizontally and grate the flesh side of the tomatoes on the large holes of a box grater, discarding the skins. We strain the pulp to remove the seeds, fill resealable plastic bags with the sauce along with a few fresh basil leaves, then into the freezer they go. We use the raw sauce throughout the year, and amazingly, it tastes as fresh as the day we make it. Use this pure sauce or our other Raw Tomato Sauce (page 159) and toss it with hot rigatoni, lots of grated Parmigiano-Reggiano, some salt and freshly ground black pepper, and a good drizzle of extra-virgin olive oil.

## PEACHES & TOMATOES

White peaches have a very short season, so we gorge while we can. We like to pair them with peeled wedges of ripe tomatoes and the sheerest slices of prosciutto di Parma, then drizzle everything with a very good extra-virgin olive oil and add a little cracked black pepper.

## PESTO ↬ makes about 1 cup

This fragrant sauce is more flavorful and the texture silkier when the tender basil leaves, garlic, and pine nuts are crushed together until smooth (crushing releases the essential oils) with a mortar and pestle rather than minced to a smooth purée in a blender. We offer both methods; the choice is yours.

2 garlic cloves, sliced
Coarse sea salt
2 cups tightly packed fresh
  smallest basil leaves
2 tablespoons pine nuts
½ cup finely grated
  Parmigiano-Reggiano
½ cup extra-virgin olive oil

To make pesto with a mortar and pestle: Put the garlic and a large pinch of salt into a mortar and crush to a paste with the pestle. Add the basil, a small handful at a time, bruising, crushing, and stirring it into a wet, green, fine paste. Be patient, this will take longer than you think. Add the pine nuts and a pinch of salt and finely crush them into the paste. Add the parmigiano, stirring and crushing it in. Add the oil in a slow steady stream, stirring with the pestle. The paste will loosen and become a thick spoonable sauce. Adjust the seasonings. Lay a sheet of plastic wrap directly on the surface of the pesto to keep it from oxidizing and losing its bright green color.

To make pesto in a food processor or electric blender: Put the garlic, a pinch of salt, and the pine nuts in the bowl of a food processor fitted with a metal blade or into the blender. Pulse several times or blend to make a paste. Add the basil and, with the motor running, drizzle in the oil until the paste is smooth. Scrape down the sides of the processor or blender with a rubber spatula as needed. Transfer the paste to a bowl and stir in the parmigiano. Adjust the seasonings. Lay a sheet of plastic wrap directly on the surface of the pesto to keep it from oxidizing and losing its bright green color.

## PASTA WITH PESTO

Cook 1 pound dried spaghetti or small square sheets of Fresh Pasta (page 178) in a large pot of boiling salted water over medium-high heat until just cooked through, about 12 minutes for the dry pasta and 1 minute for the fresh pasta. Drain the pasta, reserving ¼ cup of the cooking water. Toss the pasta in a large bowl with the Pesto (above), loosening the sauce with some of the reserved cooking water. Serve with grated Parmigiano-Reggiano, if you like.—*serves 4–6*

*Spaghetti with Pesto*

## FRESH PASTA ↣ makes 1 pound; enough to serve 4–6

Fresh homemade pasta, rolled out with a hand-cranked pasta machine, is easy to do and very gratifying. Follow our step-by-step pictures to help you through the process.

2 cups "00" or unbleached
  all-purpose flour, plus more
  for dusting
4 large eggs
Large pinch of salt

Sift the flour into a medium mixing bowl and make a well in the center of the mound. Add the eggs and salt and beat with a fork (1). Continue gently beating the eggs while gradually stirring in the flour, little by little, from the inside rim of the well. When the dough is too lumpy to work with the fork, turn it out onto a lightly floured surface. Using a bench scraper and your hand (2), knead the shaggy dough into a rough ball. With clean dry hands, knead the dough, dusting it with flour as you work (3), until it becomes a smooth, supple ball and is no longer tacky. Press your thumbs into the center of the dough (4); if the center feels tacky, knead in a little more flour. Wrap the dough in plastic wrap and let it rest at room temperature for at least 30 minutes and up to several hours.

Cut the dough into quarters (5) or eighths and keep it covered until ready to use. Working with one piece of dough at a time, flatten the dough a bit into a rectangle, then feed the narrow end through the smooth cylinders of a hand-crank pasta machine set on the widest setting. Fold the flattened dough into thirds like a business letter (6). Feed the narrow end of the dough through the cylinders (7). Do this two or three times to make the dough uniform. Decrease the setting on the machine by one notch and feed the narrow end of the dough through the cylinders again. Repeat this process, decreasing the setting by one notch each time. Roll the pasta as thin as you like; you do not have to roll to the thinnest setting (8). Lay the sheets of pasta out on a lightly floured surface and cover with damp kitchen towels to keep them from drying out until you're ready to cut them.

CUTTING PASTA: Cut the sheets crosswise into 12-inch lengths for lasagne (page 165) and 4–5-inch squares for loose ravioli (page 180). Or run the sheets of pasta through your pasta machine's attachment for cutting sheets into strands. Dust pasta strands with flour to keep them from sticking (9).

## LOOSE RAVIOLI

These are essentially uncrimped ravioli made with large square sheets of fresh pasta. Graceful and sensuous, they are easier to assemble than closed ravioli. Have your filling ready before cooking the pasta so it is hot when you make the ravioli. Work quickly so the pasta is hot when served. Bring a large pot of salted water to a boil over high heat. Cook 4–5-inch square sheets of Fresh Pasta (page 178), a few sheets at a time, until tender, 1–3 minutes. Using a slotted spatula, transfer pasta to a large bowl, letting most of the water drain off. Toss with some softened butter or olive oil to coat the sheets and keep them from sticking. Then use as directed in the recipes that follow to finish making the loose ravioli.—*make as much as you want*

## OYSTER MUSHROOMS & LEMON-RICOTTA LOOSE RAVIOLI ☞ serves 4

Oyster mushrooms are delicate, and meaty when cooked. If you cannot find them at your market, you *could* serve this dish without them—the ricotta filling has plenty of flavor (see illustrations on pages 182–183).

For THE FILLING:
1 cup fresh ricotta or fromage blanc
6 tablespoons softened butter
Finely grated zest of ½ lemon
Salt and freshly ground black pepper
1 large spring onion or medium yellow onion, trimmed, peeled, and finely chopped
2 scallions, trimmed and finely chopped
¾ pound oyster mushrooms, divided into 4 "clumps"
½ cup heavy cream, plus a splash
Parmigiano-Reggiano

For the filling, mix the ricotta, 1 tablespoon of the butter, and lemon zest together in a mixing bowl. Season with salt and a big pinch of pepper. Divide into quarters and set aside (1).

Melt 4 tablespoons of the butter in a large skillet over medium heat. Add the spring onions and scallions (2) and gently cook until soft and translucent but not browned, about 10 minutes. Add the mushroom clumps (3) to the skillet (4) and cook until tender, about 20 minutes. Season with salt and pepper. Add the ½ cup of cream and simmer until the sauce thickens a bit and the mushrooms are soft, about 5 minutes. Finely grate some parmigiano over the mushrooms. Cover and reduce the heat to low.

Prepare the loose ravioli following the directions above, adding a splash of cream to the bowl (5).

For each serving, put a small knob of the remaining 1 tablespoon butter in a warm, deep plate and place 1 sheet of the hot pasta on top of each. Put a big spoonful of the seasoned ricotta on each sheet of pasta. Place one clump of mushrooms along with the onions and some of the cream sauce on top (6), then

*continued*

8 sheets Loose Ravioli
(page 180)

partially cover with another sheet of hot pasta. Spoon a little more sauce on top of each ravioli and add a shower of grated parmigiano. Garnish each serving with a sprig of fresh parsley (7), if you like.

## DECONSTRUCTED CARBONARA

Cook 2 cups diced pancetta in a medium skillet over medium heat, stirring occasionally, until browned and crisp, 8–10 minutes. Add 4 tablespoons butter to the skillet and keep warm over low heat. Prepare 8 sheets of Loose Ravioli (page 180). For each serving, divide 4 sheets of pasta between four warm, deep plates. Divide 8 warm poached eggs (page 16) between each plate, placing 2 eggs on each sheet of pasta. Spoon the pancetta and some of the butter over the top of each. Drape another sheet of pasta over the filling and spoon a little more butter on top. Season with a little salt and some freshly ground black pepper. Use a vegetable peeler to shave lots of pecorino over each loose ravioli.—*serves 4*

## BUTTERNUT SQUASH & CANDIED BACON LOOSE RAVIOLI ☞ serves 4

FOR THE FILLING:
1/2 pound slab bacon,
   trimmed of rind and excess
   layer of fat, and cubed
1/4 cup dark brown sugar
2 cups 1/4 inch-thick bite-size
   slices butternut squash
Salt
8 tablespoons (1 stick) butter
1 handful fresh parsley
   leaves, chopped
Freshly ground black pepper

8 sheets Loose Ravioli
   (page 180)
Parmigiano-Reggiano

For the filling, preheat the oven to 400°F. Toss the bacon with the brown sugar in a bowl. Spread the bacon out on a foil-lined baking sheet. Bake until the pieces are glazed and crisp yet meaty, about 20 minutes. Set aside.

Put the squash into a large skillet of salted water, bring to a gentle boil over medium heat, and cook until just tender and not broken, 5–10 minutes. Drain in a colander. Melt the butter in the same skillet over medium heat. When it begins to foam, add the squash and cook until just warmed through. Add the parsley and season with salt and pepper. Keep warm over low heat.

Prepare the loose ravioli following the directions on page 180.

For each serving, divide 4 sheets of the pasta between four warm, deep plates. Spoon some of the squash and the butter in the center of the pasta. Add 1–2 spoonfuls of the candied bacon. Drape another sheet of pasta over the filling and spoon a little more butter on top. Grate cheese over the pasta.

*Overleaf, left page from top: ricotta mixture; spring and yellow onions; oyster mushrooms; adding mushrooms to the onions; right page from top: cooked pasta sheets; filling ravioli; Oyster Mushrooms & Lemon-Ricotta Loose Ravioli*

5.

6.

7.

## RISOTTO BIANCO WITH PRESERVED LEMON ⏵ serves 4

Risotto is traditionally made with the short-grain rice of the Po Valley. There are three main rice varieties: arborio, with its large plump grains that produce a starchy risotto; carnaroli, smaller grains that produce a looser (wavy) risotto; and vialone nano, with firm grains that cook up soft with a kernel of chewiness in the center, just the way Italians like it (see illustrations on pages 186–187).

4–5 cups chicken broth or water

4 tablespoons butter

1 small yellow onion, peeled and finely chopped

2 tablespoons finely chopped preserved lemon rind, optional

1 cup arborio, carnaroli, or vialone nano rice

1 cup white wine

½ cup grated Parmigiano-Reggiano

Salt and freshly ground black pepper

Bring the broth to a gentle simmer in a medium pot over medium heat. Reduce the heat to low and keep the broth hot.

Melt 3 tablespoons of the butter in a heavy medium pot over medium-high heat. Add the onions and cook, stirring with a wooden spoon, until soft and translucent, about 3 minutes (1). Stir in the preserved lemon rind, if using, then add the rice (2), stirring until everything is coated with butter. Pour in the wine (3) and cook, stirring frequently, until the rice has absorbed it.

Add ½ cup of the hot broth, stirring constantly to keep the rice from sticking to the bottom of the pot (4). Push any rice that crawls up the sides back down into the liquid. When the rice has absorbed all the broth, add another ½ cup of broth. Continue this process until you have added most of the broth, about 20 minutes.

Taste the rice; it is done when it is tender with a firm center. The fully cooked risotto should be creamy but not soupy. Add the parmigiano and the remaining 1 tablespoon of butter and stir until it has melted into the rice (5). Taste, and season with salt and pepper, if needed.

## RISOTTO WITH CHANTERELLES

Midsummer through early fall, we forage for chanterelles in the woods and at farmers' markets. Their meaty texture and fragrance of moss and apricot make them one of our favorite wild mushrooms. If you cannot find these golden beauties, try this risotto with other sliced mushrooms.

*continued*

Follow the directions for Risotto Bianco with Preserved Lemon, opposite, adding 4 cups trimmed, cleaned, small or thickly sliced chanterelles with the onions, sautéing them until tender, about 5 minutes. Season with salt and freshly ground pepper, then transfer to a bowl. Melt 2 tablespoons butter in same pot and continue with recipe, omitting the preserved lemon. Stir the mushrooms and onions into the pot just before the last addition of broth.—*serves 4*

## RISOTTO MILANESE ☞ serves 4

Arab traders were exporting rice from Sicily as early as the tenth century, that is, 500 years before it was planted in the Po Valley, now Italy's main rice-growing region. Those traders also brought traditional Arab spices to the area, saffron being one of them. Saffron imbues the rice with a golden glow; that must have thrilled the Milanese. Traditionally, marrow was added to enrich the dish; now pancetta and prosciutto stand in.

4–5 cups chicken broth
$\frac{1}{2}$ teaspoon saffron strands
4 tablespoons butter
1 small yellow onion, peeled and finely chopped
1 garlic clove, minced
2 tablespoons finely chopped prosciutto, optional
1 cup arborio, carnaroli, or vialone nano rice
$\frac{1}{2}$ cup grated Parmigiano-Reggiano
Salt and freshly ground black pepper

Bring the broth to a gentle simmer in a medium pot over medium heat. Reduce heat to low and keep broth hot. Put the saffron into a small bowl, add $\frac{1}{2}$ cup of the hot broth, and set aside to infuse.

Melt 3 tablespoons of the butter in a heavy medium pot over medium-high heat. Add the onions and garlic and cook, stirring with a wooden spoon, until soft and translucent, about 3 minutes. Stir in the prosciutto, then add the rice, stirring until everything is coated with butter.

Add $\frac{1}{2}$ cup of the simmering broth, stirring constantly to keep the rice from sticking to the bottom of the pot. Push any rice that crawls up the sides of the pot back down into the liquid. When the rice has absorbed all the broth, add another $\frac{1}{2}$ cup of the hot broth. Continue this process until you have added half of the broth, then add the saffron-infused broth. Continue adding the broth $\frac{1}{2}$ cup at a time.

The rice is done when it is tender with a firm center, 20–25 minutes. The fully cooked risotto should be creamy but not soupy. Add the parmigiano and the remaining 1 tablespoon of butter. Stir until it has melted into the rice. Season with salt and pepper, if needed.

*Overleaf, left page from top: sautéing onions; adding the rice; adding wine; adding hot broth; right page: Risotto Bianco wtih Preserved Lemon*

1.

3.

PIZZA DOUGH ✒ makes enough to make four 10-inch pizzas

This pizza dough can be made early in the day and left to slowly rise in the refrigerator until the evening; you can even leave it overnight. Use this dough with your own pizza toppings or with any of the following recipes on page 191.

One ¼-ounce envelope active dry yeast (2¼ teaspoons)
3 tablespoons really good extra-virgin olive oil, plus more for the crust
4 cups bread flour, plus more for kneading
2 teaspoons salt, plus more for the crust
Cornmeal

For the dough, dissolve the yeast in ½ cup warm water in a small bowl (1) or in a large liquid measuring cup with a pour spout. Stir in 1¼ cups water and 2 tablespoons of the oil.

Pulse the flour and salt together in a food processor. Pour the yeast mixture through the feed hole in the lid while the processor is running (2) and process until the dough comes together and forms a sticky ball, about 1 minute. Turn the dough out on a floured work surface (3) and briefly knead into a smooth ball. Put the remaining 1 tablespoon oil in a large bowl. Roll the dough around in the bowl until coated all over with oil. Cover the bowl with plastic wrap (4) and let the dough rise in a warm spot until it has doubled in size, about 2 hours (or see headnote).

To make pizzas, divide the dough into 4 equal pieces on a lightly floured surface and shape each into a ball. Place the balls at least 5 inches apart, loosely cover them with a clean, damp kitchen towel, and let them rise until nearly doubled in size, 30–60 minutes.

Place a pizza stone on the upper rack in the oven and preheat the oven to 500°F. Working with one ball at a time, stretch the dough into a 10-inch round on a floured surface (5), letting it rest and relax if resistant. Lay the dough out on a cornmeal-dusted pizza peel or a rimless cookie sheet. Prick the surface with a fork, brush with some oil, and sprinkle with salt (6). Arrange the pizza toppings of your choosing over the dough. Slide the pizza off the peel onto the hot pizza stone in the oven. Bake until the crust is puffed and golden around the edges and the topping is bubbling hot, 6–8 minutes. Use the peel to remove the pizza from the oven.

1.

2.

3.

4.

5.

6.

## MARGHERITA PIZZA

Follow the directions for Pizza Dough (page 188). For each pizza, spoon a thin film (¼–½ cup) Raw Tomato Sauce (page 159) over the prepared pizza dough, leaving about a ½-inch border. Cover with 6–8 slices fresh mozzarella and drizzle with some extra-virgin olive oil. Bake the pizza, then scatter a handful of small fresh basil leaves on top when it comes out of the oven. Cut the pizza into wedges.—*makes one 10-inch pizza*

## WHITE CLAM PIZZA

Heat ¼ cup extra-virgin olive oil; 4–5 thinly sliced, peeled garlic cloves; and 1 or 2 generous pinches of crushed red pepper flakes in a small skillet over medium heat until everything begins to sizzle, 2–3 minutes. Stir in 1 cup drained, canned baby clams and 1 or 2 splashes of the juice from the can, and season with salt to taste. Set aside. Follow the directions for Pizza Dough (page 188). For each pizza, finely grate some Parmigiano-Reggiano over the prepared pizza dough, then spoon a quarter of the seasoned clams evenly over the top. Brush the edges of the dough with more olive oil. Bake the pizza, then drizzle with a little more olive oil when it comes out of the oven. Cut the pizza into wedges.—*makes one 10-inch pizza (and enough sauce for 4 pizzas)*

## CAESAR PIZZA

For the salad, put 1 chopped garlic clove, 3–4 chopped anchovy filets, 1 teaspoon Dijon mustard, and salt and freshly ground black pepper into a medium bowl and mash with a fork into a paste. Stir in the juice of ½ lemon, 5–6 tablespoons extra-virgin olive oil, and ¼ cup finely grated Parmigiano-Reggiano. Adjust the seasonings. Toss the leaves of 2–4 hearts of romaine lettuce with the dressing in the bowl.

For each pizza, spoon a very thin film (about ¼ cup) Raw Tomato Sauce (page 159) over the prepared Pizza Dough (page 188), leaving about ½-inch border. Drizzle with extra-virgin olive oil and finely grate some Parmigiano-Reggiano over the top. Bake the pizza, then arrange some of the dressed salad leaves on top when it comes out of the oven. Garnish the pizza with anchovy filets, if you like, drizzle with olive oil, season with freshly ground black pepper, and scatter more grated parmigiano on top. Cut the pizza into wedges.—*makes 1 pizza (and enough salad for 4 pizzas with some extra to eat on the side)*

*Facing page, clockwise from top left: Margherita Pizza; White Clam Pizza; Caesar Pizza*

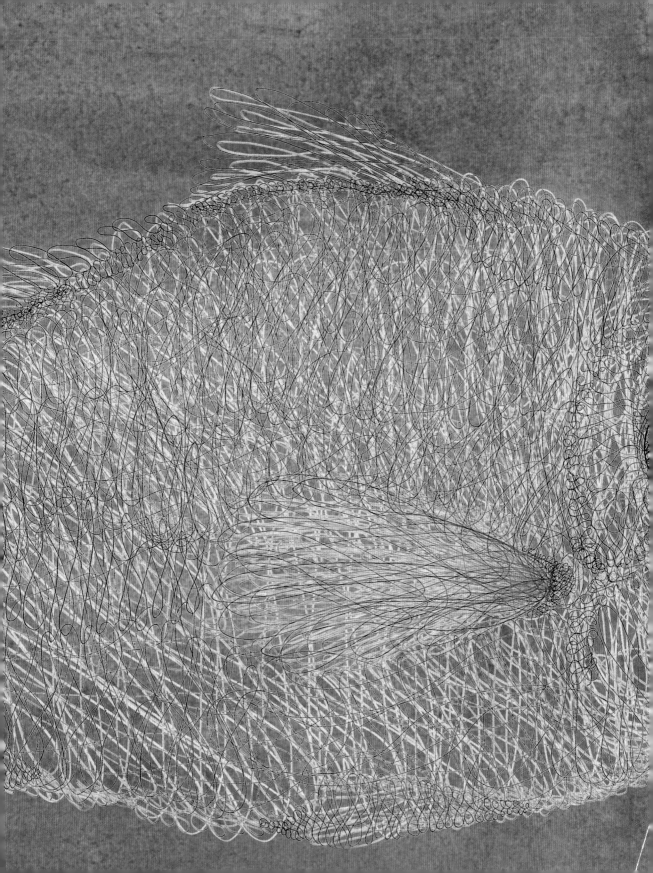

# Gifts from the Sea

*A bird may love a fish, but where would they build a home together?*— Joseph Stein,
*Fiddler on the Roof*

THERE ARE CERTAIN RITUALS WE HAVE WHEN traveling to particular parts of the world, especially those close to the water. Upon arrival, even before we unpack the car or check into our rooms, we head straight out to get a bite of the place.

In San Francisco, it's a mound of sweet, pristine Dungeness crabmeat fresh from the Pacific, buttered slices of chewy San Francisco sourdough, and a glass of crisp, cold California chablis. In Maine, it's a lobster roll from a roadside shack with wooden picnic tables outside. Though a view of the water is great, it is not essential. The soft bun, split on top, buttered, and toasted golden brown, is stuffed with big chunks of lobster salad (mayo, lemon juice, a little chopped celery, s&p). In Brittany, on the west coast of France, we order a *plateau de fruits de mer*. The towering ice-packed platter is covered with langoustine and raw briny oysters, mussels, *coquilles Saint-Jacques* (scallops in their shells), and tiny periwinkles that we lift from their shells with hat pins while sipping glasses of Muscadet or Chablis. When we land in Hawaii, it's poke made with ahi, but it could be mahi mahi. We're just so happy to have landed in paradise. In Barcelona, it's codfish *croquetas, pan con tomate,* and an order of sliced *Ibérico de Bellota* at the counter of a favorite tapas bar, washed down with a cold sparkling cava.

The ritual orients us to that particular place, its people, sounds, smells, and language. It fills our tums and gets us into the swing of things. Until we do this, we haven't really arrived.

Both of us grew up near oceans, albeit on opposite coasts. One spent summers digging for clams on Cape Cod and gathering mussels in Maine, the other eating cioppino, sand-dabs, and cracked Dungeness crab in San Francisco. But now we live in the northeast, in a lush valley on either side of the Delaware River, surrounded by fields and woods. We are lucky to have a couple of excellent seafood markets relatively close by. Over the years we've made friends with the fishmongers and seek out their advice. After all, really good seafood is really expensive, and we want to be sure. So we ask a lot of questions: what's good; what's freshest; is it wild or farm-raised; how was it caught; will frozen squid be tough (no, freezing makes it more tender); when will softshell crabs be coming in; can we get fish heads to make stock; what's that piece of sable like and how should we cook it.

We had the experience once of spending a small fortune for fish we bought at a highly regarded fancy food market in New York City, only to throw it out when we got back to the studio because it smelled so foul when we opened the package. On the other hand, when our fishmonger has the most beautiful, pristine filets of Grey sole, we gulp, then shell out the big bucks and buy two. You can bet we cook them carefully. And simply, just dusted with flour and cooked in bubbling hot, salted butter, a squeeze of lemon juice at the end. It would be a waste to mask its delicate flavor.

Whether you live by the ocean or far from it, seek out the best seafood you can afford, and don't be afraid to ask questions. Any good fishmonger will be glad to have the exchange.

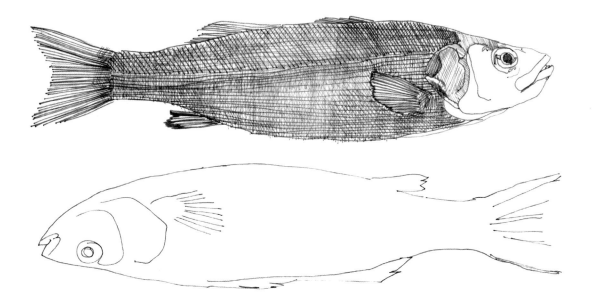

OMEGA-3 IN FISH: Omega-3 unsaturated fatty acids, found in most fish, are thought to reduce inflammation throughout the body, decrease triglycerides, lower blood pressure slightly, reduce blood clotting, decrease stroke and heart failure risk, reduce irregular heartbeats, and reduce chronic diseases involving the immune system. They encourage healthy brain function, help prevent depression, and ward off age-related macular degeneration. Sounds like snake oil, but it's fish oil! High in omega-3 fatty acids with no to low levels of mercury, sardines, mackerel, sablefish, herring, anchovies, bonito, and all kinds of salmon are great choices.

BUYING FISH: Search out a good fishmonger; they are specialists. A quality fish market will never smell "fishy". Don't be shy; ask if you can give the fish a sniff. It's the best test for freshness. Be an informed, responsible shopper; think sustainable. Ask a few questions—where, when, and how the fish was caught, and by whom. First choice is to buy local; if that's not available, buy American. We have the most highly regulated fisheries in the world with good sustainable practices. Buy wild over farmed fish. Whole fresh fish should have shiny metallic skin, clear eyes, and firm, taut flesh (1). Fresh filets and steaks should have translucent-looking dense flesh with no fissures. We buy frozen whole shrimp, well packaged with no sign of freezer burn. As for frozen fish, we demur and reach for a can of tuna instead.

WILD VS. FARMED: This has been a controversial subject with three main concerns: environmental, health of the fish, and comparative nutrition values. It is common sense to prefer wild fish caught with sustainable practices. And we do buy wild fish when we can find it and when our pocketbooks can afford it. Fish farming has been practiced, in some parts of the world, for hundreds of years. Today, half of the seafood eaten in the United States is farmed. To help meet the growing global demand for seafood, aquaculture is growing fast. When good practices are used, it's possible to farm seafood in a way that has very little impact on the environment. You can help shape the demand for, and ultimately the supply of fish that's been caught or farmed in environmentally sustainable ways by asking this simple but important question at your seafood market, grocery store, or restaurant: Do they sell sustainable seafood?

CENTER CUTS: A fairly standard restaurant portion of fish weighs 6 ounces. Steaks are portions of fish that have been cut straight through the body vertically rather than horizontally along the length. Often, but not always, they include a section of backbone, like salmon steaks do. Fish filets are cut along the entire side of the fish, removing the flesh from the spine and most of the rest of the bones (2). We request the "center cut" of fish, steaks or filets (3), because they are the meatiest and most uniform in size. Ask your fishmonger to remove the pin bones from filets. Or you can do it yourself: drape a section of filet, skin-side down, over an upside down bowl. The convex shape of the bowl will push the white pin bones out, making them more visible and easier to remove. Use a pair of tweezers or pliers to pull them out (4).

*Overleaf, clockwise from top left: scraping off fish scales; center-cut salmon filet;*
*a whole Alaskan Copper River King salmon*

1.

2.

3.

4.

1. SALMON ⊙ This fine fish may just be America's favorite. Its color can range from ivory (King salmon) to deep "salmon" red (Sockeye salmon). The main varieties of Pacific salmon are: King, Sockeye, Coho, Pink, and Chum. Atlantic salmon, wild and farmed, is from the ocean whose name it bears. We choose wild over farmed, but sometimes availability and price preclude this. Trusting your fishmonger to offer the best and most sustainable fish is the best answer. This fatty fish (in the best sense of the word) is rich in omega-3 fatty acids. Salmon has a sweet, fatty, mild ocean flavor with a creamy, firm texture. Available year-round. Grill, poach, bake, or pan roast, or serve raw or cured.

2. COD ⊙ Mild, sweet, clean tasting, with a coarse, large flake, and a silky, gelatinous texture. Poach, pan roast, or stew.

3. FLOUNDER ⊙ Flat fish (often bearing the name sole) trawled from sandy ocean bottoms. Available year-round. Mild, sweet, with delicate flavor and refined, firm, fine texture. Cook on the bone or sauté filets.

4. TUNA ⊙ Lean and meaty tasting, choose line-caught tuna varieties: yellowfin (ahi), skipjack, or albacore. (Bluefin is endangered.) Available year-round. Pan roast, grill, or poach rare, or serve raw or cured.

TAINABLE SEAFOOD

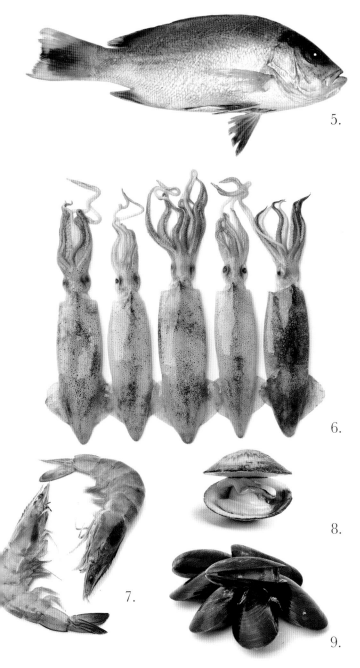

5.

6.

7.

8.

9.

5. RED SNAPPER ⊙ Line-caught in the Gulf of Mexico and southern U.S. Atlantic. Available spring through summer. Weighs 1–5 pounds; sweet, mild, yet complex flavor with a juicy, fine-flaked texture. Very versatile— sauté, grill, bake, braise, or serve raw.

6. SQUID / CALAMARI ⊙ Each calamari measures 3–5 inches long. Available year-round fresh or cleaned and frozen. Don't shy away from frozen as freezing tenderizes the chewy flesh and relieves you of the trouble of cleaning them. Delicious deep fried, stewed, or stuffed and braised.

7. SHRIMP ⊙ We prefer head and shell-on fresh or frozen wild shrimp. We use the shells to make a flavorful shrimp stock. Shrimp has its eco-problems: by-catch fish inadvertently scooped up (young hake, for example). Intensive shrimp farming can create polluted conditions. We refer to the Monterey Bay Aquarium Seafood Watch (seafood.org), which keeps a vigilant eye on fishing and farming practices.

8. CLAMS ⊙ Farmed or harvested wild, clams are available on both coasts year-round. 1½-inch little necks, briny and sweet with a firm chewy texture, are our favorite to serve raw, steamed, fried, baked, or poached in broth.

9. MUSSELS ⊙ Cultivated (or farmed) mussels are small, clean, sweet, tender, and virtually beardless. Available year-round. Steam, sauté, bake, or poach.

## POACHED SALMON WITH LEMON-BUTTER SAUCE ☞ serves 4

Salmon bathed in lemon-butter sauce with poached scallions and little boiled potatoes is kinda fancy, but actually very simple to make. This sauce makes anything taste luxurious.

FOR THE LEMON-BUTTER SAUCE
2 large egg yolks
8 tablespoons cold European-
    style high-fat butter, cut
    into 12 pieces
1 tablespoon fresh
    lemon juice
Salt

FOR THE SALMON AND POTATOES
12 small new potatoes
Salt
2 tablespoons butter
Freshly ground black pepper
1½ pounds center-cut wild
    salmon filets, cut into
    4 equal pieces
16 scallions, trimmed

For the lemon-butter sauce, whisk together the egg yolks and 1 tablespoon water in a heavy medium saucepan. Cook over low heat, whisking constantly so the yolks don't "scramble". Add the butter one piece at a time, whisking until it has melted into the sauce before adding the next. If the sauce begins to separate, remove the pan from the heat and whisk in a piece of the cold butter to cool the sauce down, and it should come back together. Return the pan to the heat and continue whisking in the butter one piece at time until it has all been incorporated. Remove the pan from the heat and whisk in the lemon juice. Season with salt. Keep the sauce warm by setting the pan in a larger pan of hot water. Cover with a piece of plastic wrap, pressing it directly on the surface of the sauce to prevent a skin from forming.

Put the potatoes into a medium pot and cover with cold water. Add 1 tablespoon salt. Bring to a boil over medium-high heat. Reduce the heat to a simmer and cook until the potatoes are tender when pierced with a paring knife. Drain; peel the potatoes, if you like. Return the potatoes to the pot, add the butter, and season with pepper. Cover and keep warm over lowest heat.

Place the salmon skin-side down in a deep, wide, medium pan. Add enough cold water to cover the fish by ½ inch. Season generously with salt. Cover and bring to a simmer over medium heat. Add the scallions. Reduce the heat to medium-low. Gently poach the salmon, uncovered, until barely opaque in the center, about 6 minutes, depending on the thickness.

Using a fish turner or slotted spatula, transfer the scallions and salmon, skin-side up, to paper towels. Gently peel off and discard the skin. Transfer the fish to individual plates, skin-side down. Add the potatoes and scallions. Spoon the lemon-butter sauce over the fish.

## BRAISED SALMON WITH ESCAROLE & PEAS ☞ serves 4

Escarole, a type of chicory, has rounded, ruffled leaves, a pale green center with darker green edges, and an intriguing, mild bitterness. Pairing it with the sweetness of English peas makes a perfectly balanced "sauce".

Four 6-ounce, center-cut
  salmon filets (each about
  1½ inches thick)
1 cup dry vermouth or
  dry white wine
Salt
2 cups shelled fresh
  (or frozen) peas
1 head escarole, trimmed,
  leaves separated
  and washed
4 tablespoons butter,
  cut into pieces
½ cup heavy cream
Freshly ground black pepper
Minced fresh chives, for garnish

Place the salmon skin-side down in a deep, wide, medium skillet. Add the vermouth and ½ teaspoon salt. Cover the skillet and bring to a simmer over medium heat.

Add the peas and escarole to the skillet. Reduce the heat to medium-low. Gently braise the salmon, uncovered, until just cooked through and barely opaque in the center, about 6 minutes, depending on the thickness. Using a fish turner or slotted spatula, transfer the salmon to a plate, skin-side up, and cover the plate with plastic wrap to keep the fish warm and moist.

Use the spatula or a slotted spoon to transfer the escarole and peas equally between 4 warm plates.

Bring the pan juices in the skillet to a gentle boil over medium-high heat. Whisk in the butter, then the cream. Simmer the sauce, whisking often, until slightly thickened, about 2 minutes.

Uncover the salmon and peel off and discard the skin. Place the salmon skin-side down on the plates with the vegetables. Spoon the warm sauce over the fish. Season with salt and pepper. Garnish with chives, if you like.

POACHED SEA BASS IN TOMATO BROTH 🐟 serves 4

This preparation is both delicate and full of flavor. Based on an Italian recipe called *acqua pazza* ("crazy water"), it refers to both the dish and the poaching broth, which is stained red from tomatoes and aromatic with garlic and herbs. We like to use black sea bass or red snapper, but any non-oily white fish will do nicely.

1 pound ripe plum tomatoes
¼ cup extra-virgin olive oil, plus more for drizzling
4 garlic cloves, thinly sliced
¼ teaspoon crushed red pepper flakes
½ cup dry white wine
3 sprigs fresh oregano
1 bunch parsley
Salt and freshly ground black pepper
4 black sea bass or red snapper filets, about 4 ounces each

Quarter the tomatoes lengthwise. Working over a sieve set over a bowl, scoop out the tomato seeds with your fingers. Put the tomatoes in the bowl with any of the strained juice and discard the seeds in the sieve.

Heat the olive oil in a large sauté pan over medium-low heat. Add the sliced garlic and crushed red pepper flakes, and cook until the oil is fragrant and well-flavored yet the garlic remains pale blonde, 3–4 minutes. Add the tomatoes and their juice, the wine, oregano, half of the bunch of parsley, and 4 cups water. Increase the heat to high and bring to a boil. Reduce the heat to medium and simmer the broth until it is slightly reduced, 15–20 minutes.

Chop the remaining parsley leaves, discarding the stems. Add the parsley, a generous pinch of salt, and some pepper to the broth. Season the fish filets with salt and place them skin-side up in the simmering broth (the fish will not be submerged). Cook until the fish is opaque, about 3 minutes. Remove the pan from the heat. Remove and discard the sprigs of oregano and parsley.

Use a fish turner or slotted spatula to transfer the fish, skin-side down, onto a deep serving platter or 4 deep plates. Season the broth to taste. Spoon the tomatoes and broth over the fish and drizzle with olive oil.

## COLD POACHED SHRIMP ☞ serves 4

This classic preparation relies on a few simple steps: using shrimp shells to make a flavorful poaching liquid; poaching the shrimp off the heat to keep them tender and succulent, and deveining the shrimp after poaching to avoid that "butterflied" look.

1 pound jumbo shell-on
   shrimp (about 16)
2 cups dry white wine
2 tablespoons salt
1 tablespoon black
   peppercorns
3 sprigs fresh thyme
1 small bunch parsley
1 yellow onion, peeled
   and sliced
1 celery stalk, sliced
1 bay leaf
Cocktail Sauce or
   Tartar Sauce
   (recipes below)
1 lemon, quartered

Peel the shrimp, reserving the shells, but leave the tail shell on. The shrimp look prettier with their pink fantails, and the tails make them easier to hold.

Put the shrimp shells, wine, salt, peppercorns, thyme, parsley, onions, celery, bay leaf, and 4 cups cold water into a medium pot. Bring to a boil over high heat. Reduce the heat to medium-low and simmer about 20 minutes. Strain the stock, return it to the pot, and bring to a simmer over medium heat.

Add the peeled shrimp to the pot and turn off the heat. Cover the pot and let the shrimp poach until just cooked through, about 2 minutes. Drain the shrimp (reserve the stock for another use), transfer the shrimp to a sheet pan, and spread them out to cool quickly.

To devein the shrimp, run a paring knife down the center of the back of each shrimp, lift or scrape out the dark vein (rinse, if necessary). Cover the shrimp and refrigerate until well chilled.

Divide the Cocktail Sauce or Tartar Sauce between 4 cocktail glasses and perch 4 shrimp on the rim of each glass. Garnish each glass with a wedge of lemon.

## COCKTAIL SAUCE

Put 1 cup ketchup; 3 tablespoons drained, prepared horseradish; and the juice of 1 lemon into a medium bowl and stir well. Cover and refrigerate.—*makes about 1 cup*

## TARTAR SAUCE

Put 1 cup mayonnaise, 3–4 minced anchovy filets, 1 tablespoon chopped capers, 2 tablespoons minced fresh parsley, and the finely grated zest and juice of 1 lemon into a medium bowl and stir well. Season with s&p. The sauce keeps in the refrigerator, covered, for up to 1 week.—*makes about 1 cup*

## MUSSELS WITH OR WITHOUT CREAM ⮞ serves 2

It's awfully fun to harvest wild mussels, but they're a lot of work, and we don't live by the ocean. So we buy cultivated or farmed mussels. They aren't gritty, have few, if any, barnacles attached to their shells, and only a wisp of a beard, so cleaning them is a breeze. And they are more tender and sweeter tasting than the wild ones.

4 tablespoons butter
1 small yellow onion, peeled
 and chopped
1–2 garlic cloves, thinly sliced
1 pinch of crushed red
 pepper flakes
1 pinch of fennel seeds
1½ cups dry white wine
2 pounds mussels, debearded
½ bunch parsley,
 leaves chopped
1 cup heavy cream, optional
Salt

Melt 2 tablespoons of the butter in a large pot with a tight-fitting lid over medium heat. Add the onions, garlic, crushed red pepper flakes, and fennel seeds, and cook until the onions begin to soften, about 3 minutes. Add the wine and bring to a simmer. Add the mussels and cover the pot.

Increase the heat to medium-high. Steam the mussels, occasionally shaking the pot over the heat while holding the lid on tight. Cook the mussels until the shells open, about 8 minutes.

Remove the pot from the heat. Add the remaining 2 tablespoons butter, half the parsley, and the cream, if using. Taste the broth and add salt, if needed.

Spoon the mussels and broth into big warm bowls, discarding any shells that don't open. Garnish with the remaining parsley. Serve with hunks of warm, crusty bread to sop up the flavorful broth.

## FILET OF SOLE MEUNIÈRE ⇝ serves 2

This classic dish is one of our all-time favorites. So delicate, it is all about the sole, which costs the earth! But we think it is worth every penny. Treat it like a jewel; it needs very little when cooking it, just a light touch. You may find Dover sole filets a little easier to handle than Grey sole when cooking them, as they are a bit firmer. Wondra, a low-protein, finely ground, prebaked flour, gives the thinnest crunchy coating.

2 sole filets, about
   6 ounces each
Salt
⅓ cup Wondra flour or
   all-purpose flour
5–6 tablespoons high-fat
   European-style butter
1 lemon, halved, plus more
   for garnish
Freshly ground black pepper
¼ bunch parsley,
   leaves finely chopped

Season the fish filets with salt. Carefully dredge them in flour.

Melt the butter in a large nonstick skillet over medium-high heat until foaming. Reduce the heat if the butter begins to brown. Place the filets in the skillet side by side, rounded-side up. Sauté the fish, tipping the skillet so the butter rushes to one end, then baste the fish with the bubbling butter until the flesh is opaque and just cooked through, about 3 minutes. Using a fish spatula, carefully transfer the filets to a warm plate.

Squeeze some juice from ½ lemon into the skillet while swirling the pan. Add more juice, if you like. Season the butter sauce with salt and pepper to taste and add the parsley.

Serve the fish with the butter sauce spooned on top, and with more lemon, if you like.

*Overleaf, left page: Filet of Sole Meunière; right page: Fritto Misto (page 212)*

## FRITTO MISTO ✎ serves 4–6

A fritto misto is a mixed fry, anything from tiny fish to lemon slices, that has been deep-fried. Our all-purpose batter should be about the consistency of heavy cream. If it is too thick (flours differ), add a little more wine.

FOR THE BATTER
1 cup all-purpose flour
$\frac{1}{2}$ teaspoon salt, plus more
    for seasoning
1 cup white wine

FOR THE FRITTO
Safflower or peanut oil
$\frac{1}{2}$ pound cod filet, cut into
    2-inch pieces
$\frac{1}{2}$ pound medium shrimp,
    (about 15), peeled and
    deveined
$\frac{1}{2}$ pound cleaned squid,
    tentacles separated from
    the body, body sliced into
    thick rings
2 lemons, one sliced into
    $\frac{1}{4}$-inch thick rings, one cut
    into wedges for garnish

For the batter, sift the flour into a mixing bowl. Whisk in the salt. Gradually add the wine, whisking until the batter is smooth. Give it a quick whisk again just before you're ready to use it. There will be about $1\frac{1}{2}$ cups of batter.

Add enough oil to a heavy medium pot to reach a depth of about 2 inches. Heat the oil over medium heat until hot but not smoking, ideally to a temperature of 350°F (use a candy thermometer to check the temperature or dip a wooden chopstick into the hot oil so that the tip touches the bottom of the pot; if lots of bubbles form right away around the tip, the oil should be ready for frying).

Use paper towels to dry the fish, shrimp, squid, and lemon rings (moisture will cause the oil to splatter).

Working in small batches, dip the fish, shrimp, squid, and lemon into the batter, shake off any excess, and carefully lower them into the 350°F oil. (Be careful not to burn your fingers or splatter the oil!) Fry in small batches, turning frequently for even browning. Remove the fritto misto when it is golden or a pale brown (you'll get the hang of it as you go). Use a fish turner or slotted spatula to lift the fritto misto out of the oil and drain on a wire rack set over a paper towel–lined tray. Skim any frying debris out of the oil between batches.

Season the fritto misto with salt while it is still hot. Serve with wedges of lemon as you fry and be sure to keep some for yourself. It's the cook's job to maintain quality control!

## GAMBAS A LA PLANCHA ☞ serves 2–4

This Spanish *tapas* dish is good and messy, to eat with your fingers while sipping a glass of fino sherry. There are some salty, lemony pan juices to mop the shrimp in, and if you're a shrimp lover and not squeamish about head-on shrimp, eat the shells and all, sucking the briny juices out of the heads. Searing shrimp in their shells makes the shells crisp and keeps the shrimp juicy.

¼ cup olive oil
1 pound (about 30) medium
  shrimp, preferably head-on,
  unpeeled
2–3 garlic cloves, thinly sliced
Coarse salt
1 lemon, halved

Heat the oil in a large cast-iron or other heavy skillet over high heat until very hot but not smoking. Add the shrimp and garlic. Season with a few generous pinches of salt.

Sear the shrimp, shaking the skillet frequently, until the shrimp turn pink and shells are golden, 2–3 minutes. Squeeze the juice from the lemon over the shrimp. Serve the shrimp in the skillet.

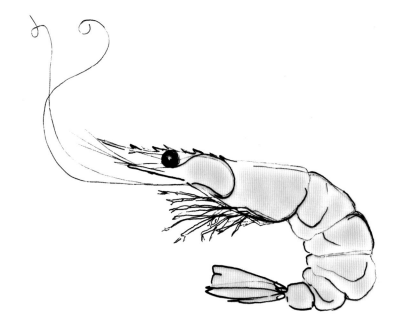

## SEARED TERIYAKI TUNA

Buy thick pieces of tuna loin (yellowfin or ahi is best) and sear them very quickly in a very hot skillet for a rare, essentially raw, interior (see page 217). Heat 1 tablespoon safflower or peanut oil in a medium nonstick skillet over high heat until very hot. Generously season two 1½-inch thick, 6-ounce tuna steaks with salt and freshly ground black pepper. Sear the tuna on both sides, about 45 seconds per side. Serve the tuna with teriyaki or soy sauce spooned on top and with watercress and thinly sliced scallions on the side.—*serves 2*

## TUNA CARPACCIO ☞ serves 4

This recipe was inspired by one served at the celebrated Harry's Bar in Venice, where they make it with thinly sliced raw beef. Here, we make it instead with sushi-grade tuna loin. Ask your fishmonger to cut ¼-inch thick slices, weighing 2 to 3 ounces each.

FOR THE MAYONNAISE SAUCE
2 large egg yolks
Salt
Juice of ½ lemon
¼ cup canola oil
¼ cup extra-virgin olive oil
1 teaspoon Worcestershire
    sauce
1–2 tablespoons whole milk
Freshly ground black pepper

FOR THE TUNA
Twelve ¼-inch thick slices
    sushi-grade tuna loin,
    2–3 ounces each

For the mayonnaise sauce, whisk together the egg yolks, 1 pinch salt, and half of the lemon juice in a medium bowl. Combine both the oils in a measuring cup with a spout. Whisking constantly, add the oil to the yolks, a few drops at a time. The sauce will thicken and emulsify. After adding about ¼ cup of the oil, begin to slowly drizzle in the remaining oil as you continue to whisk, until you have a thick, glossy mayonnaise. Add more of the remaining lemon juice, if you like. Add the Worcestershire sauce. Stir in enough of the milk to thin the sauce. Season to taste with salt and pepper. Transfer to a covered container and refrigerate until ready to use. The sauce will keep for up to 1 week in the refrigerator. This makes about ⅔ cup.

For the tuna, evenly divide the sliced tuna between 4 chilled plates, arranging the slices like a mosaic in a single layer. Drizzle the sauce over the tuna à la Jackson Pollock. Serve cold.

## CRAB CAKES ✍ makes 12–18 small cakes

There are two tricks to making these crab cakes. The first is to mix all the ingredients except the crab together, then fold the meat in ever so gently and always by hand. The second is to use buttery Ritz crackers instead of bread crumbs. Keeping these crab cakes small makes them easier to fry without falling apart.

3 tablespoons butter
3 celery stalks, minced
3 scallions, trimmed and
   minced
1 egg
½ teaspoon dry mustard
2 teaspoons Old Bay
   Seasoning
½ teaspoon salt
½ teaspoon freshly ground
   black pepper
3 tablespoons mayonnaise
1 tablespoon fresh
   lemon juice
1 teaspoon Worcestershire
   sauce
8 Ritz crackers, crushed into
   coarse crumbs (⅓ cup)
1 pound jumbo lump
   crabmeat, drained
1 tablespoon safflower oil

Melt 2 tablespoons of the butter in a medium skillet over medium-low heat. Add the celery and scallions and cook until soft, 5–8 minutes. Set aside to cool.

Whisk together the egg, dry mustard, Old Bay Seasoning, salt, pepper, mayonnaise, lemon juice, and Worcestershire sauce in a large bowl. Stir in the cracker crumbs and the cooled celery and scallions. Add the crabmeat and mix together very gently with a rubber spatula. Try not to break up the crabmeat too much.

Make 12–18 crab cakes, each about 2 inches wide, gently pressing each cake together in your hands, and arrange the cakes on a parchment paper–lined tray. Loosely cover the tray with plastic wrap and refrigerate for 1–2 hours. It may seem like the crab cakes are in danger of falling apart, but chilling them will hold them together.

To cook the crab cakes, heat the remaining 1 tablespoon of butter and the safflower oil together in a large nonstick skillet over medium-low to medium heat. Working in batches, fry the cakes until golden brown on each side, 4–5 minutes. They are very tender, so turn them gently. Serve with lemon wedges, Tartar Sauce (page 207), and saltine crackers, if you like.

## LOBSTER WITH BROWNED CREAM ☞ serves 2

Use the thickest (ideally 35 percent butterfat), most "natural" cream you can find.

One 2-pound lobster
Salt
¼–½ cup heavy cream
1–2 tablespoons cold butter,
  cut into small pieces
Freshly ground black pepper

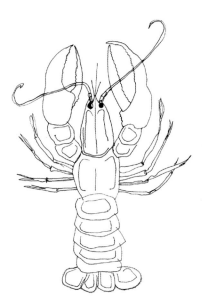

Plunge the lobster head first into a large pot of salted boiling water over high heat. Cook for 3 minutes. Use tongs to remove the lobster from the pot and allow it to drain on several thicknesses of paper towel.

When the lobster is cool enough to handle, split it lengthwise with a heavy large knife. (Be careful, we don't want you to sever an artery!) Cut through the back, splitting the head and body in two. Continue to cut through the tail with the knife or a strong pair of kitchen shears. Separate the halves and place them meat-side up in a large ovenproof skillet or shallow baking pan. Remove and discard the stomach sac between the eyes. Twist off the claws. Cover the claws with a towel and use the handle of the knife to crack them open on the top side. Remove the pieces of cracked shells. Add the claws to the skillet, cracked side up.

Pour the cream into the two lobster halves, around and over the meat in the tail, into the body and the cracked claws, and into the skillet. Use as much cream as the lobster will accept. Tuck the pieces of butter into the claw and body and tail pieces. Season with salt and pepper.

Preheat the broiler. Broil the lobster until the cream is bubbling and brown, about 5 minutes. Transfer the lobster to two plates, taking care not to spill out the delicious juices. Serve with warm crusty bread to sop up the cream, if you like.

*Facing page, clockwise from top left: Seared Teriyaki Tuna (page 214); Tuna Carpaccio (page 214); Crab Cakes (page 215); Lobster with Browned Cream*

# Perfect Bites

⊙ preserved fish & eggs ⊙

We like a selection of pickled, smoked, cured, and tinned fish, and use some or all of the following:

BELLY LOX: This is the midsection of a salmon, cured in salt brine. We love its tingly saltiness.

CHUB: These smoky North American lake fish are tender and moist.

SMOKED SABLEFISH: An appetizing classic, this buttery smoked fish, also known as black cod or simply sable, is line-caught in the waters of the North Pacific.

PICKLED, SMOKED, SALTED, AND MATJES HERRING: We love them all, from the classic briny pickled herring, to the smoky French herring, to the salted schmaltz, and the clovey matjes.

SMOKED OR CURED SALMON: With so many available, the best way to choose is simply to taste your way through, though we avoid those with an artificial-looking pink or orange hue, and ultimately settle on smoked salmon with a good pedigree and a silky, buttery texture, well balanced in the salt and smoke world.

SMOKED STURGEON: This freshwater white-fleshed fish, whose roe is turned into the priciest kind of caviar, has a distinctly earthy, sweet flavor.

FISH ROE: Big orange salmon eggs or beautiful smaller (also orange) trout eggs add a pop-in-your-mouth texture and saltiness, plus they have a jewel-like beauty. Look for Malossol quality.

CANNED SARDINES: We like them packed in olive oil. The plump Spanish sardines from Matiz Gallego (three to a can) are excellent.

## EMERGENCY RATIONS—A CAN OF TUNA & SOME LEMONS

*Is this chicken, what I have, or is this fish? I know it's tuna, but it says "Chicken of the Sea."*—Jessica Simpson

Good canned tuna needs little more than its friend, the lemon. We buy the best tuna we can find, always packed in olive oil, usually albacore, ventresca (Italian tuna belly), ventrèche (the same, but in French), or bonito (a dark-fleshed tunalike fish from Spain). We serve it simply: a toothsome hunk of tuna on a cracker or grilled toast with a squeeze of lemon juice. We can't resist big handsome cans (like those 4-pounders) of imported tuna for serving to a crowd. We just pry off the lid, tip out some of the oil, and set the tuna out with lots of crackers or toast and plenty of lemons for everyone to help themselves.

*Smørrebrød of various preserved fish & eggs*

# Chickens & other birds

# Thirteen Ways of Looking at Chicken

We were inspired to look at chicken the way the Wallace Stevens poem looks at a blackbird.

I. Last week, we made chicken thighs braised in their juices with a spoonful of homemade tomato sauce and a handful of Castelvetrano olives. We served it on a mound of soft polenta. Heaven!

II. At the market this morning, we found a bin full of bright green, marble-sized Brussels sprouts that we just had to buy. We roasted them alongside a plump chicken breast. With a little pan sauce and a handful of celery leaves to add more green to the plate, we had ourselves a pretty and most delicious lunch.

III. A good day for a pimentón-rubbed roast chicken. We each chose our favorite piece and tucked in. One prefers a leg and thigh, the other goes for the breast. We have the perfect partnership.

IV. MH had a little dinner party, so she brought the remains to the studio today in her big orange Le Creuset pot: poached chicken with turnips, parsnips, carrots, and leeks. CH sliced the meat off a whole breast and reheated it in the jellied pan juices. She sautéed the veggies in butter with some fresh parsley and thyme. Hope MH has another party soon.

V. Uber-popular, boneless, skinless chicken breasts have no flavor, so we rarely buy them. But today, while out shopping for local asparagus, there were two delicate breasts that spoke to us. Into our shopping bag they went, along with a big handful of fat spears. We dusted the chicken in Wondra flour and quickly pan-fried them in butter and a splash of olive oil until they were just browned and still juicy inside. We piled on warm asparagus then a tender salad of dandelion leaves, tendrils of micro arugula, chives, and pansy petals on top. Chicken breasts never tasted so good all dressed up for spring!

VI. We made chicken salad with lots of lemon zest, piled it on mayonnaise-smeared toast with crisp bacon slices, then added asparagus and scallions dressed with olive oil and s&p.

VII. On a stormy afternoon, we had an indoor picnic of fried chicken with pickled onions and bread & butter pickles. Crisp and crunchy meets sweet and sour.

VIII. A handful of golden chanterelles that we foraged this morning went into the pan with two chicken thighs, along with some peeled summer tomatoes, thyme freshly snipped from the garden, and a few crushed pepperoncini. When the chicken was fork-tender, we napped the braised thighs with heavy cream—our chicken cacciatore (for those mushrooms we "caught"). It was so good, we licked our plates clean (let's keep that between us).

IX. We're down to one chicken breast to split between us. *Pas de problème.* We sliced the breast into four paillards, dusted them in flour, and pan-fried them in butter and olive oil. We served them with a lemony caper pan sauce and a warm chanterelle, lemon, and parsley salad. One breast could have served four, but we were feeling somewhat gluttonous today.

X. We roasted tomatoes with a spatchcocked chicken in a very hot oven until their skins blistered and they gave up their juices to make a rich sauce. Then we threw in a handful of little zucchini to roast in the pan with the bird.

XI. We never seem to tire of chicken. Last night, one of us made a dinner of pot-roasted (braised actually) chicken, its rich broth spooned over cannellini beans, with chicken liver toasts for crunch. Too good not to share, so we're having the leftovers for lunch. Sometimes, food tastes even better the next day after the flavor has had time to develop.

XII. Snow is sliding off the roof and landing with a crescendo onto the towpath below. Inside, we sat by the fire and ate bowls of chicken and rice with collard greens.

XIII. We wanted to take a little break from chicken. So the other day we went to grab a duck from the market. No duck! We bought a big ham instead and now we're set for eternity. We coated it with Dijon mustard and brown sugar and baked it for dinner one night. We're eating ham sandwiches for breakfast, lunch, and dinner. Still lots of ham left. Don't tell chicken.

## CHOOSING, BUYING & BRINING

Like the rest of America, we eat a lot of chicken. Packaged in seemingly endless forms, chicken dominates the refrigerated cases at the supermarket. Here's a guide to buying our favorite bird.

SIZE MATTERS: Chickens of different ages and weights need to be treated differently. These are the various types at most markets and their uses:

(ROCK) CORNISH GAME HEN: a hybrid of the Cornish and White Rock breeds; younger than 5 weeks old. Weight: 1–2 pounds. Meaty; good for stuffing, roasting, broiling, and grilling.

POUSSIN OR SPRING CHICKEN: baby chicken between 4 and 6 weeks old. Weight: ¾–1 pound. Great little party bird; good for a single serving. Use as you would Cornish game hen.

BROILER OR FRYER: less than 10 weeks old. Weight: 2½–5 pounds. Tender meat. Good all-purpose chicken. Use for broiling or frying, or for roasting, grilling, sautéing, or poaching.

ROASTER: 8–12 weeks old. Weight: 5 pounds or more. Flavorful bird with more fat to keep it moist. Large cavity for stuffing; great roasted, but fine for stewing, grilling, broiling, and poaching.

CAPON: a young castrated (which improves the quality of the meat) rooster 4–8 months old. Weight: 4–10 pounds. Tender meat; has large cavity for stuffing; full breasted; use as you would a roaster. An excellent alternative to turkey.

AIR-CHILLED: The United States Department of Agriculture (USDA) requires poultry be chilled immediately after slaughter. "Air-chilled" chickens (and turkeys) have not been water-chilled en masse in a chlorinated bath, and they haven't absorbed any water during processing. (Water-chilled birds can retain up to 14 percent water—which must be printed on the label—diluting flavor and inflating cost.) Instead, individual birds hang from a conveyor belt and circulate through cold, purified-air rooms.

CERTIFIED ORGANIC: The seal "USDA Organic" is considered the gold standard for organic labeling. This label ensures that poultry eat organic feed that doesn't contain animal byproducts, are raised without antibiotics, and have access to the outdoors (how much access, however, isn't regulated).

KOSHER: Approved poultry that have been "made fit" by processing according to methods set forth by Jewish law, kosher birds are soaked in salted water after "harvest" to draw out and thoroughly drain them of their blood. This method, in effect, brines the birds. Therefore, kosher chickens and turkeys taste mildly seasoned and the meat is more moist and tender when cooked.

YOUR LOCAL FARM-RAISED CHICKEN: Friends of ours raise and sell naturally pastured chickens; every bird is their darling. They move them daily to different pastures to scratch around for insects; their diet is supplemented with local grain. The dressed birds are a thing of beauty: big and fat with thick, tight skin. Roasted, they are full of flavor, toothsome but tender. And though they are not certified organic, they taste better than the organic birds we get from our supermarket. They cost a little more, too. We always go for the best-tasting ingredients available. Sometimes that means buying local, even if it is not organic. Check out your local farm markets. Chances are, they are selling great-tasting birds, too.

WHOLE VS. PARTS: There is an economy to buying a whole bird, satisfaction at being able to inspect and choose the best-looking one, and then knowing how to cut it up. You're in control and wing tips and backs can be saved for making stock. But buying parts comes in handy when you want more than two of a specific part—say, wings for roasting or making a rich stock, or thighs because you love the dark juicy meat as much as we do and two is never enough. We don't buy boneless, skinless breasts, because while they are convenient, they don't have much flavor. But buy what you like. We're just so glad you are interested in cooking and eating.

DRY BRINE VS. WET BRINE: Years ago, when we first started brining our chickens and turkeys (and cuts of pork as well), we would haul out a large bowl or stock pot, fill it with cold water, add copious amounts of kosher salt and half that amount of sugar, then stir the bath until the granules dissolved. In went the bird, with something heavy on top, like a plate or pan, to keep the darned thing submerged. During the cooler months, we would leave the pot outdoors on our back porch "fridge". The rest of the year, we would try to make room inside our narrow refrigerator. We love the virtues of brining. It makes meat more flavorful and juicy. But wet brining is a cumbersome process. Judy Rogers, in her award-winning tome, *The Zuni Café Cookbook*, taught us all about dry brining. Same benefits; tender, juicy meat; no hassle. We've been following her lead ever since.

We make a 2:1 mixture of kosher salt to granulated sugar, then rub this directly on the surface of the bird. Whole chickens and turkeys can brine for up to 3 days this way. But even one hour of dry brining will improve the flavor and texture of the meat. Before cooking, brush off any of the salt mixture and pat the bird dry with paper towels. Don't season with any more salt.

## ROAST CHICKEN ☞ serves 4–6

For flavorful, juicy meat, we dry-brine the chicken (see page 225). To keep the skin taut and crisp, roast the bird in two phases: first at a high temperature, then at a lower one after a brief rest out of the oven.

One 3–5-pound chicken,
    rinsed and patted dry
1 tablespoon kosher salt
1½ teaspoons sugar
2 tablespoons butter, melted

Put the chicken breast-side up in a wide dish. Combine the salt and sugar, and gently rub it all over the outside of the bird. Refrigerate, uncovered, for at least 1 hour, but up to 12 hours is preferable.

Preheat the oven to 475°F with a rack set in the middle of the oven. Brush off any of the salt mixture and pat the chicken dry with paper towels (don't rinse the bird). Put it breast-side up on a roasting rack set in a roasting pan. Tie the legs together with kitchen string. Tuck the wing tips under the back. Brush the chicken all over with some of the melted butter. Add 2–3 cups water to the pan.

Roast the chicken until the skin is golden and taut, 20–30 minutes, brushing it with butter halfway through. Remove the bird from the oven. Brush it with the remaining butter. Let it rest for 15 minutes.

Reduce the oven temperature to 350°F. Return the chicken to the oven and finish roasting it until the skin is deep golden brown and the thigh juices run clear when pierced, about 30 minutes, depending on the size of the bird. (The internal temperature of the thigh meat should register 165°F on an instant-read thermometer.) Remove the chicken from the oven and let it rest for 10–15 minutes before carving. Serve the chicken with the pan drippings.

ROASTING BIGGER BIRDS: Large, plump chickens, like roasters and capons (see page 224), are beautiful birds for serving a small flock of guests (6 to 12); they just take a little longer to roast. For a 5–10-pound chicken, follow the directions above, brining the bird with 2 tablespoons kosher salt and 1 tablespoon sugar. Brush the bird with 3 tablespoons melted butter. The second stage of roasting the chicken at 350°F will take about 1 hour for the thigh meat to reach an internal temperature of 165°F.

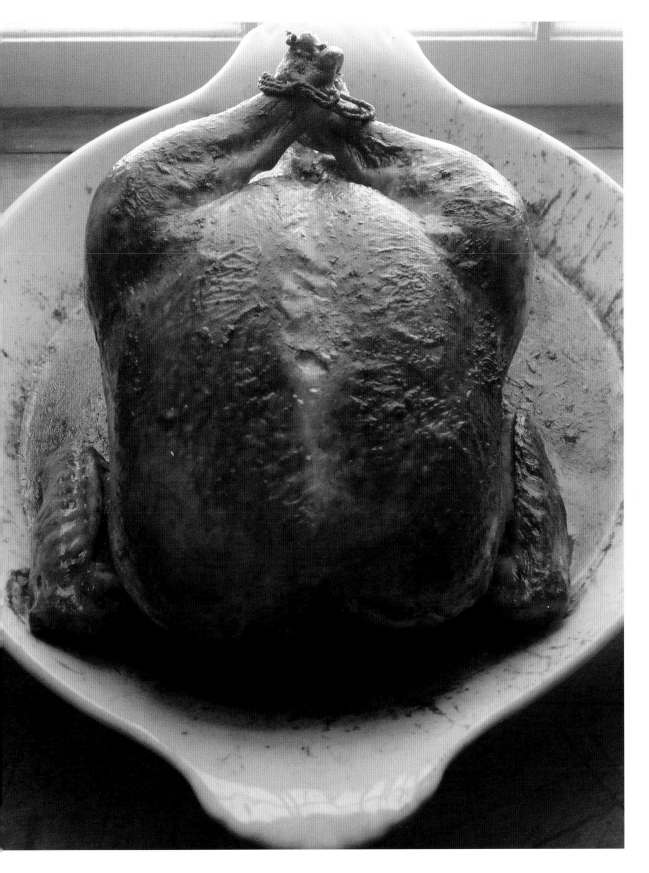

## OVEN-BRAISED CHICKEN WITH SPRING ONIONS ☞ serves 4–6

Spring onions are deliciously mild and make their appearance beginning in April with a growing season that extends all the way into August. They are sold in bunches, the thick green stalks gathered together just above the white or blush purple bulbs. For this brothy dish, use small yellow onions if spring onions are not available.

1 whole chicken, rinsed and patted dry
2 tablespoons extra-virgin olive oil
Salt and freshly ground black pepper
12 spring onions with green stems, root end removed
4–6 sprigs parsley
2–3 garlic cloves, crushed
2–4 tablespoons butter

Preheat the oven to 375°F. Put the chicken into a wide heavy pot with a lid that holds it easily. Drizzle the bird with the olive oil and season with salt and pepper. Tuck the onions, parsley, and garlic into the pot around the chicken. Add the butter and 1–2 cups cold water to the pot. Cover the pot.

Transfer the chicken to the oven to braise for 30 minutes for a 3–4-pound bird, 45 minutes for a 4–5-pound bird. Remove the pot from the oven and baste the chicken with the brothy juices.

Increase the oven temperature to 400°F. Return the pot to the oven, uncovered, and finish cooking the chicken until the skin is golden and the thigh juices run clear when pierced, 15–30 minutes, depending on the size of the chicken. (The internal temperature of the thigh meat should register 165°F on an instant-read thermometer.)

Let the chicken rest for 10–15 minutes before carving. Adjust the seasonings of the broth with salt and pepper. Serve the chicken and onions in wide bowls with a big ladleful of broth in each bowl.

## CHICKEN & RICE

Melt 3 tablespoons butter in a wide heavy pot with a lid over medium heat. Add 1 cut-up chicken (2 wings, tips removed, 2 drumsticks, 2 thighs, and a quartered breast; see page 241), cover and cook until they've released their juices, about 10 minutes. Add 1 finely chopped, peeled yellow onion and 3 finely chopped celery stalks with their leaves, and season well with salt and freshly ground black pepper. Add 1 cup water, cover, reduce the heat to low, and cook for 20 minutes. Uncover the pot, add 1 cup short- or long-grain rice, pushing the rice into the spaces around the chicken. Increase the heat to medium-low, add 1 cup water, cover, and cook until the rice absorbs all the broth, about 20 minutes.—*serves 4–6*

*A spring onion*

## OVEN-BRAISED CHICKEN WITH GNOCCHI ❧ serves 6

1 whole chicken, rinsed and
   patted dry
4 tablespoons butter, softened
Salt and freshly ground
   black pepper
3 sprigs fresh sage
4 medium carrots, peeled and
   sliced into rounds
1 pound freshly cooked
   gnocchi or other pasta

Preheat the oven to 375°F. Put the chicken into a wide heavy pot with a lid that holds it easily. Rub the bird all over with the butter and season with salt and pepper. Add the sage and 2 cups water. Cover the pot and transfer to the oven.

Braise the chicken for 30 minutes for a 3–4-pound bird, 45 minutes for a 4–5-pound bird. Remove the pot from the oven, baste the chicken with the juices, and scatter the carrots around the chicken. Return the pot to the oven, uncovered. Cook the chicken until the skin is golden and the thigh juices run clear when pierced, 15–30 minutes, depending on the size of the chicken.

Use a slotted spatula to remove the chicken from the pot. Let it rest for 10–15 minutes before carving. Season the juices with salt and pepper. Serve the chicken and warm gnocchi together in wide bowls with the carrots and brothy juices spooned on top.

## MAKING GNOCCHI

Bake 2 pounds russet potatoes in a 400°F oven until tender, about 1 hour. Scoop out the hot flesh and push it through a potato ricer (1) onto a clean work surface. Spread out the potatoes to cool completely. Pile the potatoes into a mound and make a well in the center. Add 1 beaten egg (2) and sift ¾ cup flour over the mound (3). Use a pastry scraper to scrape and fold everything together to form a shaggy dough. Knead, adding more flour, until the dough is soft, smooth, and slightly tacky. Cut the dough into 8 equal pieces. Using a light touch, roll the pieces of dough into ½-inch thick ropes. Cut the ropes into ¾-inch pillow-shaped pieces.

To shape the gnocchi, put the cut edge of a gnocco against the convex side of the tines of a fork. Using your index finger, gently roll the dough against the tines, making grooves on one side and a small dent from your finger on the other side (4). Dust the fork and your finger with flour as you work.

Cook the gnocchi in batches, in a large pot of simmering salted water. Scoop out the gnocchi with a slotted spoon after they have floated on the surface for about 10 seconds. Transfer them to a warm bowl as they finish cooking and toss with melted butter.—*serves 4–6*

## SPATCHCOCKING

Traditionally, a spatchcocked chicken or small bird is grilled. The bird is butterflied, or split open so it lays flat, like an open book. It makes the bird easier to handle and carve, and helps it cook more evenly. It gives more surface area for basting or slathering on compound butter. And it allows more room for stuffing seasonings under the skin. Why stop at grilling? We spatchcock chicken for roasting and broiling, as well. The process is simple, but we take precautions.

To split a whole chicken or small bird open, use a pair of sturdy kitchen or poultry shears (1). A heavy, sharp knife or cleaver work, too, but neither offers quite the control that shears do. Place the chicken breast-side down on a cutting board. Use the shears to cut out the backbone (2). Open up the chicken like a book and press on it to flatten it. Save the backbone for making stock (3).

## PORCHETTA-STYLE CHICKEN ☞ serves 4–6

The traditional herbs used in porchetta, the famous Italian pork roast, are wild fennel, rosemary, and garlic—big, bold flavors we think also go well with chicken. We gild the lily and add sage and lemon (4).

1–2 teaspoons fennel seeds, lightly toasted
1 garlic clove, chopped
1 large sprig fresh rosemary, leaves chopped
1 large sprig fresh sage, leaves chopped
Salt and freshly ground black pepper
Finely grated zest of 2 lemons
One 3–5-pound chicken, spatchcocked (see above), rinsed, and patted dry
1 tablespoon extra-virgin olive oil

Crush the fennel seeds in a mortar and pestle. Add the garlic, rosemary, sage, and a generous pinch of salt and pepper, and crush to a paste. Stir in the lemon zest.

Use your fingers to loosen the skin from the chicken breast and thighs, taking care not to tear the skin. Rub the herb paste under the skin all over the flesh. Season the bird all over with salt and set aside at room temperature for 1 hour. Or, cover with plastic wrap and refrigerate for up to 12 hours.

Preheat the oven to 450°F. Set the chicken skin-side up on a wire rack set in a roasting pan and rub all over with the olive oil. Add 1–2 cups water to the pan. Roast the chicken until golden brown and the thigh juices run clear when pierced, 40–45 minutes. Remove from the oven and let the chicken rest for 10–15 minutes before cutting up and serving.

1.

2.

3.

4.

## ROAST CHICKEN WITH TOMATO BUTTER ☞ serves 4–6

This savory emulsified-butter sauce can be made ahead and refrigerated. When you are ready to use it, don't warm it up, just slather it on the roasted chicken and let it melt.

FOR THE CHICKEN
One 3–5-pound chicken, spatchcocked (page 232), rinsed, and patted dry
Salt and freshly ground black pepper
1 handful chopped fresh parsley leaves for garnish
2 sprigs fresh rosemary, leaves chopped for garnish

FOR THE TOMATO BUTTER
2 anchovy filets
6 sprigs fresh thyme
¾ cup dry sherry
2 big tablespoons tomato paste
8 tablespoons (1 stick) cold butter, cut into 8 pieces

For the chicken, preheat the oven to 400°F. Set the chicken skin-side up on a wire rack set in a roasting pan and rub all over with salt and pepper. Add 1–2 cups water to the pan.

Roast the chicken until golden brown and the thigh juices run clear when pierced, 45–60 minutes. (The internal temperature of the thigh meat should register 165°F on an instant-read thermometer.)

Meanwhile, for the tomato butter, put the anchovies, thyme, and sherry in a heavy medium saucepan. Bring to a simmer over medium heat and simmer for 10 minutes. Strain the sherry through a fine-mesh sieve into a bowl; discard the solids. Return the sherry to the pan. Boil over medium-high heat until the sherry has reduced to about ¼ cup.

Reduce the heat to medium. Whisk in the tomato paste, and add the butter one piece at a time, whisking until it has melted before adding the next piece. Whisk until all the butter is melted and the sauce is smooth. Remove the pan from the heat and cover to keep the tomato butter warm.

Remove the chicken from the oven and let it rest for 10–15 minutes. Cut the chicken into pieces, arrange on a platter, and spoon the tomato butter all over. Garnish with the chopped parsley and rosemary.

## FRIED CHICKEN WITH STRING BEANS VINAIGRETTE

After soaking rains, our garden is a jungle, the plants heavy with fruit and flowers. The green and wax beans, in particular, called to us to pick them for lunch today. Fat and meaty, we boiled 2 big handfuls in a pot of salted water until tender, drained them once, cooled them off in cold running water, and drained them again. We tossed the beans in about ¼ cup Canal House Classic Vinaigrette (page 128) studded with a minced, peeled shallot and a small handful of chopped fresh parsley. We each had a dainty piece of cold fried chicken (page 242) to go with it. Now we have to figure out what to do with the out-of-control zucchini hiding under the leaves; we fear they are the first of many. Maybe we could start a Canal House baseball team that uses gigantic zucchini instead of baseball bats.—*serves 2*

## ROASTED CHICKEN WINGS

It's a pile of meaty, sticky chicken wings, eaten with our fingers, for lunch today. We marinated 4 pounds (about 20) chicken wings, tips trimmed, in the juice of 2 lemons, ¼ cup extra-virgin olive oil, 2 tablespoons Dijon mustard, 2 teaspoons dried tarragon leaves, and salt and freshly ground black pepper to taste in a large bowl for about an hour and preheated the oven to 375°F. Then we put the wings out on a roasting pan in a single layer, meaty-side up, and drizzled the remaining marinade over them. The wings roasted until they were well browned and the skin papery crisp, about 1 hour. The pan juices and marinade caramelized and some of the wings stuck to the pan. But that's what always makes them so finger-lickin' good.—*serves 4*

## SPATCHCOCKED CHICKEN WITH LENTILS & MINT

CH brought a whole chicken to the studio today. And a package of tiny green lentils. MH found a fat carrot in the vegetable drawer and a preserved lemon from the batch we made a few months ago. While the lentils and finely diced, peeled carrots cooked together in gently boiling salted water on top of the stove, the spatchcocked chicken (page 232), rubbed with extra-virgin olive oil and some fennel salt rub (page 332), roasted in a hot oven. We drained the lentils and carrots, tossed them with the diced rind of the preserved lemon, some extra-virgin olive oil, and freshly ground black pepper, and served them with the roasted chicken and torn fresh mint leaves, mingling all their flavors.—*serves 4–6*

*Overleaf, left page, clockwise from top left: Fried Chicken with String Beans Vinaigrette; Roasted Chicken Wings; Spatchcocked Chicken with Lentils & Mint*

## POACHED SPRING CHICKEN

Now that local asparagus and English peas are here, our farm markets are in full spring mode. We couldn't be happier. To honor the new season, we poached 2 skin-on, split chicken breasts with ribs (page 250) with 4 unpeeled garlic cloves. While the chicken poached, we put 1 large handful of tiny fingerling potatoes into another pot, covered them with cold water, added a generous pinch of salt, and gently boiled them until fork-tender. In another pot of salted boiling water, we added 1 bunch trimmed, peeled fat asparagus. Just before the asparagus finished poaching (about 4 minutes), we tossed in 1 cup shelled peas and 1 handful shelled, peeled favas to the simmering water for 1 minute, then drained the vegetables. We served the poached breasts (boned and skinned) thickly sliced in a deep platter, cut the potatoes in half and arranged them around the chicken along with the asparagus, favas, peas, and garlic (slipped out of their skins), and spooned some of the flavorful chicken poaching broth over all. A sprinkle of salt, a drizzle of extra-virgin olive oil, and some sliced fresh mint leaves finished seasoning the dish. We sure wish asparagus season lasted longer.—*serves 2–4*

## ROASTED DUCK LEGS & BRAISED SHIITAKES

On hot, muggy days we work in the splendor of air conditioning. So much so, that instead of a cold summer salad (a more appropriate lunch), we are feasting on roasted duck legs (page 262) with shiitake mushroom caps and small spring onion bulbs braised in a little duck stock (we had some on hand, but chicken stock would also be good). We considered pouring ourselves glasses of 2007 *Liber Pater Bordeaux,* but instead went with good old Milford tap water with a couple of ice cubes. We have to cut back somewhere!—*serves 2*

## TOMATO & ONION BRAISED TURKEY

Our local market sells boneless turkey breast roasts—the boneless breast halves tied together into a neat package. We love these roasts. But instead of roasting it, we keep the turkey moist by braising it. Here's how we do it: add a few glugs of extra-virgin olive oil, 1–2 sliced, large peeled yellow onions, and 3 cups of Simple Tomato Sauce I or II (page 156) to a deep enameled cast-iron or other heavy pot. Add a turkey breast roast seasoned with salt and freshly ground black pepper, and 2 cups of water. Put the covered pot in a preheated 350°F oven and braise until the internal temperature registers 155°F on an instant-read thermometer, about 90 minutes. The flavorful sauce is good enough to eat with a spoon, but better yet, cook some orecchiette and add it to the pot just before serving.—*serves 6*

*Overleaf, right page, clockwise from top: Poached Spring Chicken; Roasted Duck Legs & Braised Shiitakes; Tomato & Onion Braised Turkey with orecchiette*

1.

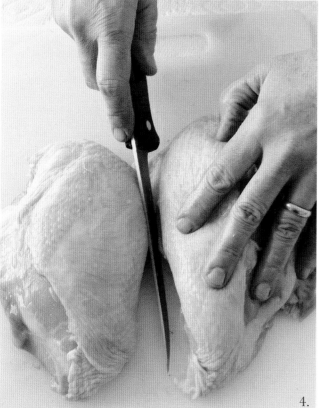

4.

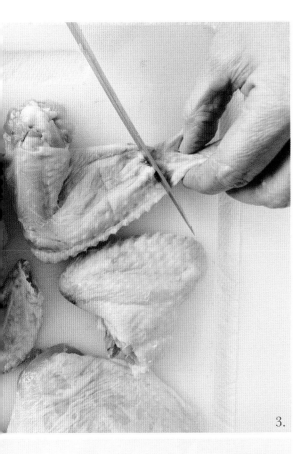

3.

6.

## THIS IS THE WAY WE CUT UP A CHICKEN

1. CUTTING OFF THE LEGS ⊙ Place the chicken breast-side up on a cutting board. Pull the leg away from the breast. Using a sharp kitchen knife, cut through the skin between the leg and breast. Pull the leg back further, away from the breast, until the thighbone begins to pop out of its socket. Cut between the thighbone and socket, separating the leg completely from the rest of the bird. For drumsticks and thighs, turn the leg skin-side down. Beginning where the fat meets the drumstick meat, cut between the thigh and drumstick joint, separating the leg into two pieces. Repeat with the other leg.

2. CUTTING OFF THE WINGS ⊙ Pull the wing back away from the breast, wiggling it to feel where the joint is. Cut through the skin at the joint, then pull the wing back further until the wing bone begins to pop out of its socket. Cut between the joint, separating the wing completely. Remove the other wing.

3. REMOVING THE WING TIPS ⊙ There's not much meat on the wing tips, so we trim them off at the joint and save them for making stock. Then we cut the wings in half. Cut through the joint between the paddle (aka wingette or flat) and drumette, separating each wing into two pieces.

4. HALVING THE BREAST ⊙ Turn the chicken over and cut off the rib cage and back, cutting through the rib cage and the sturdy shoulder joints, releasing the back. Save these pieces for making stock. Turn the breast skin-side down. Break the sturdy center bone at the wider end of the breast with a gentle whack with the knife. Turn the breast skin-side up. Press down on the breast to crack the center bone and flatten the breast. Cut down the center of the breast, through the breast plate, sternum, and wishbone, separating the breast into two pieces.

5. QUARTERING THE BREASTS ⊙ For easy serving, make all the chicken parts about the same size. Since the breasts are large, we cut each breast half in half, crosswise and slightly on the diagonal, into manageable pieces.

6. ONE CHICKEN, TWELVE PIECES ⊙ Though we could buy chicken parts, we like the economy of cutting up our own bird *and* making stock with the extra parts.

## FRIED CHICKEN 🗝 serves 4

We dry brine the chicken before frying it to help protect the meat from drying out in the hot oil. It also makes the chicken more flavorful. Draining the fried chicken on a rack instead of directly on paper towels keeps the chicken crisp all over.

One 3–5-pound chicken,
  cut into 12 pieces: 4 breast
  pieces, 4 wing pieces (tips
  removed), 2 drumsticks, and
  2 thighs (see page 241)
½ cup kosher salt, plus more
  for seasoning
¼ cup sugar
1½ cups flour
1 teaspoon baking powder
½ teaspoon freshly ground
  black pepper
Safflower or peanut oil

Arrange the chicken pieces on a parchment paper–lined baking pan in an even layer. Combine the ½ cup salt and the sugar in a small bowl, and season the chicken all over with the mixture (1). Refrigerate, uncovered, for at least 1 hour, but up to 8 hours is preferable. Rinse the chicken and pat the pieces dry with paper towels.

Whisk together the flour, baking powder, ½ teaspoon salt, and the pepper in a wide bowl. Dredge the chicken in the seasoned flour one piece at a time, making sure each piece is well coated (2). For an extra crunchy coating, dredge them again 10 minutes or so later. Set the dredged pieces of chicken on a wire rack (3).

Pour enough oil into a large cast-iron skillet to reach a depth of 2 inches. Heat the oil over medium heat until it registers 350°F on a candy thermometer, or dip a wooden chopstick into the hot oil until the tip touches the bottom of the skillet; if bubbles form right away around the tip—lots of bubbles, like Champagne—the oil is ready for frying.

Fry the chicken in the hot oil, larger pieces first, skin-side down, working in batches if all the pieces don't fit at the same time. Turn once, and fry until golden and crispy, about 8 minutes per side (4). Transfer the fried chicken to a wire rack set on top of paper towels to drain. Season to taste with salt while still hot.

*Overleaf: Fried Chicken*

1.

2.

3.

4.

## VINEGAR-BRAISED CHICKEN & ONIONS ☞ serves 6

For this braised chicken recipe, balsamic vinegar (use the salad version, not expensive *aceto balsamico tradizionale*) adds the sweetness needed to balance the sharp flavor of red wine vinegar.

2 pounds cipolline or
    pearl onions
Salt
3 tablespoons olive oil
8 ounces pancetta, cut into
    ¼-inch pieces
4 garlic cloves, crushed
One 4–5-pound chicken, cut
    into 10 pieces:
    4 breast pieces, 2 wings (tips
    removed), 2 drumsticks, and
    2 thighs (see page 241)
Freshly ground black pepper
¾ cup balsamic vinegar
¾ cup red wine vinegar
2 cups chicken stock
½ cup golden raisins
2 bay leaves

Cook the onions in a large pot of boiling salted water until tender, 5–8 minutes. Drain and let cool. Trim the root ends and peel the onions. Set aside.

Meanwhile, heat the oil in a heavy large pot over medium heat. Add the pancetta and cook, stirring occasionally, until browned, 8–10 minutes. Using a slotted spoon, transfer the pancetta to a large bowl.

Add the onions to the same pot and cook, stirring occasionally, until just browned, 8–10 minutes. Add the garlic and cook for 2–3 minutes. Transfer the onions and garlic to the bowl with the pancetta.

Season the chicken with salt and pepper. Working in batches, add the chicken to the pot skin-side down and cook, turning, until browned all over. Transfer to the bowl with the onions and pancetta.

Carefully drain the fat from the pot and return the pot to medium-high heat. Add both vinegars and bring to a boil, scraping up any browned bits stuck to the bottom of the pot. Add the stock, raisins, bay leaves, and reserved chicken, pancetta, onions, and garlic to the pot. Bring to a boil, then reduce the heat to a simmer. Partially cover the pot and braise the chicken until fork-tender, 35–40 minutes.

Skim off the fat from the braising liquid. Remove and discard the bay leaves. Adjust the seasonings.

## CHICKEN & PROSCIUTTO WITH ANCHOVY BUTTER ☙ serves 4–6

We are crazy for anchovy butter. It has everything going for it: buttery richness, a complex saltiness, and a hit of lemon juice to cut through it all. This chicken dish is bathed in the butter and has plenty extra for sopping up with hunks of lightly toasted bread.

12 tablespoons (1½ sticks) salted butter
8 anchovy filets, minced
2 sprigs fresh sage or 1 sprig fresh rosemary, lightly crushed
One 4–5-pound chicken, cut into 10 pieces:
    4 breast pieces, 2 wings (tips removed), 2 drumsticks, and 2 thighs (see page 241)
Freshly ground black pepper
10–12 thin slices prosciutto
2 lemons, halved

Preheat the oven to 400°F. Put the butter, anchovies, and sage in a small saucepan over medium-low heat. As the butter melts, mash the anchovies with the back of a wooden spoon so they dissolve into the butter. When the butter is melted and bubbling, remove it from the heat.

Season the chicken lightly with pepper, then wrap each piece with a slice of prosciutto. Working over a roasting pan to catch any drips, brush the chicken with anchovy butter, coating it completely, then arrange the pieces in the pan. Roast the chicken, basting it a few times as it cooks, until the juices run clear when pierced, 20–30 minutes. (Check the breast pieces first; they will be done before the thighs and drumsticks.)

Transfer the chicken to a serving platter. Stir the remaining anchovy butter into the pan juices that have collected in the roasting pan, scraping up any browned bits. Squeeze in the juice of ½ lemon. Spoon the pan juices over the chicken. Garnish with the remaining lemons. Serve with thick slices of lightly toasted country bread, if you like.

## POACHED CAPON IN RICH BROTH ☞ serves 6–8

We find fresh capons at our market around the holidays, and frozen birds the rest of the year. Sometimes, we serve this dish with fresh tortellini floating in the golden broth.

1 capon (or 1 roasting chicken), 4–10 pounds
4 carrots, peeled and thickly sliced
4 celery stalks, thickly sliced
2 yellow onions, peeled and quartered
1 small bunch parsley
1 tablespoon black peppercorns
Salt
Parmigiano-Reggiano

Remove the breast from the capon, carving out 2 boneless breast halves from the carcass; set aside. Cut up the remaining bird into 8 pieces (see page 241) and put them into a heavy large pot over medium heat. Cover and cook, turning occasionally, for 15–20 minutes. Add the carrots, celery, onions, parsley, peppercorns, and 6 quarts (24 cups) cold water. Bring to a boil over high heat, skimming any foam. Reduce the heat to medium-low. Add the reserved breasts and poach until just tender, 20–30 minutes.

Transfer the breasts to a plate; discard the skin. Cover the meat and refrigerate. Continue simmering the broth until the dark meat is tender, about 1 hour.

Strain the broth through a fine-mesh sieve into a large bowl. Pull out the thighs and drumsticks, and separate the meat from the bones, discarding the bones, skin, and aromatics. Cover and refrigerate the meat. Strain the broth a second time into a large clean pot, leaving any debris behind. Boil the broth over medium-high heat until reduced by half (12–14 cups), about 1 hour. Season with salt.

Thickly slice the breasts and add to the broth along with the reserved dark meat, and warm through over low heat. Serve the capon and broth in wide soup bowls, garnished with grated parmigiano.

## CHICKEN POACHED IN CREAM ☞ serves 4

Poaching chicken breasts on the bone and with the skin in cream (rather than using boneless skinless breasts) gives this luxurious sauce more flavor.

6 tablespoons butter
3 celery stalks, sliced,
  leaves reserved
1 medium yellow onion,
  peeled and sliced
4 skin-on split chicken
  breasts with ribs, rinsed
2 cups heavy cream
Salt and freshly ground
  black pepper
3 egg yolks
½ lemon

Melt the butter in a heavy medium pot over medium heat. Add the celery and onions and cook, covered, until they soften, 3–5 minutes. Add the chicken, then pour in the cream. Season well with salt and pepper. Bring to a simmer. Cover the pot and reduce the heat to low. Poach the chicken, turning the pieces from time to time, until the juices run clear when pierced (the internal temperature should register 150°F–165°F on an instant-read thermometer), about 30 minutes. Transfer the chicken to a large plate.

Strain the cream sauce through a fine-mesh sieve into a bowl, pressing on the solids; discard them. Clean the pot and return the sauce to it. Whisk the egg yolks into the sauce and squeeze in some of the lemon juice. Simmer the sauce over medium-low heat, stirring constantly, until slightly thickened, about 5 minutes. Season with salt. Strain the sauce again into a bowl and return it to a clean pot.

Remove and discard the skin and bones from the chicken breasts. Slip the breasts back into the pot with the cream sauce. Heat over the lowest heat until the breasts are warmed through. Serve them with the cream sauce in a deep serving dish garnished with celery leaves, along with rice or buttered egg noodles, if you like.

## SIMPLE POACHED CHICKEN BREASTS

Put 4 rinsed, skin-on, split chicken breasts with ribs into a wide medium pot. Add 1 quartered, peeled yellow onion; 1 quartered celery stalk; 1 bay leaf; and 1 big pinch of salt. Add enough cold water to cover the chicken by at least 1 inch. Bring to a simmer over medium heat. Reduce the heat to low. Cover and poach the chicken until the juices run clear when pierced (the internal temperature should register 150°F–165°F on an instant-read thermometer), about 30 minutes. Transfer the chicken to a plate to cool. Remove the skin and bones. (Return the skin and bones to the pot and continue to simmer the stock until it is rich and flavorful; strain the stock and save for another use.)—*makes 4*

*Chicken Poached in Cream*

## HOW WE COOK CHICKEN THIGHS

Chicken thighs have it all. Lots of dark juicy meat and plenty of skin. The next best thing to *fried* chicken thighs (see page 242), is pan-fried thighs—so easy to cook, so versatile. The trick to cooking them is to get all that delicious skin crisp. Searing thighs in a hot skillet burns the skin. Rather, we go low and slow. We cook thighs like we do duck breasts, arranging them skin-side down in a heavy skillet (cast-iron or nonstick are best) over moderate heat, and leave them alone, resisting the urge to move or turn them until the fat has rendered and the skin is golden brown and crisp. Then we turn the thighs skin-side up to finish cooking. We eat them seasoned simply with salt or embellish them with any number of other seasonings. Here are some of our favorites.

## CHICKEN THIGHS WITH PANCETTA & GREEN OLIVES  ☞  serves 4

8 whole chicken thighs,
  rinsed and patted dry
Salt and freshly ground
  black pepper
6 ounces pancetta, diced
1 garlic clove, sliced
Splash of white wine vinegar
1½–2 cups green olives,
  preferably Castelvetrano,
  pitted or not

Season the chicken thighs all over with salt and pepper and arrange them in a heavy large skillet in a single layer, skin-side down. Cook them over medium heat without moving them until the fat has rendered out and the skin is deep golden brown and crisp, about 30 minutes. Fiddle with the heat, reducing it to medium-low if the skin begins to burn before it gets evenly golden brown.

Scatter the pancetta into the skillet around the thighs. Turn the thighs over and continue cooking them until the meat closest to the bone is cooked through and the juices run clear when pierced, 10–15 minutes. Stir the pancetta as it cooks so it browns evenly. Add the garlic, vinegar, and olives to the skillet about 5 minutes before the thighs are finished cooking. Adjust the seasonings. Serve the thighs with the pancetta, olives, and pan drippings.

*Overleaf, left page: Chicken Thighs with Pancetta & Green Olives; right page, clockwise from top left:*
*Chicken Thighs with Preserved Lemon; Chicken Thighs with Sherry &Mushrooms;*
*Chicken Thighs with Kale & Golden Raisins*

## CHICKEN THIGHS WITH PRESERVED LEMON

Season 8 whole chicken thighs all over with salt and freshly ground black pepper and arrange them in a heavy large skillet in a single layer, skin-side down. Cook them over medium heat without moving them until the fat has rendered out and the skin is deep golden brown and crisp, about 30 minutes. Fiddle with the heat, reducing it to medium-low if the skin begins to burn before it gets evenly golden brown. Turn the thighs over and stir the finely chopped rind from ½ preserved lemon into the fat in the skillet. Continue cooking the thighs until the meat closest to the bone is cooked through and the juices run clear when pierced, 10–15 minutes. Serve the thighs and lemony pan drippings with lemon wedges.—*serves 4*

## CHICKEN THIGHS WITH SHERRY & MUSHROOMS

Season 8 whole chicken thighs all over with salt and freshly ground black pepper and arrange them in a heavy large skillet in a single layer, skin-side down. Cook them over medium heat without moving them until the fat has rendered out and the skin is deep golden brown and crisp, about 30 minutes. Fiddle with the heat, reducing it to medium-low if the skin begins to burn before it gets evenly golden brown. Transfer the thighs to a plate, skin-side up. Add 10 ounces sliced white mushroom caps to the skillet. Return the thighs to the skillet skin-side up. Cook the mushrooms and thighs over medium heat until the mushrooms are tender and the thigh meat closest to the bone is cooked through and the juices run clear when pierced, about 15 minutes. Add ½ cup dry sherry and cook for a few minutes, then add 1 cup heavy cream. Simmer until the sauce has thickened a bit, 5–10 minutes. Adjust the seasonings. Garnish with lots of chopped fresh chives or dill. Serve with hot, buttered, wide egg noodles, rice, or potatoes, if you like.—*serves 4*

## CHICKEN THIGHS WITH KALE & GOLDEN RAISINS

Macerate 1 cup golden raisins in ½ cup white wine. Blanch 8 ounces chopped kale in boiling salted water for 2 minutes. Drain and set aside. Season 8 whole chicken thighs all over with salt and freshly ground black pepper and arrange them in a heavy large skillet in a single layer, skin-side down. Cook them over medium heat without moving them until the fat has rendered out and the skin is deep golden brown and crisp, about 30 minutes. Fiddle with the heat, reducing it to medium-low if the skin begins to burn before it gets evenly golden brown. Transfer the thighs to a plate, skin-side up. Add 1 pinch crushed red pepper flakes to the skillet along with the reserved raisins, wine, and kale, stirring everything into the fat. Return the thighs to the skillet skin-side up. Cook over medium-high heat until the juices in the skillet have almost evaporated and the thigh meat closest to the bone is cooked through and the juices run clear when pierced, about 10 minutes. Adjust the seasonings. Serve the thighs with the kale and raisins.—*serves 4*

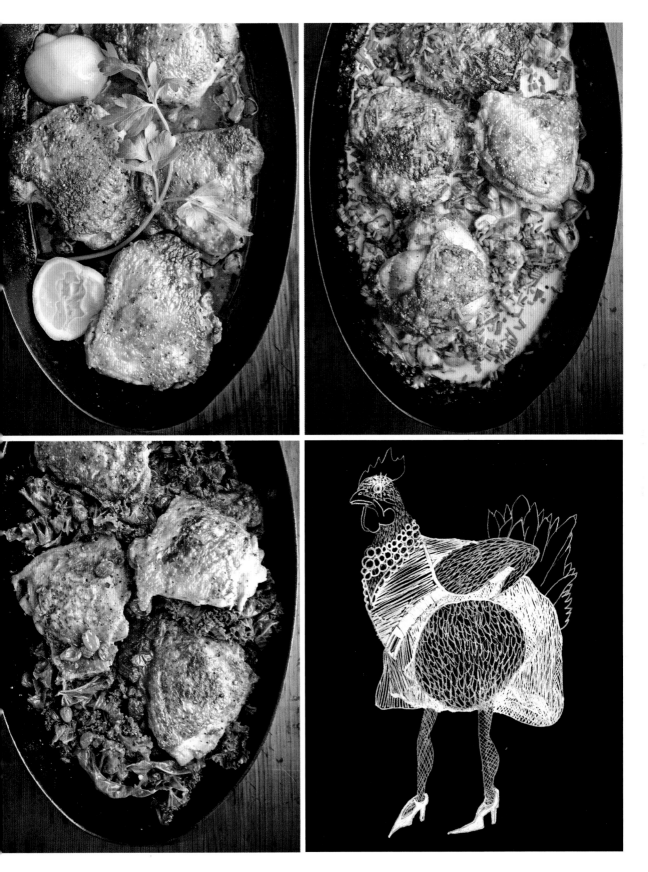

## ROAST TURKEY ✂ serves 10–16

Plan ahead and dry brine the turkey for the most flavorful, juicy bird. Just be sure to buy a turkey that has not been injected or pre-brined. See page 225 for more on brining.

One 14–16-pound fresh
  turkey
3 tablespoons kosher salt
1½ tablespoons sugar
3–4 tablespoons butter,
  softened

Remove the bag of giblets and neck from the turkey neck cavity. Reserve the liver for another use, and the rest for making stock, if you like. Rinse the turkey inside and out and pat dry with paper towels. Combine the salt and sugar and gently rub onto the breasts, legs, and thighs. Tightly wrap the turkey completely in plastic wrap or slip it into a very large resealable plastic bag, pressing out the air before sealing it. Set the turkey on a pan breast-side up and refrigerate it for 3 days. Turn the turkey every day, massaging the salt into the skin through the plastic.

Unwrap the turkey and pat it dry with paper towels (don't rinse the bird). Return the turkey to the pan breast-side up and refrigerate it, uncovered, for at least 8 hours or overnight.

Remove the turkey from the refrigerator and let it come to room temperature, at least 1 hour. Preheat the oven to 325°F. Tie the legs together with kitchen string. Tuck the wings under the back. Rub the turkey all over with the softened butter. Place the turkey breast-side up on a roasting rack set into a large roasting pan. Add 1–2 cups water to the pan.

Roast the turkey until it is golden brown and a thermometer inserted into the thigh registers 165°F, about 3 hours. Transfer the turkey to a platter, loosely cover it with foil, and let it rest for 20–30 minutes before carving.

TURKEY GRAVY: Transfer the cooked turkey from the roasting pan to a cutting board or a large platter. Put the roasting pan on the stove top straddling two burners. Bring the pan drippings to a simmer over medium heat, stirring and scraping the bottom of the pan with a whisk or wooden spoon to loosen any browned bits stuck to the bottom. Sprinkle ½ cup flour into the pan and whisk until smooth and thickened, about 1 minute. While whisking constantly, pour in 8 cups hot turkey or chicken stock. Simmer, whisking occasionally, until the gravy is thick and smooth, 10–15 minutes. Season with freshly ground black pepper. Serve hot in a gravy boat.—*makes 6–8 cups*

## DUCK À L'ORANGE ✂ serves 4

This magnificent French dish sank to a cloyingly sweet cliché back in the 1970s. Eventually, it went out of style. But we've always loved the old classic. Here is our updated, brighter-tasting version. It's a bit of work, but a special dish to serve your guests.

1 Pekin (Long Island) duck (about 5½ pounds)
1 yellow onion, peeled and coarsely chopped
3 sprigs fresh thyme
1 celery stalk, coarsely chopped
1 medium carrot, peeled, cut lengthwise and crosswise into 4 pieces
5 whole black peppercorns
3 navel oranges
Salt and freshly ground black pepper
¼ cup Port

Set the giblets from the duck aside; reserve the liver for another use. Trim the skin from both openings of the duck cavity and set aside for rendering. Cut both leg-thigh pieces off the duck. Cut the wings from the breasts. Carve the breasts from the carcass for 2 boneless breasts. Trim off the wing tips and flats and set aside. Cut the carcass into quarters. Cover and chill the leg, breast, and wing pieces.

Heat the reserved duck skin in a heavy large pot over medium heat. Cook, stirring, until about 2 tablespoons of fat is rendered, then discard the skin. Add the giblets, wing tips and flats, carcass pieces, onions, and thyme. Cook, stirring occasionally, until lightly browned, about 15 minutes. Add the celery, carrots, peppercorns, and 6 cups water. Bring to a boil over high heat, skimming any foam that rises to the surface. Reduce the heat to medium, and simmer the duck stock for 1 hour.

Meanwhile, using a sharp knife, cut all peel and white pith from 1 orange; set peel aside. Working over a medium bowl, cut between the membranes to release the orange segments into the bowl; set aside. Add the orange peel to the simmering stock. Juice the remaining 2 oranges and set the juice aside.

Strain the stock through a fine-mesh sieve into a medium bowl (you should have about 2 cups). Transfer the orange peel to a clean work surface; discard remaining solids in the sieve. Slice the peel into thin strips (remove white pith for a more refined look, if desired); set aside.

*continued*

*Overleaf, left page, clockwise from top: a whole duck; Cook's Treat; a duck cut into six pieces plus extra skin for making cracklings; right page: Duck à l'Orange*

Prick the duck pieces all over with a sharp knife. Season with salt and pepper. Arrange them in a single layer in a heavy large skillet (use two if needed), skin-side down, and cook over medium heat, occasionally pouring off the fat from the skillet into a heatproof bowl, until the skin is deep golden brown, about 20 minutes. (Cover and chill the fat; save for cooking potatoes or stir-fried rice.)

Turn over the duck pieces. Cook the breasts, skin-side up, until an instant-read thermometer inserted horizontally into the thickest part of the breast registers 125°F for medium-rare, about 2 minutes. Transfer the breasts to a large rimmed baking sheet. Continue cooking the legs and wings until well browned on both sides and the thigh juices run clear when pierced, 10–15 minutes. Transfer to the baking sheet with the breasts. Pour off the fat from the skillet, leaving the browned bits behind.

Preheat the oven to 450°F. Return the skillet with browned bits to medium-high heat. Pour in the port and cook, scraping the skillet with a wooden spoon (the browned bits will add extra flavor to the sauce) until reduced and syrupy, about 2 minutes. Add the reserved orange juice and duck stock. Boil, stirring occasionally, until the sauce is smooth and thickened, about 20 minutes. Season the sauce to taste with salt and pepper. Cover and keep warm.

Place the baking sheet with the duck pieces in the oven. Bake until the duck is just heated through, 5–8 minutes. Pour the warm sauce onto a deep platter. Scatter the orange segments and strips of peel on top. Arrange the duck pieces on top.

COOK'S TREAT: Whole poultry are typically sold with a bag of giblets (liver, neck, heart, and gizzard) tucked into the bird's cavity. Everything but the liver is good for making stock. The liver, too livery tasting for stock, is delicious sautéed in a little butter or olive oil, seasoned with salt and freshly ground black pepper, and served on a cracker or piece of toast. It's a little reward for the cook, since there's only one liver per bird.

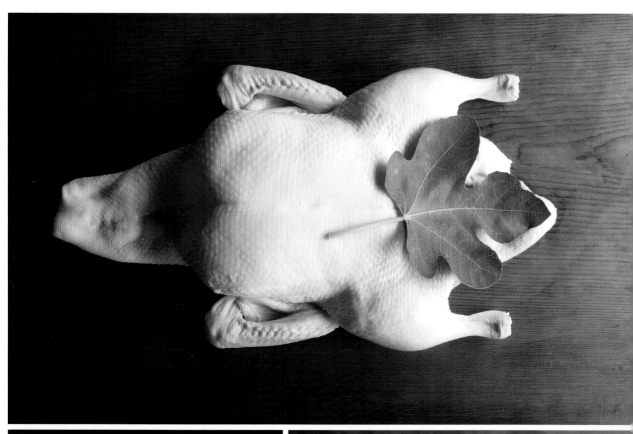

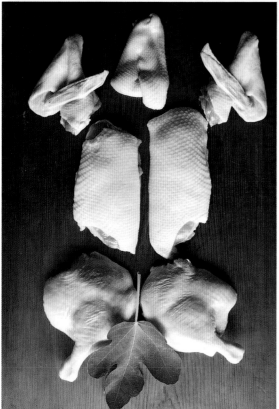

## DUCK BREASTS WITH APPLES & CARAWAY ☞ serves 4

2 boneless duck breasts,
  trimmed
Salt and freshly ground
  black pepper
1 tablespoon duck or goose
  fat, or olive oil
½ teaspoon caraway seeds,
  lightly crushed
2 apples, such as Honeycrisp,
  peeled, cored, and cut into
  thick wedges
Leaves from 1 small sprig
  fresh thyme
1 teaspoon sugar

Prick the skin of the duck breasts all over with the tip of a sharp paring knife, and season with salt and pepper. Heat the duck fat in a heavy large skillet over low heat. Sprinkle the caraway seeds over the bottom of the skillet. Place the duck breasts skin-side down in the middle of the skillet. Arrange the apples in a single layer around the duck. Sprinkle the apples with the thyme and sugar. Cook the breasts without moving them until the skin is deep golden brown and crisp, 60–70 minutes. Use a fork to turn the apples as they cook so they brown on all sides. Turn the breasts over and cook for about 5 minutes.

Transfer the duck breasts to a plate and let them rest for 5–10 minutes. While the duck breasts rest, continue to gently cook the apples until they are tender and golden brown all over.

To serve, slice the duck breasts and arrange on a platter with the apples.

## ROASTED DUCK LEGS & BEANS

We had been traveling, a week-plus of driving and eating our way through the ravishing English countryside—Lancashire, Cheshire, Wales, Shropshire, Worcester, Gloucester, Somerset, Devon and Dorset—then on to London. Our first day back at Canal House was the first day of autumn, and chilly. So we seasoned 2 duck legs with salt and freshly ground black pepper and roasted them skin-side down in an ovenproof nonstick skillet in a 350°F oven until golden and crisp, about 90 minutes. We served them atop tender Great Northern beans cooked in rich chicken stock with lots of thyme, and scattered toasted bread crumbs on top.—*serves 2*

*Duck Breasts with Apples & Caraway*

Braises & Stew

# Cook until Tender

*I can't drink a bottle of Châteauneuf-du-Pape Vieux Télégraphe without revisiting a hotel bistro in Luzerne, Switzerland, where I ate a large bowl of a peppery Basque baby goat stew. A sip and a bite. A bite and sip. Goose bumps come with the divine conjunction of food and wine.*—Jim Harrison

WE INHERITED A LARGE FLAME-COLORED LE CREUSET DUTCH OVEN from our late Canal House neighbor. He was a fervent cook and his beloved enameled cast-iron pot is all banged up to prove it. There is a crack on one side, chips in the enamel, and permanent scratches, stains, and black baked-on spatters all over. It had one lifetime of service and it's not finished yet. Now it sits at the ready on our shelf, tucked in among our colorful collection of similar *cocottes*. These hefty pots with their tight-fitting lids are the ones we reach for every time we braise meats or vegetables, make hearty stews or thick soups, or pot roast a fat chuck roast or plump bird. Just hauling one down off the shelf inspires us, sharpens our purpose, and readies us for serious cooking.

For braises and stews, we use tough, relatively inexpensive cuts of meat like brisket, chuck, shanks, or shoulder: working muscles that are full of collagen and flavor. We trim away the gristle (which never softens), but leave most of the fat, which does. We braise larger cuts of meat in small amounts of liquid (wine, broth, tomato sauce, even water is fine) and make stews with large cubes of meat and just enough liquid to cover.

The more complex stews and braises, ones with deep, rich sauces, come from building the flavors step by step. Carefully browning and caramelizing the meat, onions, and any aromatics; toasting the seasonings in the fat; adding a flavorful liquid. The simpler, pale or "blonde" stews and braises forgo the caramelization steps but can be just as flavorful.

Once everything is nestled into the pot, we put the lid on and slide it into a slow oven, where the heat is even and envelops the dish as it cooks. This is when things get seriously good. As the meat cooks in this moist, gently heated environment, these impossibly chewy cuts are coaxed into supple tenderness, the cooking liquid thickens, and the flavor deepens into a magnificent sauce. The transformation is magical. And the aroma as a good braise or stew cooks is heavenly.

We use beef chuck roast a lot for our braises and stews. It's a big hunk of meat that we'll often share half of for a simple steak-and-potato dinner for our families. The other half we use to make beef stew for lunch at the studio. We slowly simmer browned cubes of chuck and sautéed onions and garlic in red wine and beef broth in a covered heavy pot in a 325°F oven until the meat is tender. Then we enrich the sauce with flour and butter to give it body and shine, and yes, more flavor. Lacking carrots, peas, or egg noodles, we'll boil a couple of potatoes to serve with the stew. So it often is beef and potatoes back to back, but the meals couldn't taste more different. And we love the economy of one steak that feeds four one night and two for lunch the next day.

Whenever the temperature outside dips to chilly (or well below that), our appetites build and we crave deep, complex flavors, the kinds that come from slowly and gently cooked braises and stews. Then we know it is time to haul down off the shelf our thick-walled, heavy pots with their tight-fitting lids and start cooking. Amen.

# HOW WE BUILD FLAVOR IN STEWS

1. SEASONING AND FLOURING THE MEAT ⊙
Before browning meat for stew, be sure to dry the meat with paper towels. Wet/damp meat will never brown. Season the meat with salt and pepper (and sometimes paprika, which adds flavor and a rosy rich color). Keep seasoning as you cook, so the flavor is deep and not just on the surface of the sauce. Dredge the seasoned meat in flour, shaking off any extra. When floured meat is seared in hot oil, the flour mixes with the fat in the pot and adds thickness and body to the finished sauce.

2. BROWNING THE MEAT ⊙ Add a thin glaze of safflower or vegetable oil with a high smoking point to the pot—just enough to keep the meat from sticking. Brown the meat in batches, leaving about 1 inch between the pieces of meat. If you crowd the pot, the meat will steam rather than brown. Remove the meat from the pot and set aside. Now you have the most important "ingredient", the brown bits stuck on the bottom of the pot. They are the caramelization that adds flavor to the stew.

3. BROWNING THE ONION; ADDING TOMATO PASTE ⊙
Sauté the onions (and any other aromatics) in the same pot and oil that you used for the meat. Add more oil if you need to. When they are soft and translucent, push them to the edge of the pot. Add a dollop of tomato paste and allow it to "toast". More flavor.

4. DEGLAZING WITH WINE ⊙ A sticky brown glaze will have built up on the bottom of the pot. Pour in red or white wine (or even cognac). As it boils, the brown glaze will begin to melt. Use a wooden spoon to release any of the brown bits stuck on the bottom.

5. REDUCING TO THE RIGHT CONSISTENCY ⊙ As the wine cooks it will reduce and thicken into a sauce. At this stage, watch it carefully. Don't take it too far.

6. COOKING THE STEW ⊙ Return the meat to the pot. Add any cut vegetables (like carrots or potatoes) and more liquid (stock or water). Bring to a simmer. Cover and cook in the oven, where heat will evenly surround the pot. Check the tenderness of the meat after about 1½ hours. When the meat is tender, the vegetables should be too.

2.

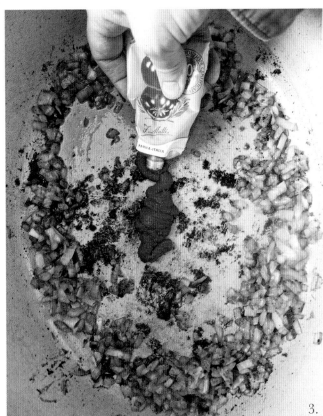

3.

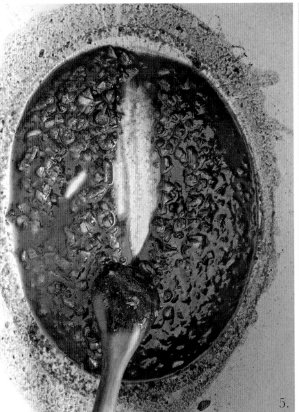

5

6.

## BEEF WITH CARROTS ☞ serves 4

*Boeuf aux Carottes* is a classic French dish as simple as its name implies. In our version we add anchovies for their deep, salty (not fishy) flavor and golden raisins for their sweetness. *C'est encore mieux!*

One 2-pound chuck roast, cut into about 12 pieces

Salt and freshly ground black pepper

½ cup flour

3 tablespoons safflower or vegetable oil

2 medium yellow onions, peeled and sliced

1 garlic clove, sliced

4 anchovy filets, minced

1 cup red wine

½ cup golden raisins

1 handful chopped fresh parsley leaves

2 pounds carrots, peeled and cut into 1-inch pieces

2 cups chicken stock

Preheat the oven to 325°F. Dry the meat with paper towels. Season with salt and pepper. Dredge the meat in the flour and shake off any excess. Heat the oil in a heavy large ovenproof pot with a lid over medium-high heat. Working in batches to avoid crowding the pot (which can cause the meat to steam rather than brown), add the meat in a single layer, turning the pieces as they brown on all sides. Transfer the meat to a large plate and set aside.

If the pot is too dry, add a little more oil. Add the onions, garlic, and anchovies to the pot and cook until the onions are soft and translucent, about 10 minutes.

Add the wine and stir with a wooden spoon, scraping up any browned bits on the bottom of the pot. Bring to a boil, and cook until the wine has reduced slightly, about 2 minutes.

Return the beef to the pot and add the raisins, parsley, carrots, and chicken stock. Bring it to a simmer over medium-high heat, cover, put it in the oven, and cook until the meat is tender, 2–3 hours. Remove from the oven. Use a slotted spoon to transfer the meat and vegetables to a bowl.

Reduce the sauce left in the pot over medium-high heat until it thickens slightly, about 10 minutes. Return the meat and vegetables to the pot. Adjust the seasonings. Serve with mashed potatoes (page 360) and garnish with chopped parsley, if you like.

RED STEW  ☞  serves 6–8

This simple stew came to us through CH's grandmother, whose Irish-American parents died in San Francisco in 1906 when she was still a child. She and her sisters were taken in by kindly Italian cousins. Perhaps in an effort to cook something familiar to the girls, Red Stew was born, marrying Irish meat and potato stew and Italian tomato sauce. That was more than a century ago and we still make this wonderful recipe, remembering those little girls and that kind-hearted cook.

4 ounces pancetta, chopped
2 medium yellow onions,
    peeled and sliced
2 garlic cloves, sliced
1 generous teaspoon
    dried oregano
1 tablespoon ground
    fennel seeds
1 tablespoon sugar
1 large pinch of crushed red
    pepper flakes
Freshly ground
    black pepper
1 cup red wine
One 3-pound chuck roast,
    cut into large pieces
One 28-ounce can whole,
    peeled plum tomatoes
4–6 carrots, peeled and cut
    into pieces
4 potatoes, peeled and
    quartered
2 cups (more or less) shucked
    English peas, fresh or frozen
Salt

Preheat the oven to 325°F. Fry the pancetta in a heavy large ovenproof pot with a lid over medium-high heat until lightly browned, about 10 minutes. Add the onions, garlic, oregano, fennel, sugar, and crushed red pepper flakes to the pot. Season with black pepper. Cook, stirring often with a wooden spoon, until the onions have softened, about 10 minutes.

Add the wine and stir, scraping up any browned bits on the bottom of the pot. Bring to a boil, and cook until the wine has reduced slightly, about 2 minutes.

Add the beef, then add the tomatoes, crushing them with your hand as you drop them into the pot, along with any juices. Rinse out the can with about 1 cup of water and add the water to the pot. Bring to a simmer, cover, and transfer the pot to the oven.

Braise the stew for 1½ hours, then add the carrots and potatoes and cook until the meat is very tender, about 1½ hours. Add the peas about 15 minutes before you are ready to serve. Taste and season with salt and pepper, if needed.

## GOULASH CANAL HOUSE–STYLE  ⪦ serves 8

2 thick beef chuck roasts
  (about 3 pounds each)
Salt and freshly ground
  black pepper
1 cup flour
3 tablespoons safflower or
  vegetable oil
4 medium yellow onions,
  peeled and sliced lengthwise
4 garlic cloves, sliced
2 tablespoons tomato paste
2 cups red wine
1½ teaspoons caraway seeds
2 tablespoons paprika, sweet
  or hot, or a combination
½ cup passata di pomodoro
  or tomato purée
4 cups chicken stock or water
2–3 bay leaves
Chopped fresh parsley leaves,
  for the noodles, optional
Cooked and buttered egg
  noodles, optional
Sour cream, optional

Trim the meat with a sharp knife, pulling the meat apart into naturally shaped pieces, and cutting away all fat and sinew. (You may have as much as 1 pound of trimmings.) Discard the trimmings. Cut the meat into 2–3-inch pieces, and pat it dry with paper towels. Season with salt and pepper. Dredge the meat in the flour.

Preheat the oven to 300°F. Heat 2 tablespoons of the oil in a heavy large ovenproof pot with a lid over medium-high heat. Working in batches to avoid crowding the pot (which can cause the meat to steam rather than brown), add the meat in a single layer, turning the pieces as they brown on all sides. Transfer the meat to a large plate and set aside.

Add the remaining 1 tablespoon oil to the pot and return the pot to medium-high heat. Add the onions and garlic, and stir to coat. Season with salt and pepper. Cook, stirring once or twice, until the onions soften, about 5 minutes. Push the onions to the edge of the pot.

Add the tomato paste in the center of the pot and "toast" it for 1–2 minutes. Add the wine and, using a wooden spoon, loosen any browned bits on the bottom of the pot. Bring to a boil and cook until the wine has reduced slightly and the alcohol has cooked off, about 3 minutes. Stir in the caraway seeds, paprika, passata, and stock, and cook until hot, about 2 minutes. Taste and season with salt and pepper.

Return the meat to the pot. The sauce should just barely cover the onions (add a little water, if needed). Add the bay leaves. Cut a round of parchment paper, using the pot lid as a template, and place it directly on top of the stew. This will keep everything moist.

Cover the pot, transfer it to the oven, and braise until the meat is very tender when pierced with a fork, 2½–3 hours. Discard the bay leaves. Season to taste with salt and pepper. Serve over parsleyed egg noodles with a big dollop of sour cream, if you like.

LAMB STEW 🖙 serves 6

Lamb shoulder is a tough but flavorful cut of meat that needs long, gentle cooking. Lamb neck, typically sold on the bone and cut into pieces, is an excellent substitute for this recipe. Keep the meat on the bone while it cooks but pull it off and discard the bones before serving. Use four pounds of lamb neck instead of three of boneless shoulder to make sure there's enough meat for your guests.

3 pounds boneless lamb shoulder, trimmed of excess fat, meat cut into 2- to 3-inch pieces

Salt and freshly ground black pepper

2 tablespoons safflower or vegetable oil

2 medium yellow onions, peeled and thickly sliced lengthwise

6 carrots, peeled, trimmed, and cut into 2- to 3-inch pieces

4–6 medium waxy or all-purpose potatoes, peeled and quartered

2–3 large sprigs fresh thyme

1 large handful fresh parsley leaves, chopped

1 small handful fresh mint leaves, chopped

Preheat the oven to 300°F. Pat the lamb dry with paper towels and season with salt and pepper.

Heat the oil in a heavy large ovenproof pot with a lid over medium-high heat. Working in batches to avoid crowding the pot, add the lamb in a single layer, turning the pieces as they brown. Transfer the browned meat to a large plate, and set aside.

Add the onions to the pot and stir with a wooden spoon to scrape up any browned bits stuck on the bottom. Cook, stirring once or twice, until the onions begin to soften, 3–5 minutes. Return the meat and any accumulated juices to the pot. Add the carrots, potatoes, and thyme. Add enough cold water to barely cover the meat and vegetables, 4–5 cups. Season with salt and pepper. Cover the pot and bring just to a simmer.

Transfer the stew to the oven and braise until the meat is very tender or easily pulls apart when pierced with a fork, 2–2½ hours. Adjust the seasonings. Skim off most of the fat from the surface of the stew. Garnish with parsley and mint just before serving.

## BRAISED BEEF BRISKET ☞ serves 4–6

We have a friend who wrote a whole book on brisket, it seems with every grandmother's, mother's, and aunt's recipe. It is a great sociological study on one recipe. People complain that brisket is usually too dry, then exclaim that their recipe is the best ever. We find that the ultimate secret to a tender, juicy brisket is lots of time in a low oven with some liquid to add moisture: low and slow. Long cooking is important. It breaks down the connective tissue in the meat, and liquid helps convert the meat's collagen to gelatin. We add flavor with pimentón (smoked Spanish paprika) and good old ketchup, and cook the roast on a bed of onions.

2 tablespoons safflower or vegetable oil
4 medium yellow onions, peeled and sliced into thick rounds
3 garlic cloves, crushed
One 3-pound beef brisket with a nice layer of fat
1 tablespoon pimentón
Salt and freshly ground black pepper
1 cup ketchup
2 tablespoons sherry vinegar or red wine vinegar
1 cup dried currants or raisins

Preheat the oven to 300°F. Heat the oil in a heavy large enameled cast-iron or other heavy ovenproof pot with a lid over medium-high heat. Add the onions and garlic, and cook until softened and slightly collapsed, about 5 minutes. Remove the pot from the heat.

Rub the brisket all over with the pimentón and a generous seasoning of salt and pepper.

Put the brisket in the pot fat-side up on top of the onions. Stir together the ketchup, 1/2 cup water, the vinegar, and the currants in a small bowl, and pour over the brisket. Cover the pot and transfer it to the oven.

Braise the meat until it is very tender, about 3 hours. Remove the pot from the oven and transfer the meat to a cutting board. Skim off the fat from the sauce. Slice the meat and serve with the sauce.

## CINNAMON & CHILE-RUBBED BRISKET

We sometimes cook a cinnamon and chile-rubbed brisket long and slow with onions and garlic and a little tomato paste. It quietly simmers away in the oven until it is so tender we can shred it with a fork. We eat the meat with rice, avocados, and limes dusted with cayenne.—*serves 4–6*

*Braised Beef Brisket*

## CORNED BEEF & CABBAGE ☞ serves 6–8

Corned beef and cabbage is an Irish-American invention. In the late nineteenth century, Eastern European Jewish and Irish immigrants lived side by side on the Lower East Side of Manhattan. The Irish bought their meat from kosher butchers and bought what they found—brisket. Since brisket is a tough cut, they employed their tradition of corning (salting, think an extreme dry brine) the meat. After a long, slow simmer, the brisket was transformed into the extremely tender, flavorful corned beef that we know today. If you prefer a leaner cut of corned beef, with slices that hold their shape when carved, choose "flat" or "first cut". The thicker "point" cut is marbled with fat and will be more tender and flavorful. Add a second brisket to the pot so you have enough for Corned Beef Hash (opposite).

1 corned beef brisket (3–4 pounds), rinsed
2 bay leaves
12 black peppercorns
8 large waxy potatoes, peeled
1–2 bunches carrots, peeled
1 head savoy cabbage, cut into 8 wedges
1 handful fresh parsley leaves, chopped
1 bunch fresh chives, minced

FOR THE HORSERADISH CREAM
2 tablespoons peeled, finely grated fresh horseradish or drained prepared horseradish
Juice of ¼ lemon
1 bunch fresh chives, minced
1 cup whipped cream
Salt and freshly ground black pepper

Put the meat, bay leaves, and peppercorns into a large pot and cover with cold water. (Keep the meat submerged by weighing it down with a heavy lid.) Bring just to a boil, skimming any foam. Reduce the heat to maintain a gentle simmer. Partially cover the pot with a lid and simmer until the meat is very tender when pierced with a skewer, about 4 hours. Transfer the meat to a platter and cover with plastic wrap.

Strain the broth, returning it to the pot. Put the vegetables into the pot and gently cook over medium heat until quite tender, 30–45 minutes for the potatoes; 20–30 minutes for the carrots and cabbage. Transfer the vegetables as they finish cooking to the platter with the corned beef. Reserve the cooking broth in the pot and keep hot over low heat.

For the horseradish cream, fold the horseradish, lemon juice, and chives into the whipped cream in a medium bowl. Season with salt and pepper.

Reheat the corned beef in the hot broth. Transfer the meat to a cutting board, thinly slice, and arrange on a warm serving platter. Reheat the vegetables in the hot broth and arrange on the platter. Ladle some of the broth over all. (Reserve the broth to make Corned Beef Hash (opposite), if you like.) Garnish with parsley and chives. Serve with the horseradish cream.

*Overleaf, left page: Corned Beef; right page: Corned Beef Hash*

## CORNED BEEF HASH ❧ serves 6

This hash is a two-step process, but nothing about it is difficult. Start by cooking the corned beef the day before (if you also want to have it for dinner that night, just double the recipe). The next day, return the pot with the cooked corned beef and reserved broth to the stovetop to reheat. Add the potatoes and onions. By the time the corned beef is hot and easy to shred, the vegetables will be cooked and the hash ready to throw together. The eggs can be poached two hours ahead; place in a bowl of ice water and chill. Reheat in barely simmering water for one minute just before serving.

1 cooked corned beef brisket (opposite), with reserved cooking broth
2 medium russet potatoes, peeled and halved
2 medium yellow onions, peeled and halved
1 small handful fresh parsley leaves, chopped
Salt and freshly ground black pepper
4 tablespoons butter
6–12 poached eggs (page 16)

Put the corned beef and broth into a large pot. Add the potatoes and onions and gently boil over medium heat until tender, about 25 minutes. Transfer the meat to a cutting board and the vegetables to a bowl. If the onions are not tender enough, continue boiling them until they are, then add them to the bowl with the potatoes. Discard all but about ¼ cup of the cooking broth.

Use two forks to shred the corned beef into bite-size pieces, then put the shredded meat into a bowl. Coarsely chop the potatoes and slice the onions, and add them to the corned beef. Stir in the parsley and moisten it all with some of the reserved cooking broth. Taste the hash and season it with salt and pepper.

Preheat the oven to 200°F. Melt 2 tablespoons of the butter in a large nonstick skillet over medium heat. Spoon half of the corned beef mixture into the skillet, shaping it into a flat cake with a metal spatula. Cook undisturbed until the bottom is browned and crisp, 6–8 minutes. Set a plate over the skillet and carefully invert the hash onto the plate; slide it back into the skillet, pressing it back into shape if needed, and cook until browned and crisp on the second side, 6–8 minutes. Transfer the hash to a cookie sheet and keep it warm in the oven. Brown the remaining corned beef mixture in the remaining 2 tablespoons of butter in the same manner. Transfer it to the oven.

Divide the hash between six warm plates. Season with pepper. Place 1 or 2 eggs on each portion of hash and serve.

## PORK STEWED IN GUAJILLO CHILE MOLE ✒ serves 6–8

Mildly hot guajillo chiles carry the flavor in this stew. The leathery skins, after soaking and puréeing (along with spices, nuts, and raisins), are transformed into this intensely flavored, velvety mole.

12 whole guajillo chiles, wiped with a damp paper towel

5 cups hot chicken stock

⅔ cup blanched almonds

1 tablespoon ground cumin

1 tablespoon dried oregano

2 teaspoons ground cinnamon

10 black peppercorns

Salt

1 cup raisins

3 garlic cloves

4 tablespoons safflower or vegetable oil

6 pounds boneless pork butt or Boston butt, cut into 1-inch cubes

3 medium yellow onions, peeled and sliced

Freshly ground black pepper

½ bunch scallions, trimmed and chopped

Large handful fresh cilantro leaves, chopped

Remove the stems from the chiles and shake out the seeds. Heat a heavy large skillet over medium heat. Toast the chiles in the skillet, pressing them down with tongs and turning once or twice, until they are fragrant and turn slightly darker, 30–60 seconds. Transfer the chiles to a medium bowl. Pour 2 cups of the hot chicken stock over the chiles and set aside to soak until soft and pliable, about 30 minutes.

In the same skillet, toast the almonds over medium heat, stirring frequently, until pale golden brown, 6–8 minutes. Transfer to a plate to cool completely. Add the cumin, oregano, cinnamon, and peppercorns to the skillet and toast the spices over medium heat, stirring, until fragrant, about 30 seconds. Add to the almonds. Finely grind the almonds and spices with 1 teaspoon salt in a food processor or blender. Add the chiles and their soaking liquid, raisins, and garlic. Purée to a smooth paste.

Heat 2 tablespoons of the oil in the skillet over medium heat. Add the spice paste and fry, stirring to keep it from burning, until it becomes a shade darker and is very fragrant, about 5 minutes. Remove the skillet from the heat and set aside.

Dry the pork with paper towels. Heat the remaining 2 tablespoons of oil in a heavy large pot with a lid over medium heat. Working in batches, brown the pork all over, about 5 minutes. Transfer the browned meat to a plate and set aside. Add the onions to the pot and cook, stirring often, until soft, about 5 minutes.

Return the pork and any juices to the pot. Add the spice paste. Add 2 cups of the stock and season with salt and pepper. Bring to a simmer. Cover the pot and simmer the stew over low heat, stirring occasionally, until the pork is tender, 2–3 hours. Add a little more stock to the pot if the stew begins to dry out. Serve the stew garnished with scallions and cilantro.

## BRAISED LAMB SHANKS ✒ serves 4

The meat from the shank, a working muscle, is tough. It needs long, gentle cooking in liquid to be coaxed into supple tenderness. And, like most braised dishes, the flavor is better the next day. The braising juices from the lamb shanks is plentiful and full of flavor. There will be more than you need to spoon over each serving. Strain it and have it hot as a nourishing morning broth, or use it for soups, risottos, or any recipe calling for a rich, flavorful meat broth.

FOR THE LAMB SHANKS
4 lamb shanks
Salt and freshly ground black
    pepper
2–4 small yellow onions,
    peeled and quartered
    lengthwise
4–8 garlic cloves, peeled
2 cups white wine
2–3 bay leaves
6 cups chicken stock or water
4 tablespoons butter

FOR THE SPRING ONIONS
16–20 young spring onions
    or 2–3 bunches scallions,
    trimmed
8 tablespoons (1 stick) butter
¼ cup white wine
Salt

For the lamb shanks, preheat the oven to 375°F. Season the lamb shanks with salt and pepper and put them into a large heavy ovenproof pot with a lid. Add the onions, garlic, wine, bay leaves, stock, and butter to the pot. Season with salt and pepper. Bring to a simmer over medium-high heat on top of the stove.

Cover the pot with the lid and transfer it to the oven. Braise the shanks until just tender when pierced with a fork and the meat begins to pull away from the bone, about 2½ hours.

Uncover the pot and continue cooking the shanks in the oven until they are so tender the meat nearly falls off the bone and the braising juices have reduced a bit, about 1 hour. Remove and discard the bay leaves before serving.

For the spring onions, while the lamb shanks are finishing their last hour of cooking, put the onions in an even layer in a deep, wide pan with a lid. Add the butter and wine and season to taste with salt. Cover the pan and bring to a simmer over medium heat. Reduce the heat to medium-low and gently braise the onions until tender, 20–30 minutes. (The braising juices can be added to the pot with the lamb shanks, if you like.)

Serve the lamb shanks, onions, garlic, and spring onions on warm serving plates with some of the braising juices spooned on top.

## BAKED HAM WITH GOLDEN BREAD CRUMBS ☞ makes enough for a village

The sweet, crunchy bread-crumb crust is the part everyone always wants when we serve this ham. Make extra toasted bread crumbs to serve sprinkled on the sliced ham or serve the ham with Golden Bread Crumbs with Pancetta & Prunes (page 289). A bone-in ham will feed 3–4 people per pound.

One 16-pound bone-in smoked ham
2 cups packed dark brown sugar
½ cup Dijon mustard
¼ cup extra-virgin olive oil
3 cups coarse fresh bread crumbs made from crusty white bread
1 small handful fresh sage leaves, chopped
1 small handful fresh rosemary leaves, chopped

Preheat the oven to 300°F. Using a sharp knife, remove the rind from most of the ham, leaving a band around the end of the shank bone and a thin layer of fat all over. Score the fat on top of the ham in a ¾-inch diamond pattern. Place the ham in a large roasting pan. Pour 3 cups of water into the pan. Bake the ham for 2 hours.

Meanwhile, stir the brown sugar and mustard in a medium bowl to make a thick paste and set aside.

Heat the olive oil in a large skillet over medium heat. Add the bread crumbs, sage, and rosemary, and toast, stirring frequently, until crisp and golden, 5–10 minutes. Set the bread crumbs aside.

Remove the ham from the oven and increase the temperature to 350°F. Spread half of the sugar-mustard paste over the scored top of the ham. Bake the ham for 1 hour.

Remove the ham from the oven and increase the temperature to 400°F. Spread the remaining half of the sugar-mustard paste over the ham and pack the bread crumbs all over the top. Add 1 cup water to the roasting pan if the pan juices have dried out.

Return the ham to the oven to bake until the bread crumbs are deep golden brown, about 15 minutes. Transfer the ham to a serving platter or a carving board and let it rest for about 10 minutes before carving.

*Overleaf, left page: Golden Bread Crumbs; right page: artist's rendition of Baked Ham*

## GOLDEN BREAD CRUMBS WITH PANCETTA & PRUNES

We love these bread crumbs so much that we make a big batch of them to sprinkle over cooked vegetables, toss into pastas, and add to green salads to give them a little crunch. Melt 4 tablespoons butter in a heavy large skillet over medium heat. Add about 2 cups finely diced pancetta and cook, stirring often, until lightly browned, about 15 minutes. Stir in 8 cups fresh bread crumbs, and toast, stirring frequently, until deep golden brown, about 15 minutes. Remove the skillet from the heat. Stir in 2 pinches of crushed red pepper flakes and 1 cup finely diced pitted prunes, using the back of a spoon to break up the prunes and evenly mix them throughout the crumbs. Season with salt and freshly ground black pepper. Allow to cool completely and store in an airtight container in the refrigerator. Warm in a skillet over medium heat before using. —*makes about 8 cups*

## SLOW-ROASTED BONELESS PORK SHOULDER ☞ serves 6–8

We learned this way of cooking pork shoulder in Italy where it is called *porchetta*. Ours is a home-style version using pork shoulder instead of skin-on pork belly. No cracklings, but easier to cook and all the flavors are the same.

One 6–7-pound boneless
   pork shoulder/butt
1 handful fresh herb leaves
   (rosemary, parsley, or other
   herbs), finely chopped
4 garlic cloves, thinly sliced
Salt and freshly ground
   black pepper
½ lemon, thinly sliced

Lay the meat out on a clean work surface, fat-side down. Season it with the chopped herbs, garlic, and plenty of salt and pepper. Arrange the slices of lemon on top. Gather the loose folds of the pork together to enclose the seasonings, and make a neat package by snugly trussing the roast with kitchen string. Rub salt and pepper all over the roast. Cover the meat and refrigerate it for a few hours, or, for more flavor, overnight.

Preheat the oven to 200°F. Put the roast into an enameled cast-iron pot with a tight-fitting lid. Cover the pot and put it in the oven. Roast the pork (resisting the urge to check on it as it cooks) until it is fully tender and a lot of juices have accumulated in the pot, about 8 hours. Remove the lid and continue cooking the roast until it is golden brown on top and the juices have reduced a bit, 30–60 minutes.

Let the roast rest for 10–15 minutes before carving. Serve with the fragrant juices.

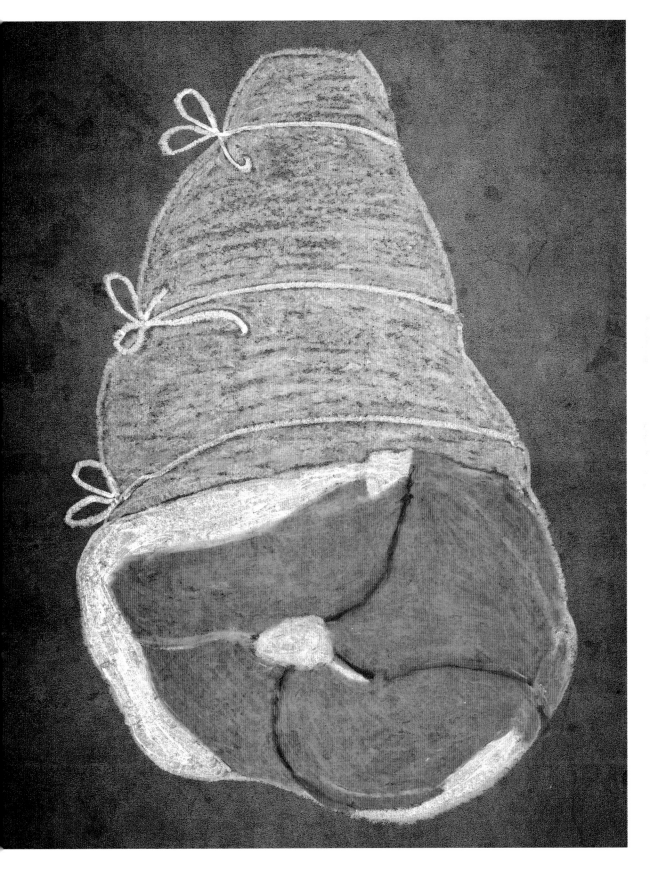

## ROAST PRIME RIB OF BEEF ✏ serves 8–10

Prime rib is a luxury these days—expensive, but oh, so delicious. Both of us serve it for Christmas dinner or New Year's Eve supper. It makes a spectacular presentation standing tall on a big platter. Actually, this recipe requires very little preparation or tending to as it cooks. If there are any leftovers, what is better than a cold roast beef sandwich with horseradish mayonnaise? This is one of those miracle recipes. How can such a large roast cook at such a low temperature? But it works every time. The gentle heat cooks the roast evenly throughout, which means beautifully rosy pink slices of beef.

One 8–12-pound prime rib roast of beef, tied between the ribs
Salt and freshly ground black pepper

Preheat the oven to 200°F. Generously season the roast all over with salt and pepper. Heat a heavy skillet large enough to accommodate the roast and sear the meaty sides of the roast until nicely browned, 5–10 minutes.

Transfer the roast to a large roasting pan, rib-side down, and roast in the oven until the internal temperature reaches 120°F for rare, 130°F–135°F for medium-rare, and 140°F for medium, 3–4½ hours.

Transfer the roast beef to a carving board or a warm serving platter and let it rest for 30 minutes. Remove string before carving the roast. Serve with Horseradish Cream, if you like.

### HORSERADISH CREAM

Dissolve 2 large pinches of sugar in 2 tablespoons cider vinegar in a bowl. Stir in ¼ cup Dijon mustard, then add 1⅓ cups whipped heavy cream and about ¼ cup finely grated, peeled fresh horseradish or drained prepared horseradish. Season with salt.—*makes about 2 cups*

### HORSERADISH MAYONNAISE

If you are lucky enough to have leftover Horseradish Cream, just stir a few tablespoons into some mayonnaise. Make as much or as little as you like. Or, spoon ½ cup of mayonnaise into a small bowl. Stir in 1 tablespoon Dijon mustard and 1 tablespoon drained prepared horseradish. Season with freshly ground black pepper and adjust the seasonings.—*makes about ⅔ cup*

## ROAST LEG OF LAMB ☞ serves 8

For us there is nothing better than a leg of lamb. We serve it on birthdays, graduations, any time there is a celebration. And it also shows up on the menu of most of our Sunday dinners. We often throw some peeled, sliced potatoes into the pan to cook along with the roast. And for a rich brown gravy, we pour strong black coffee into the roasting pan to add flavor and color to the pan juices.

1 leg of lamb, 4–5 pounds,
   tail, pelvic, and thigh bones
   removed, shank bone and
   heel left attached, at
   room temperature
Salt and freshly ground
   black pepper
3 garlic cloves, chopped
3 anchovy filets
Large handful fresh
   parsley leaves
3 tablespoons Dijon mustard
2 cups freshly brewed
   black coffee
2 tablespoons flour
2 cups chicken stock, or more

Preheat the oven to 350°F. Season the lamb with salt and pepper. Put the garlic, anchovies, parsley, and a pinch of salt and pepper in a pile on a cutting board and chop it into a fine paste. Using the tip of a paring knife, make several 1-inch deep slits all over the meaty parts of the lamb. Push the paste into the slits with your finger. Some of the paste will smear on the surface of the lamb, but that's fine. Slather the mustard all over the lamb. Season with salt and pepper.

Put the lamb on a roasting rack in a roasting pan. Pour the coffee into the pan. Roast the lamb until it is nicely browned on the outside, rosy pink on the inside, and the internal temperature reaches 130°F for medium-rare, about 1½ hours. Add a splash of water to the pan as the lamb roasts if the pan juices begin to dry out. Transfer the lamb to a warm serving platter or cutting board, loosely tent it with foil, and let the roast rest for 15–20 minutes before carving.

To make the pan gravy, put the roasting pan with the drippings on top of the stove and heat over medium heat. Add the flour and cook, whisking constantly to prevent it from getting lumpy, until the flavor is toasty rather than raw, 3–4 minutes. Whisk in the stock and cook, whisking constantly, until the gravy is smooth and thickened, about 5 minutes. Season with salt and pepper. Thin the gravy with a little more stock if it's too thick. Strain the gravy through a sieve into a gravy boat and serve with the roast.

*Facing page, top, left to right: strong black coffee; seasoned lamb slathered with mustard before roasting; bottom: Roast Leg of Lamb*

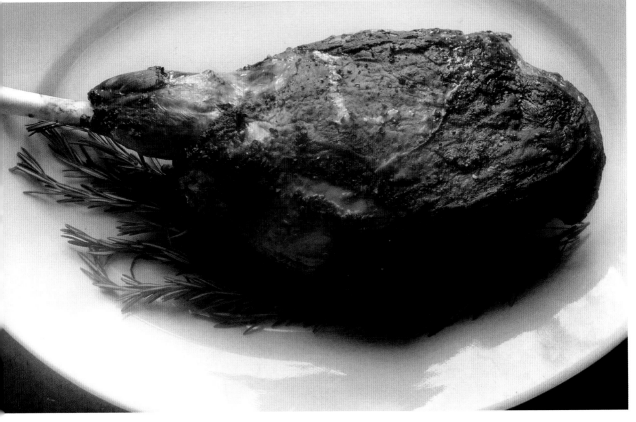

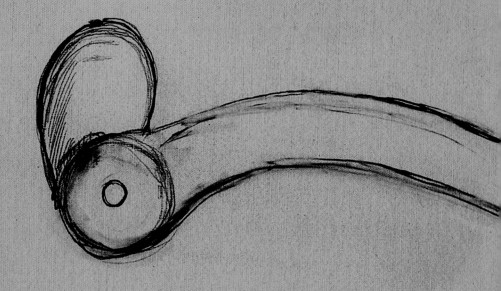

# Ground Meat

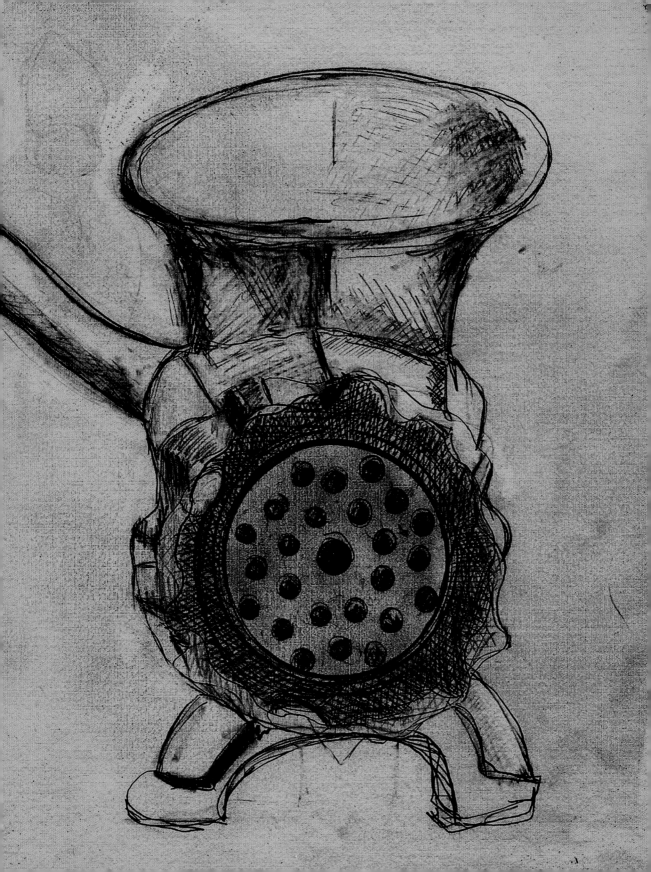

# The American Way

*The tree was all covered, / All covered with moss, / And on it grew meatballs, / And tomato sauce.*—
"On Top of Spaghetti"

IN 1950S AND 1960S AMERICA, SUPERMARKETS WERE REPLACING SPECIALTY FOOD SHOPS, like
grocery stores, cheese shops, fishmongers, and butcher shops. And though these large
markets promoted self-service, each department was still staffed with knowledgeable clerks who
could assist and advise. Growing up, we often accompanied our mothers and grandmothers on
their shopping expeditions. Since home refrigerators were smaller than today's, they couldn't
hold a week's worth of groceries, so people shopped more often. That's where we learned to be
discerning shoppers, expecting premium brands, the freshest fish, and, like our matriarchs, to
ask butchers to grind our hamburger fresh, watching to see what went into the grinder. Purvey-
ors respected customers with high expectations and standards.

In this country we have a love of the new and modern. So in postwar America, convenience
eclipsed tradition, and in the kitchen, our version of the casserole as a one-dish meal was born. It
seems so American that the individual parts blend together into one whole thing. Ground meat,
usually hamburger, often replaced the traditional meat of authentic ethnic dishes.

Take beef stroganoff, named after the aristocratic Russian Stroganov family. Tender beef was
cooked in a mustard sauce with sour cream—a marriage of French and Russian cuisine—and
served with fried straw potatoes. At the time of the Russian revolution, aristocrats fled into
China. Perhaps this is when the potatoes were lost and became rice or noodles. Over time,
onions and mushrooms were added. Finally, Peg Bracken Americanized it into Skid Row
Stroganoff: hamburger, bouillon, paprika, mushrooms, and cream of chicken soup over
noodles. Or Hungarian goulash (*gulyás*): cubed beef, sometimes heart and liver, simmered with

onions, seasoned with paprika and caraway seeds, with tiny dumplings (*nokedli*). The Hungarian-American version is a one-pot favorite of hamburger, tomato sauce, and elbow macaroni. Mexican tacos, Italian spaghetti and meatballs, and Chinese ground beef lo mein shared similar fates.

We love ground meats for their texture and flavor and prefer to keep things simple by making meatballs and meatloaf. Even more elemental, the old-fashioned chopped steak, an economical ringer for steak, is lean ground round enriched with egg yolk, shallots, and fresh herbs; shaped into flat oval patties; and marked on both sides with crosshatching to catch a seasoning of salt and pepper. Sometimes we fancy it up with a *marchand de vin* sauce.

The trick for meatballs is holding the delicate orbs together with minimal binding so they are tasty and tender. We always add eggs, sometimes fresh bread crumbs softened in half-and-half, or ricotta cheese and grated pecorino. It's easy and fun to make big batches. We'll pull up chairs to the kitchen table and roll the mixture into hundreds of small balls. Often we'll freeze them on cookie sheets, then store the frozen meatballs in resealable bags. Then the hardest part is done. When we want to serve them, all we have to do is to make a sauce—dill, Tetrazzini, cream, or ginger-soy—or float them in a rich broth with tiny pasta. For classic Italian-American spaghetti and meatballs, we double their size. Bigger is better in the United States.

Our meatloaf uses beef, pork, and veal; eggs, heavy cream, ricotta, and fresh bread crumbs; and Beau Monde seasoning. This retro seasoning is mostly celery salt and onion powder, and some secret ingredient that gives it that *je ne sais quoi*. We are always looking for ways to add salt and flavor and this does the trick for us. Sometimes we forgo softened bread crumbs, replacing them with crumbled tofu. An older friend remembers when pantries were stocked with tapioca for weeknight dessert puddings, and using those tiny white pearls as a binder. We are going to try that! Once the mixture is patted into a loaf pan, a sweet, tangy, ketchup sauce is slathered on top and bakes into a sticky glaze. We always make extra to serve alongside.

And of course, we both love good ole cheeseburgers. As magazine editors we used to travel far and wide for our work. On the drive home from the airport, we would always swing into a drive-through for a salty, juicy, fast-food burger—such a classic taste. After all, we are American women.

## CHOOSING & BUYING GROUND MEAT

When we have the opportunity, we seek out a trusted butcher for ground meat. They grind any blend we ask for, guaranteeing the freshest and most flavorful. We also buy from local, small-scale farmers who grind their own meat and poultry. We take comfort in knowing the meat's provenance. When we are feeling virtuous, we haul out our heavy metal Universal hand-crank meat grinder to get the meat the way we like it. But nine times out of ten, we pick up packaged ground meat and poultry from the supermarket. It's a convenient and affordable purchase, but we trust the quality and handling of what our store carries. Seek out what's best for you.

Most ground meat and poultry sold at the supermarket these days is finely ground, and with beef, pork, and veal, the meat typically comes from the trimmings of larger cuts like roasts, briskets, and steaks. Package labels often, but not always, indicate the cut of meat or poultry used, and include its lean-meat to fatty-meat ratio. The more information on the label, the better. (We avoid buying "hamburger" and "ground beef"—they come from unspecified cuts.) Remember, fat equals flavor and adds juiciness. The leaner the blend you use, the drier and less flavorful it will be. Check sell-by dates. Ground meat is perishable. Choose the freshest available, keep it cold, and use it right away. Or wrap the package well in a resealable plastic bag and freeze it. Defrost it in the fridge.

## OUR FAVORITE GROUND MEATS

BEEF: 80 percent lean ground chuck (from the chuck roast, a neck/shoulder cut) is our all-purpose choice. It is tender, flavorful, juicy, and readily available. Specialty blends that include brisket, short ribs, rib eye and/or hanger steak are worth trying. Choose bright, fresh, rosy-red meat with defined white flecks of fat. Medium-grind meat makes great burgers.

PORK: The pork shoulder, well-marbled with fat, is the standard cut used for ground pork. It's about 85 percent lean. It's tender and juicy. Choose pale pink meat with defined white flecks of fat.

VEAL: Mild, palest pink ground veal, often used in delicate forcemeats, is included in meatloaf and meatball mixes to help retain moisture and lend a gentle flavor to ground pork and beef.

LAMB: Lamb has lots of fat, which gives it lots of flavor. We tend to like the sweeter, milder flavor of domestic ground lamb with an 80 percent lean meat to 20 percent fat blend.

TURKEY: Lean ground turkey breast is dry and flavorless. So we use ground turkey (a combination of dark and light meat) or ground thigh meat with a more delicious lean-to-fat ratio.

MEATLOAF MIX: You'll find the classic meatloaf and meatball combination (equal parts ground pork, beef, and veal) in one convenient package. Some are premixed. We'd rather mix our own, gently (and not too much) for a more airy, tender texture. Plus, we like the option of checking the quality of the individual ground meats before making our purchase.

ground beef (chuck roast)

ground pork

ground veal

ground lamb

ground turkey

meatloaf mix: ground pork, beef, veal

## CLASSIC MEATBALLS ☞ makes about 70

Everyone loves good ole meatballs, including us, and this big batch can feed a crowd. This is our all-purpose meatball, tender and delicate, with just enough fresh bread crumbs to bind the rest of the ingredients together. When it comes to size, we are partial to little ones, about 1 ounce or the size of a walnut. We use a tablespoon to keep the size uniform. But when making these meatballs for Spaghetti & Meatballs (page 306), we go big, and double the size. These meatballs are deliciously versatile whether little or big; baked, browned in a skillet, or dropped directly into simmering water, broth, or tomato sauce. For making and shaping meatballs, see pages 304–305.

6 tablespoons extra-virgin olive oil
2 medium yellow onions, peeled and finely chopped
1 garlic clove, minced
2½ teaspoons salt
1½ teaspoons freshly ground black pepper
Freshly grated nutmeg
2 large eggs
½ cup half-and-half
1½ cups fresh bread crumbs
1 pound ground chuck
1 pound ground pork
1 pound ground veal
Safflower oil for frying

Heat the olive oil in a large skillet over medium heat. Add the onions and garlic and cook, stirring often, until the onions are soft and translucent, about 15 minutes. Season with salt, pepper, and lots of nutmeg. Remove from the heat and set aside to cool (1).

Put the eggs and half-and-half into a large mixing bowl (2) and whisk until well combined. Add the bread crumbs and the cooled onions (3) and stir together. Add the beef, pork, and veal and mix everything together with your hands until well combined, taking care not to overhandle the meat (4). Scoop 1 heaping tablespoon of the meat mixture (about 1 ounce) into your hands (5) and gently roll it into a ball. The meatballs will be soft. (They hold their shape better if the meat mixture is cold, and they are easier to roll with clean, damp hands.) Arrange them in a single layer on parchment paper–lined baking pans as you work (6). You can do this a few hours ahead, cover them with plastic wrap, and refrigerate until you are ready to cook them.

Preheat the oven to 375°F. Bake the meatballs until just cooked, about 20 minutes. Or to pan-fry them, pour safflower oil into a heavy medium skillet to a depth of ½ inch and heat over medium-high heat until hot. Working in batches to avoid crowding the skillet, cook the meatballs in a single layer, turning them delicately with two forks so they cook evenly, until browned all over and cooked inside, about 8 minutes per batch.

*Overleaf, left page, clockwise from top left: sweated onions with seasonings; eggs with half-and-half; mixing Classic Meatball mixture together; bread crumbs, half-and-half, and onions*

## MEATBALLS WITH MINT & PARSLEY ✍ makes about 55

Fresh ricotta keeps these herb-flecked meatballs tender and moist and their flavor delicate. Use the best quality fresh, whole-milk ricotta you can find (Italian markets, farmers' markets, and grocery stores with a well-stocked cheese or dairy section are good bets). These meatballs can be rolled larger or smaller, depending on what they're to be used for. We like a walnut size (about 1 ounce) to serve with cocktails or to put in soups, and bigger ones (about 2 ounces) to go with buttered noodles or rice. For making and shaping meatballs, see illustrations on pages 304–305.

1 pound ground pork
1 pound ground veal
¼ pound prosciutto, finely chopped
1 cup best quality whole-milk ricotta
1 cup finely grated pecorino romano
2 eggs, lightly beaten
2 teaspoons salt
1 teaspoon freshly ground black pepper
½ nutmeg, grated
2 handfuls fresh mint leaves, finely chopped
2 handfuls fresh parsley leaves, finely chopped
Safflower oil for frying

Put the pork, veal, prosciutto, ricotta, pecorino, eggs, salt, pepper, nutmeg, mint, and parsley in a large mixing bowl (7). Gently mix everything together with your hands until well combined, taking care not to overhandle the meat (4). Scoop 1 heaping tablespoon of the meat mixture (about 1 ounce) into your hands (5) and gently roll it into a ball. (Meatballs will hold their shape better if the meat mixture is cold, and they will be easier to roll with clean, damp hands.) Arrange them in a single layer on a sheet pan or tray as you work (6). You can do this a few hours ahead, cover them with plastic wrap, and refrigerate until you are ready to cook them.

Pour the safflower oil into a heavy medium skillet to a depth of ½ inch and heat over medium-high heat until hot. Working in batches to avoid crowding the skillet, cook the meatballs in a single layer, turning them delicately with two forks so they cook evenly, until browned all over and cooked inside, about 8 minutes per batch. Transfer cooked meatballs to a platter, loosely cover with foil, and keep warm in an oven at its lowest temperature until ready to serve.

*Overleaf, right page, clockwise from top left: shaping meatballs; meatballs ready for cooking; Meatballs with Mint & Parsley mixture*

1.

3.

## SPAGHETTI & MEATBALLS ☞ serves 4

This dish is as classic Italian-American as it gets. Use this sauce or substitute with either of the tomato sauces on page 156. The meatballs and sauce can be made ahead and stored in the fridge for up to three days, or frozen for up to three months.

FOR THE TOMATO SAUCE
4 tablespoons butter
2 tablespoons extra-virgin olive oil, plus more for finishing
1 medium yellow onion, peeled and finely chopped
1 garlic clove, minced
Salt and freshly ground black pepper
Freshly grated nutmeg
1 bay leaf
1 sprig fresh rosemary, leaves minced
One 28-ounce can whole peeled plum tomatoes, crushed

FOR THE MEATBALLS
Twelve 2-ounce Classic Meatballs (page 302)
1 pound spaghetti
Parmigiano-Reggiano

For the tomato sauce, melt the butter with the olive oil in a wide medium saucepan with a lid over medium heat. Add the onions and garlic and cook until soft and translucent, about 10 minutes. Season to taste with salt, pepper, and nutmeg. Add the bay leaf and rosemary. Add the tomatoes and rinse out the can with 1 cup water, adding it to the pan. Bring to a simmer, reduce the heat, and gently simmer for about 20 minutes. Adjust the seasonings. Remove the bay leaf before serving. This makes about 5 cups of sauce.

Add the meatballs to the pan of sauce, cover, and simmer over low heat until the meatballs are warmed through.

Meanwhile, bring a large pot of salted water to a boil over high heat. Add the pasta and cook, stirring occasionally, until just tender, 10–12 minutes. Drain the pasta, reserving some of the cooking water. Return the pasta to the pot. Toss the pasta with a big spoonful or two of the tomato sauce, loosening the sauce with some of the reserved cooking water.

Serve the pasta family style or on individual plates with the meatballs and remaining tomato sauce spooned on top. Drizzle with a little olive oil, if you like. Serve with grated parmigiano.

## MEATBALLS WITH DILL SAUCE ☞ serves 4

2 tablespoons butter
1 small yellow onion, peeled and finely chopped
Salt and freshly ground black pepper
4 tablespoons flour
4 cups hot chicken stock
1 small bunch fresh dill, chopped
32–40 warm 1-ounce Classic Meatballs (page 302)

Melt the butter in a heavy medium saucepan over medium heat. Add the onions and cook until soft and translucent, but not browned, 10–15 minutes. Season to taste with salt and pepper. Sprinkle in the flour and cook for about 5 minutes, stirring with a wooden spoon to prevent it from taking on any color. Add the chicken stock, 1 cup at a time, stirring until the sauce is smooth and thickened. Stir in most of the dill just before serving.

To serve, spoon the sauce over the meatballs and garnish with the remaining dill. Serve them over rice, mashed potatoes, or a tangle of buttered noodles, if you like.

## MEATBALLS WITH TETRAZZINI SAUCE ☞ serves 4

2 tablespoons butter
1 yellow onion, peeled and finely chopped
4 ounces white mushrooms, cleaned and sliced
¼ cup dry sherry
Salt and freshly ground black pepper
1½ tablespoons flour
1 cup hot chicken stock
1 cup warm whole milk
¼ cup grated Parmigiano-Reggiano
32–40 warm 1-ounce Classic Meatballs (page 302)

Melt the butter in a large skillet over medium heat. Add the onions and cook, stirring often with a wooden spoon, until just soft, 8–10 minutes. Add the mushrooms and cook until soft, about 10 minutes. Add the sherry and cook until it has just evaporated. Season to taste with salt and pepper. Sprinkle the flour over the mushrooms and cook, stirring until the flour coats them and absorbs any butter left in the skillet, about 5 minutes. Combine the hot chicken stock and milk and add it to the mushrooms, ½ cup at a time, stirring until the sauce is smooth and thick. Stir in the parmigiano.

To serve, spoon the sauce over the meatballs and serve over rice, mashed potatoes, or a tangle of buttered noodles, garnished with fresh parsley, if you like.

*Facing page, top: Meatballs with Dill Sauce; bottom: Meatballs with Tetrazzini Sauce*

## LITTLE MEATBALLS IN BROTH  ☞  serves 4–6

For this satisfying soup, use any meatballs, any broth. Scale the recipe up or down. Add a handful of peas or a shower of chopped parsley. It is simple and quick to put together once you have made the meatballs, and it's a nice way to use up any leftover meatballs.

6–8 cups chicken stock,
  preferably homemade
  (pages 84–87)
6 tablespoons *acini di pepe*
  or other tiny pasta
Twenty-four 1-ounce
  Meatballs with Mint &
  Parsley (page 303) or other
  meatballs
1–2 large handfuls baby spinach
Salt
Extra-virgin olive oil

Bring the chicken stock to a gentle boil in a medium pot over medium-high heat. Add the pasta and cook, stirring occasionally, until tender, 10–12 minutes. Reduce the heat to medium. Add the meatballs and simmer until warmed through.

Add the spinach to the meatballs and pasta, cover, and cook until it wilts and collapses, 1–2 minutes. Season with salt to taste. Serve the soup drizzled with olive oil, if you like.

## MEATBALLS WITH MINT & PARSLEY IN CREAM SAUCE

Follow the directions for Meatballs with Mint & Parsley (page 303), making them larger (about 2 ounces), if you like. They will take about 10 minutes to brown all over and cook through. When the meatballs are finished cooking, increase the heat to high and deglaze the skillet with ½ cup white wine, stirring with a wooden spoon to loosen any browned bits stuck to the bottom of the skillet. Add ¾ cup heavy cream and cook, stirring, until the sauce thickens. Taste, then season with salt, if necessary. Pour the sauce through a fine-mesh sieve over the meatballs and serve.—*makes about 2 dozen*

*Little Meatballs in Broth*

## TURKEY-SCALLION MEATBALLS WITH SOY-GINGER SAUCE ☞ makes 24

Ground turkey breast has little flavor and can be dry because it is so lean. For juicier, more flavorful meatballs, make these Asian-spiked meatballs with ground dark meat (or 85 percent lean) turkey.

FOR THE SAUCE
¼ cup dark brown sugar
¼ cup soy sauce, preferably
  Japanese or reduced
  sodium
¼ cup mirin (sweet rice wine)
2 tablespoons chopped,
  peeled fresh ginger
½ teaspoon ground coriander
2 whole black peppercorns

FOR THE MEATBALLS
1 pound ground turkey
4–6 scallions, trimmed and
  finely chopped
1 bunch cilantro, finely
  chopped (about 1 cup)
1 egg, lightly beaten
2 tablespoons Asian sesame oil
2 tablespoons soy sauce
Freshly ground black pepper
Safflower oil for frying
Fresh mint and cilantro leaves
  for garnish, optional

For the sauce, bring the sugar and ¼ cup water to a boil in a small saucepan over medium-high heat, stirring until the sugar dissolves completely. Reduce the heat to medium-low and add the soy sauce, mirin, ginger, coriander, and peppercorns. Simmer, stirring occasionally, until reduced by half, about 15 minutes. Strain the sauce through a fine-mesh sieve into a small bowl, discarding the solids. Set aside to cool. (The sauce can be made up to 2 days ahead. Keep refrigerated.)

For the meatballs, put the turkey, scallions, cilantro, egg, sesame oil, soy sauce, and several grindings of pepper into a mixing bowl and gently mix together with your hands until well combined. (Do not overhandle.) Scoop 1 heaping tablespoon of the meat mixture (about 1 ounce) into your hands and gently roll it into a ball. (Meatballs will hold their shape better if the meat mixture is cold, and they will be easier to roll with clean, damp hands.) Arrange them in a single layer on a sheet pan or tray as you work. You can do this a few hours ahead, cover them with plastic wrap, and refrigerate until you are ready to cook them.

Pour the safflower oil into a heavy medium skillet to a depth of ½ inch and heat over medium-high heat until hot. Working in batches to avoid crowding the skillet, cook the meatballs in a single layer, turning them delicately with two forks so they cook evenly, until browned all over and cooked inside, about 8 minutes per batch.

Arrange the meatballs on a platter and garnish with some mint and cilantro leaves, if you like. Put the sauce in a small dipping bowl on the platter. Serve the meatballs with toothpicks.

## LAMB MEATBALLS WITH SAFFRON & CURRANTS ✍ makes about 24

Saffron, cinnamon, and crushed red pepper flakes give these little meatballs a distinctive warmth. The currants add sweetness. The crumb coating makes them just the right crunchy on the outside. Serve them hot or at room temperature; they're delicious either way.

2 pinches of saffron threads

2 tablespoons extra-virgin olive oil

1 small yellow onion, peeled and minced

⅓ cup dried currants, chopped

1 pound ground lamb

1 handful fresh parsley leaves, chopped

2 small garlic cloves, minced

½ teaspoon ground cinnamon

Salt

Big pinch of crushed red pepper flakes

Freshly ground black pepper

2 tablespoons flour

3 large eggs, lightly beaten

2–3 cups panko, finely crushed

Safflower oil for frying

1 lemon, cut into wedges

Lightly toast the saffron in a small skillet over medium-low heat until it turns a shade darker, about 30 seconds. Crush the saffron to a powder in a mortar and pestle. Dissolve the saffron in 2 tablespoons warm water and set aside.

Heat the olive oil and onions together in a small skillet over medium heat and cook until they begin to soften, 3–5 minutes. Add the saffron water and cook until the onions are soft, 3–5 minutes. Add the currants. Set aside to cool.

Put the lamb, parsley, garlic, cinnamon, 1½ teaspoons salt, crushed red pepper flakes, black pepper to taste, and the cooled onions in a large mixing bowl. Mix everything together with your hands until well combined, taking care not to overhandle the meat. Scoop 1 heaping tablespoon of the meat mixture (about 1 ounce) into your hands and gently roll it into a ball. (Meatballs will hold their shape better if the meat mixture is cold, and they will be easier to roll with clean, damp hands.) Arrange them in a single layer on a sheet pan or tray as you work. You can do this a few hours ahead, cover them with plastic wrap, and refrigerate until you are ready to cook them.

Put the flour in a wide bowl and add the eggs, beating until smooth. Put the panko in another wide bowl. Dip the meatballs in the egg mixture, then roll them in the panko. Arrange them in a single layer on a sheet pan or tray as you work.

Pour the oil into a heavy medium skillet to a depth of ½ inch and heat over medium-high heat until hot. Working in batches to avoid crowding the skillet, cook the meatballs in a single layer, turning them with two forks so they cook evenly, until golden brown all over, about 5 minutes. Drain on a rack set over paper towels. Season with salt. Serve hot or at room temperature with lemon wedges.

## MEATLOAF ✒ serves 4–6

A warm slice of tender meatloaf is irresistible. And a sandwich made with a cold slice or two of leftover meatloaf ranks right up there with the best of flavors. We often make two meatloaves to last us through the week.

FOR THE MEATLOAF
2 tablespoons extra-virgin olive oil
1 large yellow onion, peeled and minced
1 garlic clove, minced
Salt and freshly ground black pepper
1 egg, beaten
1 cup heavy cream
1 cup ricotta
1½ tablespoons Beau Monde seasoning, or 2 teaspoons celery salt and 2 teaspoons onion powder
1 tablespoon hot sauce, or to taste
2 cups loosely packed fresh bread crumbs
3 pounds meatloaf mix or
  1 pound ground chuck,
  1 pound ground pork,
  1 pound ground veal

FOR THE SAUCE
1 cup ketchup
2 tablespoons vinegar
2 tablespoons brown sugar
1 teaspoon Dijon mustard

For the meatloaf, preheat the oven to 375°F. Heat the oil in a medium skillet over medium heat. Add the onions and garlic, season to taste with salt and pepper, and cook, stirring from time to time, until softened, 8–10 minutes. Transfer the onions to a plate, spreading them out to cool.

Meanwhile, mix together the egg, heavy cream, ricotta, Beau Monde seasoning, and hot sauce in a large bowl. Season liberally with salt and pepper. Add the bread crumbs, folding them in with a rubber spatula. Fold in the cooled onions.

Use clean hands or a rubber spatula to mix the beef, pork, and veal into the bread crumb mixture. It will be quite loose and wet, but that is what makes the meatloaf so tender.

Pack the meat mixture into a 2-quart terrine, 4 × 13-inch Pullman loaf pan, or two 1-quart loaf pans. Pat the meat into a dome-shaped top.

For the sauce, mix together the ketchup, vinegar, brown sugar, and mustard in a small bowl. Spoon the sauce on top of the meatloaf. You may have some left over; serve it alongside the cooked meatloaf.

Set the meatloaf on a foil-lined baking pan and transfer it to the oven. Bake until the internal temperature reaches 160°F, about 1 hour. Allow the meatloaf to cool for about 15 minutes before slicing. (The longer it rests the better, as it will slice more easily.) The first couple of slices can be tricky to remove from the pan, but then it becomes easier when you have a little more space.

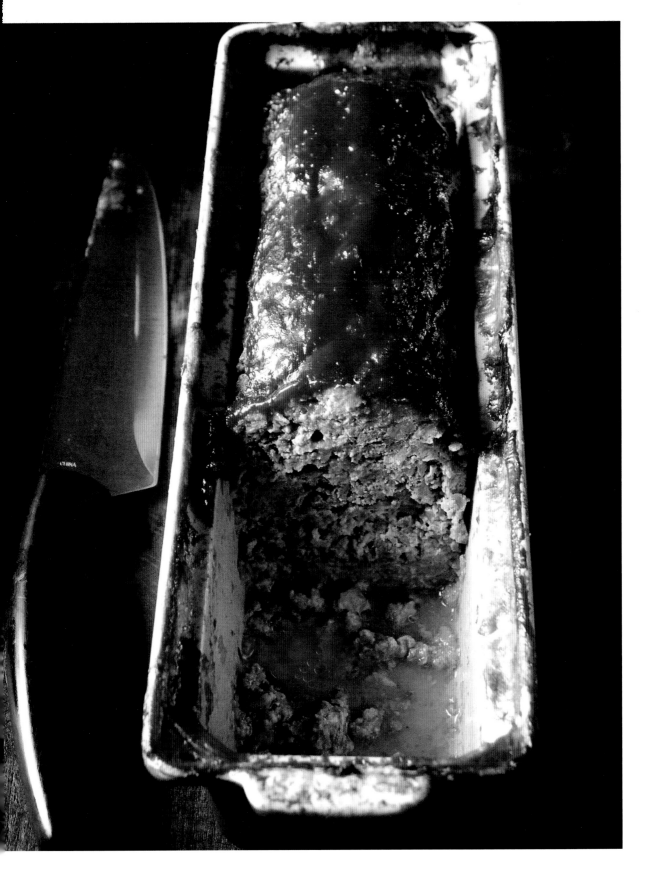

## CHOPPED STEAK MARCHAND DE VIN ☞ serves 4–6

CH was given this version of the classic French red wine–reduction sauce by friends and owners of a West Coast restaurant she took her daughters to when they were little girls. The silky sauce was served over beautiful little steaks and over chopped steak for the girls. Now we always dress up our chopped steak with this elegant sauce.

FOR THE SAUCE
3 shallots, peeled and chopped
1 cup red wine
2 cups store-bought veal demi-glace or 2 tablespoons beef bouillon paste
1 sprig fresh thyme
1 bay leaf
3 tablespoons cold unsalted butter, cut into small pieces
Salt and freshly ground black pepper
2 tablespoons minced fresh parsley

FOR THE CHOPPED STEAK
2 pounds ground beef round
2 shallots, peeled and finely chopped
2 tablespoons minced fresh parsley, plus more for garnish
1 teaspoon fresh thyme leaves, chopped
1 egg yolk
Salt and freshly ground black pepper
2 teaspoons safflower or olive oil

For the sauce, put the shallots and wine in a heavy medium saucepan and cook over medium heat until the wine has been reduced to ¼ cup and the shallots have softened, about 10 minutes. Add the demi-glace (or bouillon paste dissolved in 2 cups of water), thyme, and bay leaf, and simmer until the sauce is reduced by half and thickens slightly, 10–20 minutes. Strain the sauce through a fine sieve into a bowl, discarding the solids. Return the sauce to the pan over low heat. Add the butter one piece at a time, whisking after each addition until it is completely incorporated before adding the next. Whisk until the sauce is smooth with a lovely sheen. Season to taste with salt and pepper. Stir in the parsley. Cover and set the pan in a larger pan filled with hot water to keep the sauce warm.

For the chopped steak, put the meat, shallots, parsley, thyme, egg yolk, and salt and pepper to taste in a medium bowl. Using two forks, gently mix everything together without compacting the meat. Form the meat into 4–6 oval patties. Use a knife to crosshatch the surface of the patties on both sides. Heat the oil in a heavy large nonstick or cast-iron skillet over medium-high heat. Put the patties in the skillet and cook on both sides until brown, about 3 minutes per side for medium-rare.

To serve, spoon a little warm sauce onto a plate, place a patty on top of the sauce, and spoon more sauce on top. Repeat with the remaining patties. Garnish with chopped parsley. Serve with fries, if you like.

## SHEPHERD'S PIE ☞ serves 4

Mashed potatoes are typically used to cover the meat filling of this crustless pie. We prefer a more delicate, refined flavor, so we use a combination of parsnips, potatoes, and apples instead.

1 pound large parsnips, peeled and chopped

1 large russet potato, peeled and chopped

1 large apple, peeled, cored, and chopped

6 tablespoons butter

Salt and freshly ground black pepper

2 medium yellow onions, peeled and finely chopped

4 medium carrots, peeled and diced

4 large white mushrooms, cleaned and finely chopped

2 tablespoons tomato paste

1 tablespoon Worcestershire sauce

2 pounds ground lamb

$\frac{1}{2}$ cup chicken stock

1 tablespoon flour

Preheat the oven to 375°F. Put the parsnips, potatoes, apples, 3 tablespoons of the butter, and $\frac{1}{2}$ cup water into a heavy medium pot. Cover and cook over medium heat, stirring from time to time, until everything is very soft, about 40 minutes. Mash or purée the vegetables (don't drain them!) to the consistency that you like—it can be very smooth or quite rustic. Season to taste with salt and pepper. Set aside.

Meanwhile, melt the remaining 3 tablespoons butter in a large skillet over medium-high heat. Add the onions and carrots and season to taste with salt and pepper. Cook the vegetables, stirring now and then with a wooden spoon, until soft, about 15 minutes. Add the mushrooms and cook for about 2 minutes. Push all the vegetables to the edge of the skillet. Add the tomato paste to the center of the skillet and toast it for about 1 minute. Stir in the Worcestershire sauce.

Add the lamb to the skillet, season to taste with salt and pepper, and cook, breaking up the meat with the back of the spoon, until the meat is no longer pink, 5–10 minutes. Add the stock and sprinkle in the flour. Stir everything together.

Transfer the meat to a baking dish in an even layer. Spoon dollops of the puréed parsnips onto the meat and spread it over the meat evenly in a smooth layer. Bake until heated through and slightly golden on top, 20–30 minutes.

Grilling

# Making Friends with Fire

*Get out of your chair, and go out[side].*—Francis Mallmann, Argentine chef and live-fire champion

T HE MERCURY DOES NOT NEED TO CRAWL up past 80 degrees for us to get our grill on. It can be a freezing early spring day, a brisk fall evening, or midwinter stews-and-braises weather. What lures us outside to grill is the ritual of building a fire—striking a match and lighting crumpled paper, igniting hardwood charcoal, watching as the coals smoke, spit, and eventually glow white, orange, and red. It's the aliveness of fire, of cooking over something a little wild. It's the enjoyment of cooking something in a big way, out of the ordinary, away from the domestic environment inside the kitchen with its tame stove, oven, and pots. It is the craving we get for the sharp taste of charry meat or vegetables, sweetly perfumed with smoke, that makes us want to get our grill on.

Simple, smoke-perfumed meat and fish are sublime as is, but even for salt-and-pepper cooks like us, we occasionally want to spice things up. We'll use one of our dry spice rub mixtures. The ingredients in each blend inspire us: black Tellicherry peppercorns from India's Malabar Coast, Dutch caraway seeds, Indian cumin, fennel seeds from California, sweet paprika from Hungary, smoked paprika from Spain, and aromatic Sichuan peppercorns. We tame flavorful but tough cuts of beef, like flank or hanger steak, by lightly scoring them in a crosshatch pattern on both sides. Then we smear a spice rub into the nooks and crannies and cook the meat quickly over hot coals.

When we want to grill a "good" steak—thick-cut with the best flavor and just the right balance of tender and chewiness—we go for a fat, well-marbled rib eye. We prefer on-the-bone because the bone keeps the steak from curling as it cooks, and who doesn't like to gnaw on a meaty bone once the steak is carved?

We don't sweat the details when it comes to things like whether to put the steak on the grill straight from the fridge or at room temperature. Instead, we stick close by the grill, paying attention to the fire, adding more charcoal if needed, watching for flare-ups, snuffing them out with the grill lid, moving scallions or chickens before they char, basting spare ribs with our addictive hoisin sauce until the meat is tender enough to pull easily from the bones and lacquered a deep mahogany. And we poke and prod, fiddle and fuss over racks of lamb, moving them all around the grill, browning the delicious fat and keeping it from burning. We keep checking its internal temperature until it reaches rosy pink medium-rare.

Sometimes, when the coals are covered with a good layer of ash and not too hot, we will nestle whole eggplants in the glowing embers and wait, turning them as their skin blisters and chars. Then we pull them out when the flesh has softened and collapsed. We peel off the skin and mash the eggplant into a divinely smoky spread with garlic, lemon juice, and olive oil.

Grilling well demands making friends with fire and being a good companion. Don't be afraid. The payoff is delicious.

## COOKING WITH FIRE

We love the lively heat and distinctive smokiness from cooking over a bed of glowing red and white-hot coals any time of the year. We are partial to charcoal grilling in a kettle grill (1), but if we are short on time or feeling a little lazy, we'll fire up the gas barbie (less fun, less flavor, but more controllable). Either way, we follow a few basic tenets when we get our grill on.

Stick by the grill and pay close attention. Flare-ups happen fast, and the black carbon coating from grilling directly over fire tastes acrid. Tame unwanted flames not with a water spray bottle, but by moving the food to a cooler spot on the grill, or by taking it off the grill until the coals quiet down. Resist fussing with food on the grill until grill marks are well established; this helps reduce sticking. Use the grill's lid to increase ambient heat inside the grill and/or to tame flare-ups.

PREPARING THE GRILL GRATES: Before we begin grilling, we use a grill brush to scrub the top of the grill grate clean. Alternately, we crumple aluminum foil into a rough 3-inch ball and scrub the grate with it. Then we soak a wadded piece of cloth or paper towel in oil and lube the grate. When the coals are hot, we place the grill grate over the coals, let it get hot, then give the grate another good scrub. The heat helps loosen any charred-on bits from previous grillings. Using a pair of long-handled metal tongs, we grab the oiled cloth and wipe the grate again. A clean, well-oiled, and *hot* grate helps keep food from sticking. Scrub and oil the grill grate when finished grilling, while it's still hot. You won't need elbow grease the next time you get ready to grill.

HARDWOOD CHARCOAL: The two most common charcoals available for grilling are briquettes and lump or natural hardwood charcoal (2). Both are forms of carbonized wood. Briquettes, uniform rounded blocks of compressed charcoal with additives (some kinds come presoaked in lighter fluid), offer even, long-lasting heat, but not the smokiness that lump charcoal imparts. Hardwood charcoal (the lumps look like incinerated chunks of wood) is 100 percent natural. It spits and crackles, it smokes, and it burns clean and fiery hot. It's our charcoal of choice.

STARTING THE FIRE: We don't like lighter fluid's nasty smell perfuming our food, so we ignite hardwood charcoal or briquettes in a chimney charcoal starter (3). Fill the top of the metal cylinder with charcoal, stuff some paper underneath, and light the paper. Before long, the charcoal comes to crackling life, glowing red, *naturally*.

TOOLS: We are better grill cooks because of these tools (4). Cooking times vary depending on *everything*; we frequently check food's internal temperature for doneness with an instant-read thermometer (a). Keep the grill grate clean with a sturdy grill brush (b). When grilling over indirect heat, paint on marinades and sauces with a basting brush (c). We always use a timer (d). Long-handled, spring-loaded, metal tongs (e) make grabbing and turning food over a hot grill a cooler job.

*Overleaf: grilling a chicken off the fire*

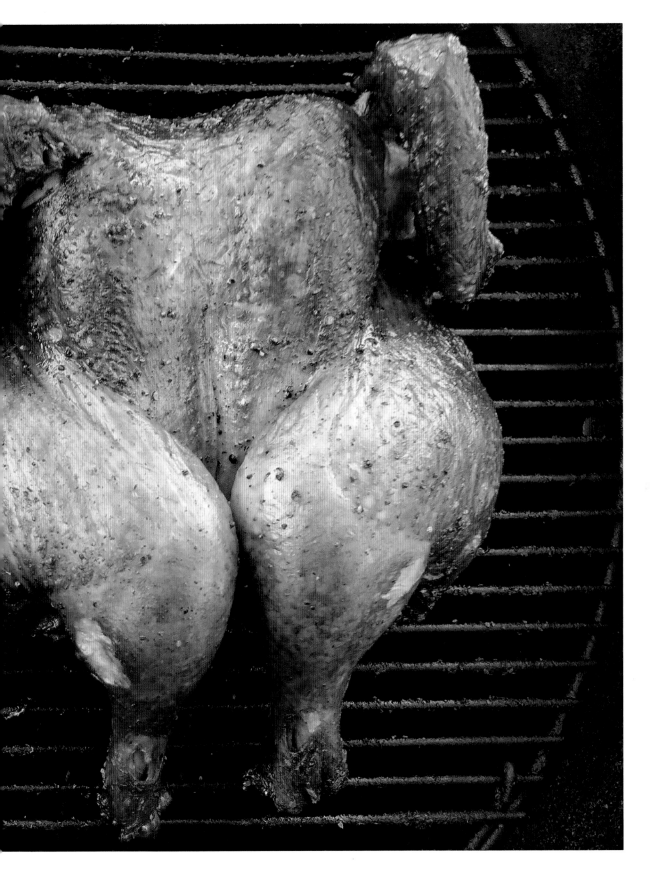

# How we build our fires

⊙ Build a fire, let it die down, then push it to the side. ⊙

It is thrilling to strike a match, light a fire, and make something so primal come to life. We love preparing hot coals and building a good fire as part of the whole grilling experience.

Whether using lump hardwood charcoal or briquettes, we start by stuffing crumpled paper in the bottom of a chimney charcoal starter. Then we set the chimney on the middle grate of a kettle grill, fill the top of the chimney with more or less charcoal, and light the paper. The chimney starts smoking and before long, the crackling sound of charcoal catching fire begins. When some of the charcoal is glowing red, we carefully dump the lively coals onto the middle grate. (Use a kitchen towel or mitt to grab the hot chimney handle.) For a hot grilling fire, we add more charcoal on top of the red coals. Hardwood charcoal spits and pops when it begins burning. The fire is ready for grilling when the coals have died down a bit, but are glowing red and covered with a thin layer of ash. The whole grill will be hot.

We create two zones of heat for grilling. Using long metal tongs or a spatula (or a fireplace shovel), push the coals to one side of the grill. This hottest spot on the grill is great when you want direct heat for lots of charry browning (think steaks). If the heat needs replenishing, add charcoal directly to the hot coals on this side. The cooler section of the grill is the spot to move food to finish cooking or when there are flare-ups (you want to avoid these as it burns the food). It's also the side used for cooking over indirect heat—just the place for grilling a whole chicken, side of salmon, or to smoke some ribs. (If using a gas grill, we fire up just the "back burner".) After the coals are pushed to the side, set the top grill grate in place and let it get hot before grilling. Want to gauge the heat of your grill? Hold your hand above the grate and you'll know in a manner of seconds!

## DRY SPICE RUBS

After years of fine-tuning our grilling techniques, we have landed on the side of dry spice rubs over wet marinades. Meat soaked in a spicy, sometimes cloyingly sweet liquid can end up tasting more like the sauce than like the meat. We use dry spice rubs two ways: We rub them into meat, poultry, and fish before grilling, and/or sprinkle them on afterwards, adding layers of flavor.

## TOASTED CARAWAY SALT RUB

Toast 2 tablespoons caraway seeds in a heavy, dry skillet over medium heat, shaking the skillet often, until fragrant, 1–2 minutes. Set aside to cool. Finely grind the seeds and ½ teaspoon whole black peppercorns in a spice mill, then transfer to a small bowl. Stir in 1 tablespoon kosher salt and 2 teaspoons sweet Hungarian paprika. This can be made 1 month ahead. Store in an airtight container.—*makes about ¼ cup*

## LEMON-PEPPER SALT RUB

Finely grind 2 tablespoons whole black peppercorns in a spice mill. Transfer to a small bowl. Stir in 3 tablespoons finely grated lemon zest and 1 tablespoon kosher salt. Rub seasoning between your fingertips to break up any clumps of zest. This can be made 3 days ahead. Store in an airtight container.—*makes about ¼ cup*

## FENNEL SALT RUB

Toast ¼ cup fennel seeds in a heavy, dry skillet over medium heat, shaking the skillet often, until fragrant, 1–2 minutes. Set aside to cool. Finely grind the seeds and 2 teaspoons whole black peppercorns in a spice mill, then transfer to a small bowl. Stir in 1½ tablespoons kosher salt and 2 large pinches of cayenne pepper. This can be made 1 month ahead. Store in an airtight container.—*makes about ¼ cup*

## SMOKY PAPRIKA SALT RUB

Toast 1 tablespoon coriander seeds and 1 tablespoon cumin seeds in a heavy, dry skillet over medium heat, shaking the skillet frequently, until fragrant, 1–2 minutes. Set aside to cool. Finely grind the seeds in a spice mill, then transfer to a small bowl. Stir in 2 tablespoons Spanish smoked paprika, 1½ tablespoons kosher salt, and ½ teaspoon cayenne pepper. This can be made 1 month ahead. Store in an airtight container.—*makes about ¼ cup*

*Facing page, clockwise from top left: Toasted Caraway Salt Rub; Lemon-Pepper Salt Rub; Fennel Salt Rub; Smoky Paprika Salt Rub*

## OUR FAVORITE STEAKS

The king of steaks in our kitchen is the bone-in rib eye, cut from a prime rib roast. Chewier cuts like the thin, wide flank steak and the surprisingly tender flatiron steak, are full of flavor. Just be sure to thinly slice these steaks across the grain for a more tender chew.

### GRILLED RIB EYE STEAKS (ON THE BONE)

Prepare a hot charcoal or gas grill (for tips, see page 330). Meanwhile, pat dry 2 rib eye steaks on the bone, 2–3 inches thick, with paper towels. Rub the steaks all over with a little extra-virgin olive oil, and season well on both sides with salt and freshly ground black pepper. Grill the steaks over the hottest spot of the grill until a good browned crust has developed on the first side, about 8 minutes. To ensure a good crust, resist the urge to move or fiddle with the steaks while they are cooking, but if flare-ups threaten to burn the meat, you've got to move it to a cooler spot on the grill. Turn the steaks and grill the second side for 5 minutes. Move the steaks to a cooler spot on the grill to finish cooking, turning occasionally, until their internal temperatures reach 120°F for rare, 130°F for medium-rare, and 140°F for medium, 5–15 minutes depending on the thickness of the steaks and the desired doneness. Pull the steaks off the grill and let them rest on a cutting board for 10–15 minutes. Cut the steak from the bone and slice the meat against the grain. Serve both the bones and the meat. (You will be fighting over the bones.)—*serves 2–4*

### GRILLED FLANK STEAK

Prepare a hot grill (for tips, see page 330). Meanwhile, pat dry 1 flank steak, about 2 pounds, with paper towels. Using a sharp knife, lightly score a 1-inch crosshatch pattern on both sides to keep the meat from curling as it cooks. Rub the steak all over with extra-virgin olive oil, and season well with salt and freshly ground black pepper. Grill the steak over the hottest section of the grill until well browned, about 3 minutes per side for medium-rare. Let the steak rest on a cutting board for 10 minutes. Thinly slice the meat across the grain.—*serves 4–6*

### GRILLED FLATIRON STEAKS

Prepare a hot grill (for tips, see page 330). Meanwhile, pat dry 2 flatiron steaks, about 8 ounces each, with paper towels. Rub the steaks all over with extra-virgin olive oil, and season well with salt and freshly ground black pepper. Grill the steaks over the hottest section of the grill until well browned, about 3 minutes per side for medium-rare. Let the steaks rest on a cutting board for 10 minutes. Slice the meat across the grain.—*serves 2–4*

*Grilled Rib Eye Steaks (On the Bone)*

## GRILLED WHOLE BEEF TENDERLOIN ☞ serves 12

When we're grilling a hunk of meat, we usually keep the seasonings quite simple to begin, then slather on some flavorful compound butter (see below) at the end.

1 whole beef tenderloin,
  6–7 pounds
1–2 tablespoons extra-virgin
  olive oil
2–3 tablespoons coarsely
  ground black pepper
Salt

Pat the tenderloin dry with paper towels. Using a sharp knife, trim off any fat. Slide the blade under the long silvery membrane, trimming it off. Fold under about 6 inches of the thin end of the meat, which should make it about as thick as the rest of the filet so it will cook evenly. Tie the tenderloin into a neat package with kitchen string, then rub it all over with oil. Rub with pepper, pressing it into the meat, and season with salt.

Prepare a medium-hot charcoal or gas grill (for tips, see page 330). Grill the filet over the hottest part of the grill, turning it once a brown and charry crust develops. Brown all over, then move it to a cooler spot on the grill to finish cooking until the internal temperature reaches 120°F for rare and 130°F for medium-rare. Grilling time will vary depending on your grill and the heat. Start checking the internal temperature after 20 minutes.

Let the tenderloin rest on a cutting board for 15 minutes. Snip off the string, slice the meat, and serve warm with a smear of Compound Herb Butter. Or let it cool, wrap, and refrigerate for up to 3 days before serving it cold and sliced.

## COMPOUND HERB BUTTER

Beat ½ pound (2 sticks) room-temperature salted butter in a medium bowl with a wooden spoon until smooth and creamy. Add ½ cup chopped fresh herbs (one or a combination of your favorite herbs), 1 small finely chopped peeled shallot or trimmed scallion, and 1 minced garlic clove, if you like. Season with salt and freshly ground black pepper, and stir until well combined.—*makes about 1 cup*

LEMON & RED CHILE BUTTER VARIATION: Omit the herbs, shallots, garlic, and black pepper. Wash and dry 2 lemons and finely grate the zest over the butter. Squeeze in juice of ½ lemon. Add 1–2 teaspoons dried red chile flakes. Season with salt.—*makes about 1 cup*

*Grilled Whole Beef Tenderloin*

## GRILLED SPARE RIBS ✂ serves 4

If you can't babysit the ribs on the grill, then cook them in the oven and finish them on the grill to add a little smoky perfume. Even though baby back or country-style ribs look meatier, we prefer spareribs for succulent pork that is finger-lickin', lip-smackin' good.

6 pounds pork spareribs
Salt and freshly ground
  black pepper

Pat the spareribs dry with paper towels. Remove the membrane on the underside of the ribs by loosening it first with a knife on one edge and by pulling it off diagonally with a pair of pliers. It may come off in pieces; that's fine. (Your butcher may be willing to do this for you.) Rub the ribs with lots of salt and pepper.

Preheat the oven to 275°F. Put the ribs in a single layer on a large, foil-lined baking sheet. Cook them in the oven until the meat is tender when pierced with a knife and the ribs bend and "flop" when you pick them up with tongs, 2–3 hours.

To finish the ribs in the oven, during the last half hour of cooking, brush the ribs with Hoisinful Sauce, if using, every 5 minutes. The ribs will have a "lacquered" glaze.

To finish the ribs on the grill, preheat a grill with a lid. If using a charcoal grill, build a small fire to one side. If using a gas grill, fire up the "back burner" to medium heat. Add a handful of soaked chips to the metal smoker box. This makes heat and smoke but not direct flame which can cause the sugary glaze on the ribs to burn. Put the ribs on the grill away from and off of the fire. Cover with the lid. Brush the ribs with the sauce every 10 minutes. Cook for 30 minutes.

Let the ribs rest on a cutting board for 15 minutes. Cut the slabs into ribs and serve with or without sauce.

## HOISINFUL SAUCE

Stir 2 cups hoisin sauce, ¾ cup bourbon, and 2 smashed garlic cloves together in a medium bowl. Set aside for the garlic to flavor the sauce, about 1 hour. Remove and discard the garlic cloves.—*makes 2¾ cups*

## GRILLED RACK OF LAMB ☞ serves 4–8

By cutting the rack in half, the lamb will be easier to cook and everyone can have one or two crispy "end chops".

Four 8-rib racks of lamb,
  halved into 4-rib pieces
Extra-virgin olive oil
Salt and freshly ground
  black pepper
2 lemons, quartered

Prepare a medium-hot charcoal or gas grill (for tips, see page 330). Meanwhile, pat the lamb dry with paper towels. Rub the lamb all over with a little oil, and season well with salt and pepper.

Grill the lamb in the center of the grill, moving it to a cooler spot if there are flare-ups, which there most likely will be. The layer of delicious fat on the outside of the chops will render and drip onto the coals. Turn the pieces as they brown. When browned all over, move the lamb to the coolest spot on the grill to finish cooking, turning often, until the internal temperature reaches 125°F for medium-rare. Let the lamb rest on a cutting board for 5 minutes.

Cut the ribs into individual chops, pile them on a big platter, drizzle with some oil, and season with salt and pepper. Serve with lemon wedges and Lemon-Mint Sauce, if you like.

### LEMON-MINT SAUCE

Whisk 1 small minced garlic clove, ⅓ cup extra-virgin olive oil, ¼ cup chopped fresh parsley leaves, ¼ cup chopped fresh mint leaves, and 3 tablespoons fresh lemon juice in a medium bowl. Season to taste with salt and freshly ground black pepper.—*makes about ¾ cup*

### A PILE OF GRILLED LAMB CHOPS SCOTTADITO WITH HARISSA SAUCE

For the Harissa Sauce, mince 2 garlic cloves into a paste and transfer to a small bowl. Stir in 2–4 tablespoons harissa, ½ cup extra-virgin olive oil, and the juice of 1 lemon.—*makes about ¾ cup*

To marinate the lamb chops, arrange four 8-rib racks of lamb, halved into 4-rib pieces, in a large pan and brush with some of the harissa sauce. Cover with plastic wrap and set aside for about an hour, or refrigerate for about 4 hours.

To grill the lamb chops, unwrap the meat and follow the instructions above for grilling, cutting the racks into chops, and serving. Spoon any remaining sauce over the lamb just before serving.—*serves 4–8*

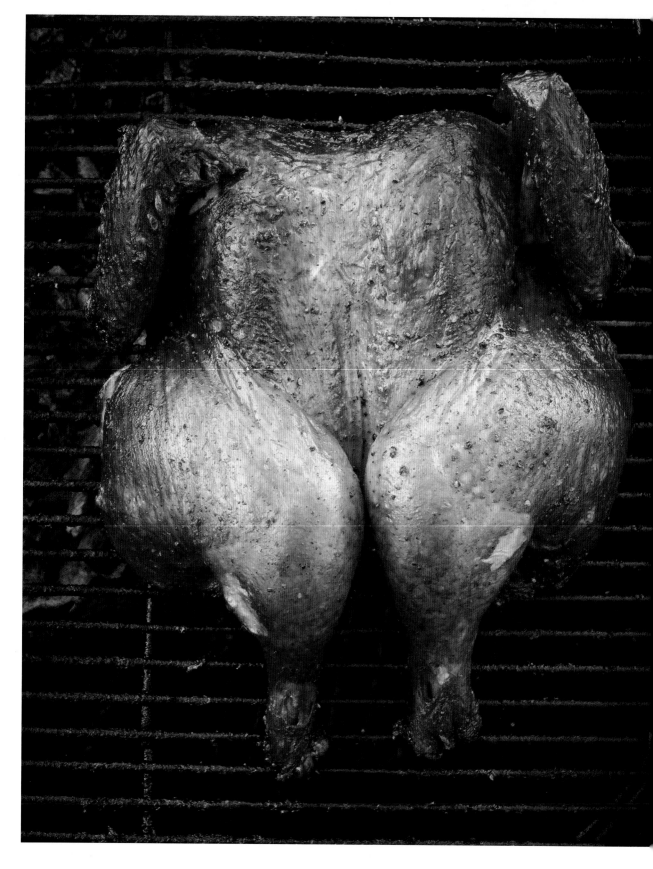

## GRILLED SPATCHCOCKED CHICKEN ☞ serves 4–6

1 chicken, 3–5 pounds
2 tablespoons extra-virgin
   olive oil, plus more for
   drizzling
Salt and freshly ground
   black pepper
1 lemon, cut in half

Rinse the chicken inside and out and pat dry with paper towels. Using poultry shears or a large, sharp knife, spatchcock the chicken (see page 232). Rinse the bird again, and dry with paper towels. Rub the bird all over with oil and season it generously with salt and pepper.

Preheat a grill with a lid. If using a charcoal grill, build a hot fire to one side and let the coals get white hot. If using a gas grill, fire up the "back burner" to a medium-hot heat (see tips, page 330).

Put the chicken on the grill skin-side up away from and off of the fire. Cover it with the lid and grill the chicken until the skin is golden brown and releases easily from the grill rack, 45–60 minutes. Keep the grill hot as the chicken cooks by adding more charcoal as needed. If flare-ups threaten to burn the bird, carefully move it to a cooler spot on the grill. The chicken is done when the thigh juices run clear when pricked with a fork.

Transfer the chicken to a platter, squeeze the lemon juice over it, drizzle with oil, and season with salt and pepper. Let the chicken rest for 15 minutes before serving.

## CHICKEN ALLA DIAVOLA

Follow the instructions above and on page 232 for rinsing, spatchcocking, and drying the bird. Season the spatchcocked chicken all over with 2 teaspoons freshly ground black pepper, 2 teaspoons crushed red pepper flakes, and salt, rubbing the seasonings into the skin until it is well coated. Put the chicken skin-side up in a large dish. Stir the juice of 2–3 lemons, ¾ cup extra-virgin olive oil, 1 teaspoon crushed red pepper flakes, and a pinch of salt in a small bowl. Pour half of the marinade over the bird. Reserve the remaining marinade. Let the chicken marinate at room temperature for 1 hour, turning it over after 30 minutes.

Follow the instructions above for grilling the bird. Spoon the reserved marinade over the chicken before serving.—*serves 4–6*

*Grilled Spatchcocked Chicken*

## GRILLED SIDE OF SALMON ☞ serves 6–8

Grilling fish can be a challenge because its fragile flesh doesn't tolerate much handling. Here we lay a side of salmon on the grill skin-side down, then don't touch it until it's done. Then we slide a cookie sheet under the whole fish to ensure it stays in one piece when we take it off the grill.

1 side of salmon, skin on,
  pin bones removed
  (see page 196)
Extra-virgin olive oil
Salt and freshly ground
  black pepper
1 lemon, cut in quarters

Preheat a grill with a lid. If using a charcoal grill, build a hot fire to one side and let the coals get white hot. If using a gas grill, fire up the "back burner" to a medium-hot heat (see tips, page 330).

Meanwhile, rub the flesh side of the salmon with oil and season well with salt and pepper. Lay the fish skin-side down on a rimless cookie sheet. Slide the fish off the cookie sheet onto the grill away from and off of the fire. Cover it with the lid and grill the fish until just cooked through, about 30 minutes.

To see if the fish is cooked through, test by putting the point of a paring knife into the center of the thickest part of the fish. Remove the point and quickly (carefully) press it to your lower lip. If it is very warm, the fish is cooked. Slide the cookie sheet under the salmon between the flesh and skin, leaving the skin stuck to the grill. Use a big spatula to scoot the fish onto the cookie sheet.

Carefully slide the salmon onto a large serving platter and drizzle with olive oil. Garnish with the lemons. Serve as is, or with either of the following sauces.

## GREEN OLIVE SAUCE

Mix together 1 cup minced, pitted green olives; minced rind of 1 small preserved lemon; 1 finely minced shallot; ½ cup finely chopped parsley leaves; 1 minced anchovy filet; and ½ cup extra-virgin olive oil in a bowl. Season with salt and freshly ground black pepper.—*makes about 2 cups*

## GREEN OLIVE MAYONNAISE

Stir together 1 cup mayonnaise; 1 cup minced, pitted green olives; 1 finely minced shallot; ½ cup finely chopped parsley leaves; 1 minced anchovy filet; and 1 tablespoon fresh lemon juice in a bowl. Stir in ¼ cup extra-virgin olive oil. Season to taste with salt and freshly ground black pepper. This mayonnaise keeps, refrigerated, for up to 1 week.—*makes about 2 cups*

## GRILLED SWORDFISH ✎ serves 4

The firm, meaty flesh of swordfish makes it ideal for grilling. To avoid tearing the flesh, resist the urge to fuss with the fish on the grill until good grill marks have developed. Three other musts for grilling: Be sure the grill grate is clean, well oiled, and really hot.

1½–2 pounds swordfish steaks, 1–1½ inches thick
Extra-virgin olive oil
Salt and freshly ground black pepper

Prepare a medium-hot charcoal or gas grill (for tips, see page 330). Meanwhile, rub the swordfish all over with oil and season it well with salt and pepper.

Grill the fish in the center of the grill until there are deep brown grill marks, 3–5 minutes. Turn the fish and grill the other side until just cooked through, 3–5 minutes. Transfer the swordfish to a cutting board and cut into 4–8 pieces. Arrange the fish on a serving platter, drizzle with oil, and garnish with tarragon sprigs, if you like. Serve hot with Tarragon Sauce on the side, or with a smear of Horseradish Butter.

## TARRAGON SAUCE

This unusual green sauce, thickened with fresh bread crumbs and brightened with a splash of vinegar, is also delicious spooned over smoky grilled chicken. It's best made just before serving.

Stir together 1 cup fresh white bread crumbs, 1 tablespoon red wine vinegar, and 2 tablespoons water in a mortar and pestle. Let soak for 5 minutes. Pound the softened bread crumbs until somewhat smooth. (If you don't have a mortar and pestle, use a mixing bowl and a wooden spoon.) Slowly drizzle in ½ cup extra-virgin olive oil, stirring and mashing the whole time to make a creamy consistency. Stir in ½ cup chopped fresh parsley leaves and chopped leaves from 5–6 fresh tarragon sprigs. Season with salt and freshly ground black pepper.—*makes about 2 cups*

## HORSERADISH BUTTER

Beat ½ pound (2 sticks) room-temperature salted butter in a medium bowl with a wooden spoon until smooth and creamy. Add 2 tablespoons drained prepared horseradish. Season with salt and a generous amount of freshly ground black pepper and stir until well combined. Slather the room-temperature butter on the hot swordfish.—*makes about 1 cup*

*Grilled Swordfish with Tarragon Sauce*

## GRILLING VEGGIES

Vegetables lack the fattiness of meat, poultry, and fish. Fat preserves juiciness and, when it drips onto hot coals, creates smoke. Simply rubbing vegetables with olive oil and a splash of lemon juice or vinegar, or tossing them in a vinaigrette or marinade, gives them the protection they need from the searing, dehydrating heat of the grill. It also helps prevent them from sticking to the grill. Here are a few tips for taking advantage of the fragrant heat when grilling vegetables.

1. Grill vegetables directly over hot coals. Some char and blistering adds lots of flavor. 2. To prevent steaming, grill veggies in a single layer, moving them to a cooler spot on the grill if they threaten to catch fire. 3. Soft vegetables that grow above ground (tomatoes, peppers, zucchini, onions, scallions, mushrooms, radicchio) grill best. They become supple, even meaty. Heaven!

## GRILLED EGGPLANT & NAAN WITH HUMMUS

We grill large globe eggplants over hot coals (and sometimes directly on a bed of medium-hot coals) until they collapse completely, then scrape out the soft flesh to make baba ghanoush or other seasoned spreads. But we grill a smaller, narrower eggplant when we want to eat them skin and all.

Prepare a medium-hot charcoal or gas grill (for tips, see page 330). Meanwhile, put some thickly sliced eggplant in a medium bowl and toss with a good glug of extra-virgin olive oil, a squeeze of fresh lemon juice, a big pinch of smoked paprika, and a generous seasoning of salt and freshly ground black pepper. Turn the eggplant until well coated. Grill the eggplant over the coals without moving them until they are well browned, with good grill marks, and can be moved without sticking to the grill, about 5 minutes. Turn them over and grill the other side until the flesh is tender, about 5 minutes. Transfer the eggplant back to the bowl.

For each serving, quickly toast 1 naan or other flatbread on the grill, turning it when slightly charred around the edges. Slather about ¼ cup hummus over the crisp, hot bread. Arrange the eggplant slices on top. Scatter 1 small handful of fresh mint, parsley, and chopped chives over the bread. Squeeze a little fresh lemon juice on top and drizzle with extra-virgin olive oil with smoked paprika. Season with salt. Serve warm or at room temperature in wedges.—*makes 1*

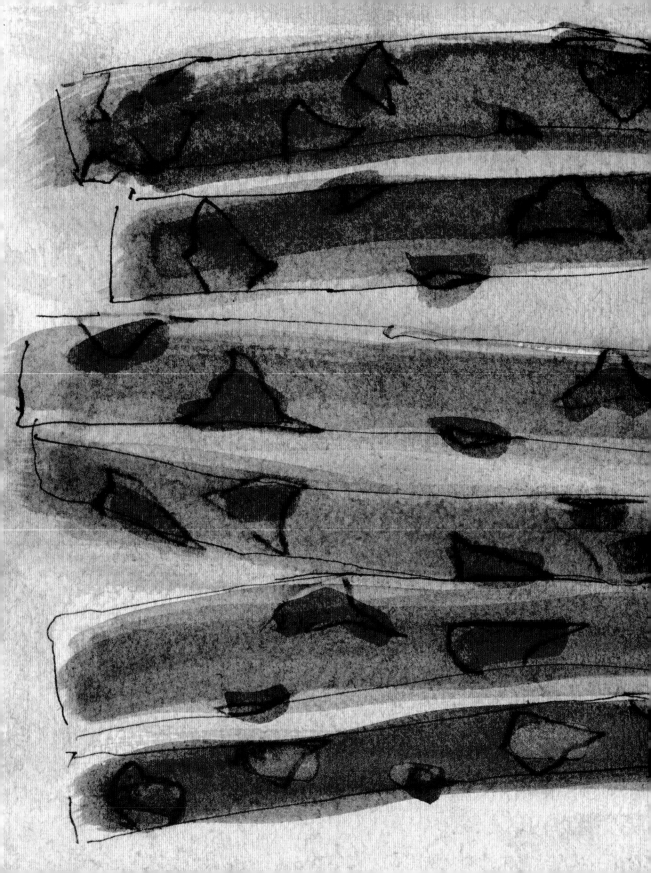

Vegetables

# Eat your Veggies

*If it came from a plant, eat it; if it was made in a plant, don't.*—Michael Pollan, *Food Rules*

NO MATTER WHERE OUR STUDIO IS, we always find a way to have a little garden of sorts: pots of herbs on a fire escape, tomatoes on a balcony, even a window box of salad greens. One year we joined our town's community garden, ambitiously renting two long raised beds. We nailed together and painted signs—Canal House South 40 and Canal House North 40. We were proud of our patches. It was wonderful to walk down the tow path in the morning with our coffee, unlock the gate, and look with pleasure at our beautiful beds. They didn't allow public drinking in the garden, but a few times in the evening we would sneak paper cups of cold rosé to sip while we watered. Watering was a joy. We'd fill up the big spouted cans, haul them across the garden, and shower the thirsty plants. And the garden gaveth: first young lettuces, chives, and radishes; next peas, scallions, spinach, and tiny zucchini with their blossoms; and then the tomatoes. By mid-August the bugs came, the heat came, but no rain came. We loved it all just the same. And besides, the farm markets were overflowing. We have a new garden now, four small raised beds for herbs, lettuces, and of course a few tomatoes. Always hopeful, we fall in love with a packet of watermelon seeds, an Italian heirloom zucchini, or stringless green beans. You dream, you plant, you cross your fingers and say a prayer, and sometimes the magic works (and sometimes it doesn't).

And all this because both of us love vegetables. We are practically vegetarians except that we also love the taste of meat, and few can argue with the fact that a little bit of meat adds a whole lot of flavor. We value our veg and cook each kind in the way it asks to be cooked. Nothing frozen (maybe the occasional English peas); everything fresh, organic, and above all, local. We like our vegetables cooked, not al dente, not crunchy. But cooked through until they are tender, so the full flavor of the vegetables comes through when you bite into them. We roast beets to concentrate their flavor. We cook carrots in a little water with a big pat of butter so the butter cloaks the carrots when the water boils away as they continue to cook. We parboil sturdy vegetables to soften them before we sauté them in the same skillet to add rich caramelized flavor. After many years, we've come to these simple ways of cooking that are economical of time and pots, and we love the delicious results.

Sometimes people think that we are "foodies" and all that the phrase implies: that we host wine dinners, know the grooviest restaurants, follow/lead the most current food trends. No, we just love food. We wake up in the morning and start planning dinner. We peruse markets until something catches our eye and inspires us. It might be a big russet potato that we could scrub, bake, and eat with a pool of melted butter in its floury flesh; or leathery collard leaves that we could braise with a ham hock until they are swimming in their own liquor; or sprightly spinach leaves to plunge into boiling water for a few seconds, then bathe in butter and vinegar. No restaurant offers this, and that's why we love to cook (and eat) at home.

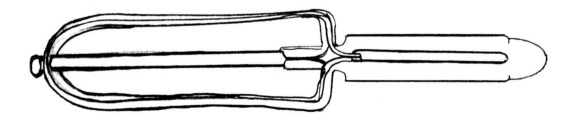

# The Onion

⊙ sweet, pungent, aromatic ⊙

*[. . .] Holding the onion vertically, slice it cleanly in half right down the center line, and look at what you have done. [. . .] Structurally, the onion is not a ball, but a nested set of fingers within fingers, each thrust up from the base through the center of the one before it. [. . .] Thus the spectrum of the onion: green through white to green again, and ending all in the brown skin you have peeled away. Life inside death.*—Robert Farrar Capon, *The Supper of the Lamb: A Culinary Reflection*

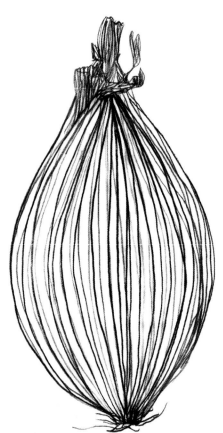

We owe a great deal to the *Allium* genus: garlic, bulb onions, shallots, leeks, scallions, and chives. Our kitchen is never without them. A big wooden bowl sits on our table, filled with onions and garlic. Scallions and spring onions (when they are in season) are stored in open plastic bags in the refrigerator's vegetable drawer. And our window boxes are brimming with chives, ready to be snipped and sprinkled.

There are white onions, mild enough to eat raw; super sweets Maui and Vidalia; vibrant red onions, for pickling; and the workhorse of the family, the yellow onion. Yellow onions sauté and braise into a sweet, rich base for so many of our recipes. We use scallions and chives as a flavorful garnish to add bright green notes.

Between the two of us, we must have cut up a million onions. After all that practice, here's how we do it. Cut an onion in half vertically. Now you have two flat surfaces to use to stabilize the onion as you proceed. For each half: trim off the top stem end and peel away the brown papery skin. Don't slice through the root end; it will help hold everything together as you work. Using a very sharp knife, slice the onions from stem almost to the root. Angle your knife toward the middle of the onion for prettier slices. For chopped onions, take it a step further. We don't bother cutting through the onion horizontally, just cut down through the slices then discard the stem. Make the slices as thin and the chopped pieces as fine as you like.

*Facing page, clockwise from top left: whole and halved spring onions; a bowl of onions and garlic; whole and halved yellow onions; slicing and chopping onions*

## BUYING & STORING & PREPARING VEGETABLES

Supermarket produce managers who allow vegetable bins to be stocked with limp, damaged, molding, or rotting vegetables should be fired. Buying and eating vegetables can be a dreary prospect. Walk through a good farm market or one whose customers' traditional foods rely on brilliant vegetables, ones that have *prana* or vitality, and it is a game changer. Seek these out.

BUYING & STORING: Choose whole vegetables that are firm and unblemished. When possible, buy in-season produce, organic and/or local, for these have the most vitality and flavor. If there is a choice between two vegetables of the same size, select the heavier one, an indication the vegetable has retained more moisture and is fresher. Pre-cut vegetables, though convenient, haven't much flavor and are sometimes treated with preservatives. Don't bother. Cool, dark root cellars were a perfect place to store sturdy potatoes, yams, onions, garlic, and the like, but they've virtually disappeared. A cool cupboard is a good substitute. Store other vegetables (carrots, greens, cabbage, scallions, peppers) in a loosely closed plastic bag or perforated vegetable bag in the vegetable drawer of the fridge. Cut off and store separately in the fridge any green tops of root vegetables. Mushrooms do best in a closed paper bag. Unwashed vegetables keep longer. Asparagus keeps especially well standing up in some water in the fridge. But rather than perfecting vegetable storage, buy less and buy more frequently. The fresher the vegetable, the better the flavor.

PEELING, TRIMMING & PREPPING: Hold off preparing vegetables until you are ready to cook them; they will have better flavor. When you are ready, trim off the ends and remove any bruised or damaged parts. Rinse or soak vegetables in cold water to rid them of dirt, dust, or silt. A vegetable brush comes in handy for sturdy, dirty vegetables. A pastry brush, with its soft bristles, works well cleaning mushrooms. (Onions and garlic do not get rinsed; their skin gets peeled off.) A swivel-blade vegetable peeler is indispensable for peeling asparagus. Start peeling just below the tips, and once the stalks are peeled, trim off the tough woody bottoms. Vegetables cut into even pieces will finish cooking at the same time. Collards and kale have a fibrous, inedible rib. Strip the sturdy leaves off the rib before slicing or chopping and cooking them.

BLANCHING: When we want to soften and take the raw edge off thick-skinned vegetables like string beans or broccoli, or loosen small onions' tight skin, we plunge them into boiling salted water for a minute or two. Then we quickly drain them. Blanching green vegetables makes them even brighter green. Plunge in cold water to keep them crisp.

*Facing page, top: peeling and trimming asparagus; bottom: prepping collards (left) and curly kale (right)*

## BOILING & POACHING

Here are a few rules and tips to make boiled vegetables taste their best. Start root vegetables in cold water. They begin cooking gradually as the water heats up. Add non-root vegetables to boiling salted water to quickly cook them from the outside in and retain shape and color. Generously salt the water. Don't crowd the pot. Boil vegetables in plenty of water in an uncovered pot so that they cook evenly. Poaching vegetables in a flavorful liquid (like broth or milk) over gentle heat deepens their flavor and makes them supple and tender throughout.

## ASPARAGUS ✍ serves 2–4

Asparagus from the supermarket usually doesn't require such cleaning, but we always peel ours for even cooking and tenderness (see page 357).

1 pound fat asparagus
Salt

Soak the asparagus in a few changes of cold water to rid them of any sandy grit. Lift them out of the water and transfer to a cutting board. Lay the spears flat on the board to keep them from snapping. Peel off their skins starting just below their tips using a swivel-blade vegetable peeler. Trim off the woody ends with a knife.

Bring a pot or wide pan of water to a boil over medium-high heat and generously season with salt. Cook the asparagus in the boiling water until tender, 4–5 minutes. Lift the asparagus out with a slotted spatula and drain them on a clean dishcloth. Eat the spears with your fingers; it's perfectly proper.

### LEMON-BUTTER SAUCE

Double the recipe if you want more of this lighter version of hollandaise sauce. Whisk together 2 large egg yolks and 1 tablespoon water in a heavy medium saucepan. Heat over low heat, whisking constantly to prevent the yolks from "scrambling". Add 8 tablespoons cold butter, one piece at a time, whisking until it has melted into the sauce before adding the next. (If the sauce begins to separate, remove the pan from the heat and whisk in another piece of cold butter to cool the sauce down. It should come back together.) Continue whisking in the butter this way until it has all been incorporated into the sauce. Remove the pan from the heat and whisk in the juice of ½ lemon, or less to suit your taste. Season with 1–2 pinches cayenne and salt. Keep the sauce warm by setting the pan in a larger pan of hot water over low heat. To prevent a skin from forming, whisk the sauce frequently or cover it with a sheet of plastic wrap laid directly on the surface.—*makes about ¾ cup*

## CARROTS GLAZED WITH BUTTER

Peel and trim about 1 pound young carrots. Put the carrots, 4 tablespoons butter, 2 tablespoons dark brown sugar, ¼ cup sherry, ¼ cup water, and salt and freshly ground black pepper into a heavy medium pan. Cover and cook over medium heat, shaking the pan occasionally, until the carrots are just tender when pierced, about 10 minutes. Uncover and cook until the sauce reduces a bit and glazes the carrots, 1–2 minutes. Serve the carrots with the buttery sauce, garnished with chopped fresh parsley.—*serves 2–4*

For a brighter-tasting version of these carrots, substitute 1 tablespoon granulated sugar for the brown sugar and water for the sherry. Add a squeeze of fresh lemon juice at the end.

## CREAMY POTATOES WITH CHIVES

Put 4 peeled russet potatoes cut into half-inch cubes into a heavy medium pot. Add 4 tablespoons butter and about 2 cups half-and-half, enough to cover the potatoes. Season with salt and freshly ground black pepper. Bring just to a simmer over medium heat, then reduce the heat to low. Poach the potatoes until they are tender and have absorbed most of the half-and-half, about 60 minutes. Stir occasionally and carefully with a rubber spatula to keep the potato pieces whole. Season with salt and freshly ground black pepper and garnish with lots of chopped fresh chives.—*serves 4–6*

## MASHED POTATOES

Peel and halve 4 russet potatoes. Put them into a medium pot, cover with cold water, add 1 big pinch of salt, and bring to a boil over high heat. Reduce the heat to medium and cook until tender when pierced, 20–30 minutes. Drain the potatoes, reserving 2 cups of the cooking water. Pass the potatoes through a ricer into a bowl and thin them with 1½–2 cups of the reserved cooking water. Season with 8 tablespoons softened butter (or as much as you like) and salt to taste.—*serves 4–6*

## BLANCHED SPINACH WITH BUTTER & VINEGAR

Rinse well 1 pound mature flatleaf spinach in cold water. Working in batches, blanch the spinach in a large pot of salted boiling water until just tender but still vivid green, about 30 seconds. Transfer the spinach with a slotted spatula to a colander and drain well. Melt 6 tablespoons butter in a medium pan over medium heat. Swirl in 1 tablespoon red wine vinegar. Remove the pan from the heat. And the spinach and toss well. Season with salt and freshly ground black pepper.—*serves 4*

*Facing page, clockwise from top left: Carrots Glazed with Butter; Creamy Potatoes with Chives; Mashed Potatoes; Blanched Spinach with Butter & Vinegar*

## BEANS & LEGUMES

Dried beans and legumes are some of the most useful, delicious, and nutritious staples to have on hand. We favor any of the dried white beans and lentils (particularly the earthy small black, green, or le Puy variety that keep their shape when tender). With cooked beans (stored in their cooking liquid) and/or legumes stashed in the fridge, you've got a jump on any meal of the day.

BUYING: Choose beans and legumes that have been recently harvested and dried. As beans age, their outer shell becomes tough and impermeable. Sometimes old beans never get tender, even after hours of cooking. Though it may be hard to spot, look for a "Best If Used By" date on the package.

SOAKING: Soaking dried beans in water hydrates and softens them, giving them a jump start, but it's not necessary. If you choose to soak your beans, they only need about 4 hours. But be sure that you cook them at the gentlest simmer so their skins don't break. Lentils do not need to be soaked.

SALTING: Adding salt to beans and legumes while they cook actually accelerates the cooking time.

COOKING: For plump, creamy beans that hold their shape, simmer them slowly over low heat in plenty of water. When they are tender, let the beans cool in the flavorful cooking liquid.

## TENDER WHITE BEANS

Rinse 2 cups dried white beans and put them into a heavy medium pot. Cover them with cold water by about 2 inches. Add 1–2 garlic cloves, 1 large sprig fresh thyme or sage (optional), 2 bay leaves, and 1 pinch of salt. Bring the beans just to a simmer over medium heat, stirring occasionally. Reduce the heat to low and very gently simmer them until they are swollen and tender, 30–90 minutes (or more), depending on the freshness of the dried beans. Remove the pot from the heat. Stir in a generous pinch of salt and pour a good glug of extra-virgin olive oil on top. To store the beans, let them cool to room temperature in the cooking liquid. The beans will keep, covered, in the refrigerator for up to 5 days.—*makes about 6 cups*

## LENTILS WITH ROASTED BEETS

Rinse 1½ cups French lentils in cold water. Put the lentils in a medium pot with 3 cups water, 1 small peeled yellow onion, 2 garlic cloves, and 1 bay leaf. Bring to a boil over medium heat, reduce the heat to low, and gently simmer until all the water has been absorbed and the lentils are tender, 30–45 minutes. Drain lentils if needed. Lift out and discard the onion, garlic, and bay leaf. Dice 4 small peeled, roasted beets (page 372), and add them to the lentils. Season to taste with salt and freshly ground black pepper. Transfer to a serving dish. Drizzle generously with a really good extra-virgin olive oil and garnish with lots of chopped fresh parsley and scallions.—*serves 6*

*Lentils with Roasted Beets*

## BRAISING & STEWING

A heavy large pot with a tight-fitting lid is essential for braising vegetables. Often, onions and garlic are first softened in fat, then vegetables are added for a long, slow simmer. Olive oil or butter, a flavorful broth, and the vegetables' own juices produce deep flavor. These vegetable dishes are so satisfyingly rich you can skip the meat and serve them with beans, pasta, or over polenta (page 375).

## BRAISED CABBAGE WITH CANNELLINI BEANS ☞ serves 4

Why is cabbage a deeply misunderstood vegetable? Because when raw it looks like a hard ball. But after braising in its own juices, it becomes supple, tender, and sweet.

1 large tomato, halved
1 green cabbage, quartered
  and cored
½ cup extra-virgin olive oil
1 cup cannellini bean cooking
  liquid or water
1 large branch fresh sage
3 pepperoncini
Salt and freshly ground
  black pepper
4 cups warm cooked
  cannellini beans (page 363)

Preheat the oven to 400°F. Grate the fleshy side of the tomatoes on the large holes of a box grater into a bowl. Discard the skins (see page 158).

Put the cabbage into a heavy large ovenproof pot with a tight-fitting lid. Pour the olive oil and grated tomatoes over the cabbage. Add the bean cooking liquid and sage. Crush the pepperoncini into the pot and season to taste with salt and pepper. Cover the pot and braise in the oven until the cabbage is golden brown and tender when pierced with the tip of a knife, about 30 minutes.

Spoon the warm beans onto a platter, arrange the braised cabbage on top, and spoon the juices over everything.

## RED CABBAGE IN CUMBERLAND SAUCE

Serve this sweet-sour cabbage condiment with sausages, grilled meats, or poultry. Or add a spoonful to a bowl of cooked beans or lentils. As with many dishes, its flavor improves after a day or two.

Core and thinly slice 1 small red cabbage. Chop 1 cored, peeled Golden Delicious apple.

Melt 4 tablespoons butter in a heavy large pot over medium-high heat. Add 1 large sliced peeled onion and 5 crushed juniper berries, and season with salt and freshly ground black pepper. Cook until soft, about 5 minutes. Add the cabbage and apples, and stir until well mixed. Stir ½ cup red currant jelly, ¼ cup Port or Marsala, 2 tablespoons Dijon mustard, and 1 tablespoon red wine vinegar together in a bowl, then stir into the cabbage. Reduce the heat to medium and braise until tender, about 30 minutes. Increase the heat to high and reduce any liquid until syrupy, about 3 minutes.—*makes 3–4 cups*

*Braised Cabbage with Cannellini Beans*

## COLLARDS & HAM ☞ serves 4

Of all the long-cooked greens, we love collards the best. Those big leathery leaves cook down into such sweet suppleness. A great Southern favorite, there is much lore on the trials of ridding them of all their sandy dirt. But the collards we buy at the market come soil-free, so a simple rinse in the sink will do it. You start out with a big pot full of leaves, and as they cook they will considerably shrink and make their lovely pot liquor.

1 big bunch collard greens, washed, with the water still clinging to them
1 large yellow onion, peeled and thinly sliced
1 garlic clove, sliced
Salt and freshly ground black pepper
½ boneless ham hock
Extra-virgin olive oil

Fold each wet collard leaf in half lengthwise (as if you were closing a book), and cut out and discard the center rib and stem. Slice the leaves crosswise into fat ribbons (see page 357).

Put the onions and garlic into a heavy large pot with a lid and season with salt and pepper. Add the ham hock and cook over medium heat to soften the onions a bit, about 5 minutes.

Add the wet collards to the pot. Reduce the heat to low, cover the pot, and cook until the greens are very soft and swimming in their pot liquor, about 2 hours. Season with salt and pepper to taste. Pull apart the ham hock and serve with the collards, drizzled with olive oil.

## BRAISED ESCAROLE

Escarole always needs a good soak in cold water to rid it of the dirt between its leaves. We wash it just before cooking so the leaves still have water clinging to them when added to the skillet. This way, when they meet the warm oil, they wilt gently. This is a quick braise.

Trim 1 head escarole of its dark green outer leaves and green tops and discard them. Separate the pale inner leaves, rinse them well, and shake off some of the water. Put ¼ cup extra-virgin olive oil and 1–2 thinly sliced garlic cloves into a large skillet and warm over medium heat until fragrant, about 1 minute. Add the escarole and braise, turning the leaves as they begin to wilt, 3–5 minutes. Season to taste with salt and freshly ground black pepper.—*serves 2–4*

FOR BRAISED ESCAROLE WITH WHITE BEANS: Add 1–2 cups cooked white beans with some of their cooking liquid (page 363) and season to taste with salt and freshly ground black pepper.—*serves 4*

*Facing page, top: Collards & Ham; bottom: Braised Escarole with White Beans*

## SUMMER VEGETABLES STEWED IN BUTTER ☞ serves 4

This delicate vegetable stew can be served warm or at room temperature with grilled fish or chicken.

2 cups white baby turnips, trimmed, larger ones halved
Salt
8 tablespoons butter
1 small yellow onion, peeled and sliced
1 garlic clove, thinly sliced
1 large handful fresh chanterelles, cleaned
1–2 large sprigs fresh tarragon
1 pepperoncini, crushed
Freshly ground black pepper
4 small zucchini, thickly sliced
4 baby zucchini, optional
2 cups fresh or frozen peas
Extra-virgin olive oil
1 ripe tomato, cored, peeled, and cut into thick wedges
Zucchini blossoms, optional

Cook the turnips in a pot of boiling salted water until just tender, about 5 minutes. Drain, reserving some of the cooking water.

Melt the butter in a heavy large skillet with a lid. Add the onions and garlic, and cook over medium heat until soft, about 3 minutes. Add the chanterelles and tarragon, cover, and simmer until just tender, about 5 minutes. Season with pepperoncini and salt and pepper.

Add the cooked turnips, zucchini, peas, and about ¼ cup of the reserved turnip cooking water. Add a few glugs of olive oil for extra richness.

Cover and stew the vegetables until tender. Remove the skillet from the heat. Add the tomatoes and bathe them with the warm vegetables and juices. Transfer to a serving platter. Remove and discard the tarragon. Season with salt and pepper. Scatter zucchini blossoms on top, if using.

## BRAISED MUSHROOMS ON POLENTA

Heat 2 tablespoons extra-virgin olive oil and 2 tablespoons butter together in a wide heavy pot over medium heat until the butter foams. Add 1 small chopped, peeled onion, and 1 minced garlic clove and cook until soft and translucent, 3–5 minutes. Add 2 pounds sliced, cleaned, mixed wild and/or cultivated mushrooms and cook, stirring occasionally, until they begin to soften, about 3 minutes. Add leaves of 4 fresh thyme sprigs, 2 tablespoons sherry, and 4 canned plum tomatoes, crushing them in your hand as you add them. Add 2 cups chicken stock or water; ½ bunch of parsley, leaves chopped; and 2 tablespoons butter.

Braise the mushrooms over medium-low heat until everything is stewy and has thickened a bit, about 20 minutes. Season with salt and freshly ground black pepper (it will most likely need it). Spoon the mushrooms and pot juices over warm polenta (page 375), if you like.—*serves 4*

## ROASTING & BAKING

The dry, enveloping heat that comes from cooking in an oven is an easy and convenient way to cook vegetables evenly and deepen their flavor. The terms *baking* and *roasting* are virtually interchangeable today. We bake potatoes uncovered and we roast beets covered. However, when we cook vegetables uncovered in a really hot oven (400°F or hotter) so the intensity of the heat browns and caramelizes the outside of the vegetable and sweetens its flavor, we're *roasting*. Sturdy root and thinner-skinned vegetables (including cauliflower, Brussels sprouts, tomatoes, eggplant, even radicchio) can handle the searing heat, but benefit with a coating of fat before roasting to encourage browning and protect the outside from drying out before the inside is done. And seasoning vegetables with salt and spices or dried herbs before they are roasted adds a whole lot of flavor.

## BAKED POTATO

The classic baked potato with its thick, dark brown skin and dry, starchy interior is thanks to one variety: the "Russet Burbank" (aka Idaho) potato. The flesh of these low-moisture, high-starch spuds (ideal for baking, frying, mashing, and thickening soups) is floury when cooked. The mouthfeel is comforting. A waxy potato, with its high moisture and low starch content (like white, new, or Yukon Gold), would never cut it, but the flesh holds its shape and remains moist when cooked, perfect for boiling, roasting, steaming, and sautéing. There's no need to wrap a russet in foil before baking it; the leathery skin provides plenty of protection for the flesh and doing so would only make it limp. One of the pleasures of eating a baked potato is the pliable, crisp skin, full of earthy flavor. Mash the flesh with a fork while the potato is still piping hot, for it won't be fluffy if you wait. Prepare and bake sweet potatoes and yams as you would russet potatoes, but rub the skin with a little oil and bake in a 400°F oven on a baking sheet to keep any juices from dripping onto the floor of the oven.

Preheat the oven to 450°F. Wash and pat dry 1 russet potato and prick in several places with a fork to allow steam to escape as it bakes. Bake the potato either on a baking sheet or directly on the oven rack. Bake until the flesh is tender and the tip of a sharp knife or a skewer easily slides into the center of the potato when pierced, 50–60 minutes.

Cut a deep slit down the center of the hot potato, being careful to avoid the escaping steam. Using both hands, squeeze the outside of the potato toward the center to loosen and break up the flesh. Mash the flesh with a fork, keeping the fluffy spuds inside the walls of the potato skin. Season the potato while still hot with one or two big knobs of softened butter, salt and freshly ground black pepper, and a big dollop of sour cream, if you like. Serve with boiled and buttered string beans (completely optional).—*makes 1*

## ROASTED BEETS ✍ serves 4

We prefer roasting beets to boiling them because they retain more of their earthy, "dirty" flavor.

12 medium beets, leaves and stalks trimmed to about 1 inch from the stem end
Butter or extra-virgin olive oil
Salt and freshly ground black pepper

Preheat the oven to 400°F. Wrap each trimmed beet in aluminum foil and arrange on a baking sheet. Roast in the oven until tender (we just pierce through the foil into the beet with a sharp knife to check doneness), 45–60 minutes. Remove the beets from the oven.

Unwrap the beets, being careful of steam. When they are cool enough to handle, trim off and discard the tops and tails and slip off the skins. Cut the beets (optional), and season with butter or olive oil, and salt and pepper, if you like.

WARM BEETS WITH BALSAMIC BUTTER: Toss roasted beets with 4 tablespoons melted butter and 1–2 tablespoons balsamic vinegar, and season with salt and freshly ground black pepper.

WARM BEETS WITH TARRAGON BUTTER: Toss roasted beets with 4 tablespoons melted butter, 1 handful chopped fresh tarragon leaves, and season with salt and freshly ground black pepper to taste.

## ROASTED CARROTS

Preheat the oven to 400°F. Put 12 trimmed, peeled, young carrots, whole or cut into equal large pieces in a shallow roasting pan. Rub the carrots all over with 2 tablespoons olive oil, season with ½ teaspoon ground coriander, ½ teaspoon ground cumin, and salt and freshly ground black pepper, and arrange them in a single layer. Roast the carrots uncovered until browned on the bottom and tender, about 30 minutes. Transfer the carrots to a serving dish and toss with the finely grated zest of ½ lemon, 1–2 tablespoons fresh lemon juice, 1–2 tablespoons extra-virgin olive oil, and some chopped fresh mint or parsley leaves, if you like. Adjust the seasonings.—*serves 2–4*

## ROASTED KABOCHA SQUASH

Preheat the oven to 400°F. Cut a 3-pound kabocha squash in half and scoop out the seeds. Quarter the halves, arrange them flesh side up in a roasting pan, and rub the flesh with extra-virgin olive oil. Season with salt and freshly ground black pepper. Roast the squash until tender, about 1 hour. Drizzle the squash with extra-virgin olive oil or melted butter, and adjust the seasonings.—*serves 4*

*A platter of roasted vegetables*

## POTATOES BAKED IN MILK & CREAM ☞ serves 6

We've made versions of this potato gratin with cheese and seasoned the milk and cream with garlic and bay leaves, but we've abandoned both for this pure version. The starchy russet potato is the only one to use; it softens as it absorbs the milk and cream and thickens the gratin like no other.

2 pounds (about 3) large
   russet potatoes, peeled and
   cut in ¼-inch thick slices
1½ cups whole milk
1½ cups heavy cream
Salt and freshly ground
   black pepper
Freshly grated nutmeg

Preheat the oven to 275°F with a rack set in the middle of the oven. Arrange the potato slices slightly overlapping in layers in an 8-cup gratin or baking dish. Mix together the milk and cream in a bowl and pour it over the potatoes to just cover them (use a little more milk and/or cream if needed). Put the dish in the oven and bake for 1 hour.

Carefully remove the dish from the oven and generously season the potatoes with salt, pepper, and nutmeg.

Return the dish to the oven and bake until the liquid is thick and bubbling and the top is golden brown, about 1 hour.

Remove the gratin from the oven and let it set up for about 20 minutes before serving.

## SOFT BUTTERY POLENTA

A plate of warm polenta seasoned with salted butter and grated parmesan cheese is a comforting meal itself. But it is delicious with a ragù or tomato sauce spooned on top, or served with braises, stews, meats, fish, game, or poultry. Use medium or coarse cornmeal stone-ground for the best flavor. Package labels vary—"cornmeal", "grits", "polenta"—they all make this beloved Italian cornmeal mush. Just avoid the premade tubes, or the "quick-cooking" or "instant" varieties. We start our polenta in cold salted water, whisking it a few times as it comes to a boil. Clumping is never a problem. Don't underestimate the time it takes to cook polenta, about 1 hour for the cornmeal to swell and fully soften. What's the rush?

Put 5 cups of cold water into a heavy medium pot. Stir in 1 cup polenta and 2 generous pinches of salt. Bring to a boil over medium-high heat, whisking often. Reduce the heat to medium-low and cook the polenta, stirring frequently, until it is thick but loose and tender, 45–60 minutes. The polenta will swell and thicken as it cooks. Stir in more water as needed if it gets too thick before it's finished cooking. Stir in 2–4 tablespoons butter and season with salt.—*serves 4–6*

*Potatoes Baked in Milk & Cream*

## SAUTÉING

To sauté is to cook food quickly in a small amount of fat over relatively high heat, shaking the pan and tossing the food to keep it from sticking and burning. The French verb *sauter*, which means "to jump", describes the action. Sometimes we "parboil" hard vegetables in a little water with butter or olive oil right in the sauté pan. When the water evaporates, fat coats the now tenderized vegetables and the sautéing begins, adding a caramelized flavor.

## RED PEPPERS & ONIONS AGRODOLCE ☞ serves 4–6

Pile these meaty peppers on crostini or serve with grilled meat, fish, or fowl. When we have the time we peel the peppers, but it's the quick sauté that adds the flavorful caramelization.

1 handful dried currants
1 tablespoon drained capers
1 pinch of crushed red
  pepper flakes
2 tablespoons red wine vinegar
¼ cup extra-virgin olive oil
Salt and freshly ground
  black pepper
1 large yellow onion, peeled
  and sliced
1–2 tablespoons tomato paste
2 large red bell peppers,
  trimmed, cored, and sliced
1 garlic clove, thinly sliced

Stir together the currants, capers, pepper flakes, and vinegar in a small bowl. Add 2 tablespoons of the olive oil, season with salt and pepper, and set aside.

Heat the remaining 2 tablespoons of olive oil in a large skillet over medium-high heat. Add the onions and sauté for about 2 minutes, stirring once or twice. Push the onions aside, add the tomato paste to the center of the skillet, and toast it for 1 minute. Add the bell peppers and sauté for about 2 minutes, stirring often. Add the garlic, season with salt and pepper, and sauté for about 1 minute. Add the currant/caper mixture and cook until the peppers are just tender, about 5 minutes. Taste and adjust the seasonings.

## GREEN BEANS WITH GINGER, SCALLIONS & CILANTRO

Melt 3 tablespoons butter in a small pot over medium heat. Add 1 tablespoon grated peeled fresh ginger and 1 grated garlic clove. Cook for 1 minute and set aside.

Put 4–6 cups trimmed green beans, ½ cup water, and 1 tablespoon butter in a large skillet. Boil over medium-high heat until the water evaporates, 7–8 minutes. Sauté the beans in the skillet, tossing them to keep them from sticking, for about 2 minutes. Add 2 chopped, trimmed scallions and the ginger butter and toss together. Mix in a large handful of chopped fresh cilantro leaves and stems. Season with salt and freshly ground pepper.—*serves 4*

*Facing page, top: Red Peppers & Onions Agrodolce; bottom: Green Beans with Ginger, Scallions & Cilantro*

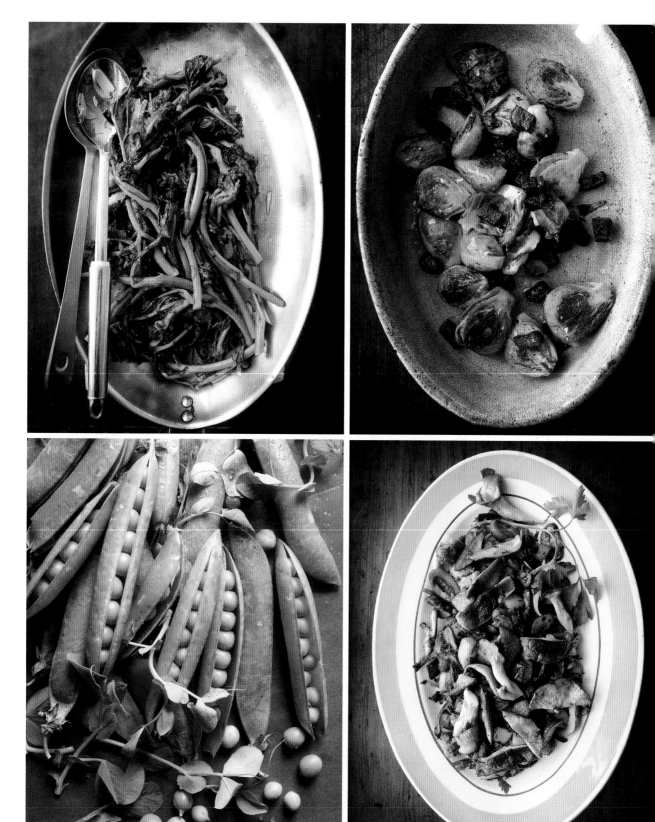

## SAUTÉED BROCCOLI RABE

This method both blanches and sautés the broccoli rabe right in the same skillet.

Put 1 bunch trimmed broccoli rabe, 2 sliced garlic cloves, ½ cup water, and a splash of extra-virgin olive oil into a large skillet. Boil over medium-high heat until the water evaporates, turning the spears with tongs so they cook evenly, about 6 minutes. Add a splash of extra-virgin olive oil and a pinch of crushed red pepper flakes, and sauté 1–2 minutes. Season with salt and freshly ground black pepper. —*serves 2–4*

## BRUSSELS SPROUTS WITH BACON

Put 1 cup (about 4 ounces) diced slab bacon into a medium skillet and cook over medium heat until browned and crisp all over, about 10 minutes. Transfer the bacon to a bowl, leaving the fat in the skillet. Add 1 pound trimmed, halved Brussels sprouts; 1 sliced garlic clove, and ½ cup water to the skillet. Increase the heat to medium-high and boil, stirring often, until the water evaporates, 5–6 minutes. Return the bacon to the skillet, add a splash of extra-virgin olive oil, and sauté, stirring often, until the Brussels sprouts are deep golden brown, about 5 minutes. Season to taste with salt and freshly ground black pepper.—*serves 2–4*

## SAUTÉED MUSHROOMS WITH POTATOES

Put 1 large diced, peeled potato; 2 sliced garlic cloves; 1 cup water; a big pinch of salt; and 1 tablespoon extra-virgin olive oil in a nonstick skillet. Boil over medium-high heat until the water evaporates, turning often, 6–7 minutes. Add 3 tablespoons olive oil and 4 cups sliced, cleaned mushrooms to the skillet and sauté until tender, about 8 minutes. Toss the vegetables to keep them from sticking. Mix in a large handful of chopped fresh parsley. Season with salt and freshly ground black pepper.—*serves 2–4*

## NILOUFER'S SUCKY PEAS

Niloufer Ichaporia King includes this recipe in her wonderful book *My Bombay Kitchen*. The idea is to pull the peas out of the pods with your teeth, just as you would eat an artichoke leaf. The charred bits of the pod and the salt stick to your lips, flavoring the tender peas.

Pour a little extra-virgin olive oil into a large cast-iron skillet. Wipe the skillet out with a paper towel, leaving the thinnest film of oil. Heat the skillet over high heat. When it's very hot, and working in batches, add 1 pound English peas in their pods in a single layer, turning them with a spatula until they turn from bright green to a blistery blackened olive color. Transfer to a plate, sprinkle with Maldon or any other coarse, flaky salt, and serve right away.—*serves 4–6*

*Facing page, clockwise from top left: Sautéed Broccoli Rabe; Brussels Sprouts with Bacon; Sautéed Mushrooms with Potatoes; fresh English peas*

# Sweeties

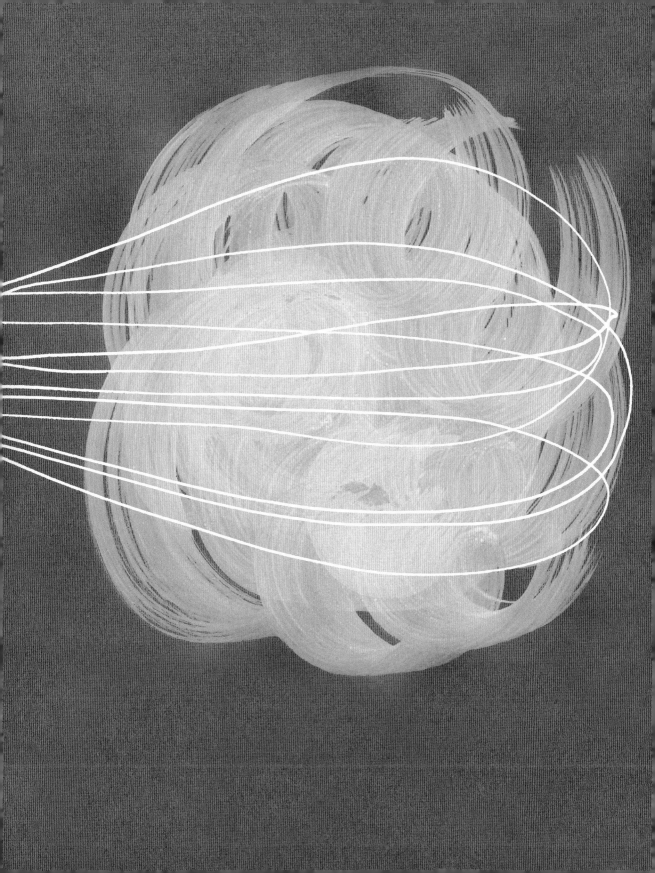

# A Savory Sweet Tooth

*I don't want a grown-up person at all. A grownup won't listen to me; he won't learn. He will try to do things his own way and not mine. So I have to have a child. I want a good sensible loving child, one to whom I can tell all my most precious candy-making secrets—while I am still alive.* —Roald Dahl, *Charlie and the Chocolate Factory*

W E ARE SALT-AND-PEPPER COOKS WITH MORE OF AN APPETITE for savories than sweets. That's not to say we don't each have a wee sweet tooth, it just means we are a little more particular about the kinds of sweets we like.

CH was eleven when she decided to teach herself to cook. Her first efforts were savories. Roast leg of veal made with a leg of lamb massaged for 30 minutes with olive oil, then slathered with mashed garlic, Dijon mustard, salt and pepper, and chopped fresh rosemary was a great success. Her chocolate chili is not as strange as it sounds. Chocolate, Mexico's gift to the world, figures in some of the classic mole sauces. And her erroneous version of Welsh rabbit (thick slices of sharp Cheddar laid on top of Ryvita crackers and sprinkled with chili powder, then grilled under the broiler), which she and her younger brother would snack on while sipping a frothy brew of hot milk with instant coffee, sweetened with lots of sugar.

Like many girls, MH began her forays into cooking with baking, mostly fruit tarts and bar cookies, gingerbread houses and sweet breads. There was satisfaction in the ta-da factor when a baking project was successful, of taking loose ingredients and transforming them into a beautiful shape, especially a sweet one. And there was pleasure in pleasing; everybody always lights up when there is dessert. Once her palate matured, she turned her attention more toward cooking with fire and salt.

So the desserts and sweets we love to eat and make today are influenced by the savory bent we both share. We roast rhubarb in red wine. Plump dried apricots in white. We add preserved lemon to our lemon meringue tart filling to intensify its flavor and bring out its sweetness. We make sure our pecan pie has more nuts than sweet jellied filling. We use unsweetened whipped cream to dull the tooth-aching sweetness of pavlovas and meringues. We spread salted butter on our biscuits and shortbreads. We don't like gooey cakes much. But we can't resist a moist chocolate one that's covered in chocolate frosting standing tall and proud.

After years of making pies and galettes, cakes and buttercreams, sabayon and soufflés, we believe that to be a good cook, you don't need to know how to temper chocolate or roll out pastry dough perfectly. A good cook feels the ingredients and tastes and adjusts along the way. We've learned to relax when rolling out dough and to use good butter. We balance sweet with salt. We do what most professional bakers do: we rely on measuring our ingredients by weight, not volume, for more consistent results. Use ripe fruit in season, nothing out of season beats it for flavor and perfume. You do not need a copper bowl for stiff, glossy egg whites. Make sure your heavy cream is really cold before whipping it, and underwhip it for soft pillowy dollops. Use the best ingredients you can afford. Master a few good recipes: a fruit pie or tart, a pudding, a handsome pound cake, a killer chocolate cake. They will serve you well.

But most of all, have confidence and have fun. Even if everything goes wrong, just put it on a plate and cover it with whipped cream. Because remember, nobody doesn't love dessert!

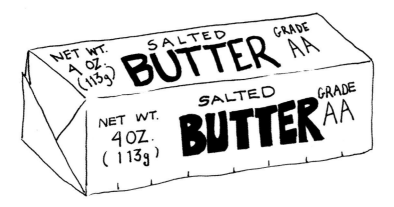

FRUIT POACHING LIQUIDS: A basic simple syrup (1 part sugar dissolved in 1 part boiling water) is a perfectly good solution in which to poach fresh and dried fruit. The formula can be adjusted to suit your taste. We're always in pursuit of flavor, and that often means substituting some or all of the liquid with wine (red, white, or rosé) and adding aromatics (fresh herbs such as rosemary, basil, or tarragon; vanilla bean; citrus zest; fresh ginger; and/or spices like black peppercorn, star anise, or cinnamon sticks). Use the following poached fruit recipes as your flavor guide, then follow your imagination.

## PEARS POACHED IN RED WINE ☞ serves 8

Poaching pears makes the flesh plump and irresistibly meaty. It hardly matters which variety you choose to cook. We use a mid-priced, medium-bodied red wine for the poaching liquid. A Pinot Noir or Côte du Rhône makes a rich garnet syrup that tastes warm and sweet.

1 bottle (750 ml) red wine
1½ cups granulated sugar
8 semifirm, ripe pears
1 lemon peel, cut into wide strips
1 vanilla bean, split lengthwise

Stir the wine and sugar together in a large bowl and set aside. Peel the pears, leaving the stems on. Use a small sharp spoon to scoop out the cores and seeds from the bottoms of the fruit, leaving the pears whole. Trim pear bottoms so each pear stands up.

Put the pears in a heavy deep pot just large enough to fit the pears in one layer. Pour the wine and sugar over the pears and tuck the lemon peel and vanilla bean into the pot. Cover the pot and bring the poaching liquid to a simmer over medium heat. Reduce the heat to low and poach the pears, turning them now and again so they poach evenly, until they feel meaty and tender when pierced, 15–30 minutes. Remove the pot from the heat. Let the pears cool in the poaching liquid, uncovered and at room temperature, for up to 12 hours, turning them occasionally.

Transfer the pears to a dish, standing them up. Discard the peel and vanilla bean. Boil the poaching liquid over medium heat until syrupy and reduced to about 1⅓ cups, about 1 hour. Remove the pot from the heat and let the syrup cool. Return the pears to the pot and turn them occasionally in the syrup until ready to serve. They will keep in the refrigerator, covered, for up to 2 days.

POACHING STONE FRUIT: Peaches, nectarines, plums, apricots—members of the stone fruit family—have a hard pit or stone in the center. We wait for these fruits to come into season as there is nothing quite like the experience of biting into the ripe and fragrant flesh and the sweet juices running down your chin. Gently cooking these fragile fruits in an aromatic poaching liquid preserves their integrity, plumps the flesh, and deepens the flavor. The trick, though, is to keep the flesh from becoming mushy. Rather than actually poaching the fruit, we pour hot poaching liquid over the peeled fruit and let it steep. This way, there's no chance of overcooking. The fruit releases its juices and perfumes the hot liquid, which in turn permeates the fruit. Once the poaching liquid has cooled to room temperature, the fruit is ready to serve. The fruit will keep in the poaching liquid in the fridge for up to two days. The flavorful liquid will keep for a week and makes a lovely addition to a cocktail or poured over ice and topped off with sparkling water.

## WHITE PEACHES "POACHED" IN LEMON VERBENA SYRUP ✍ serves 4–8

Every spring, we plant little pots of lemon verbena. By August, they are bushy enough to start clipping. We use the leaves to infuse tea, simple syrups, and poached fruit, white peaches a particular favorite.

1 cup granulated sugar
1 handful fresh lemon
    verbena leaves
4 ripe white peaches

Put the sugar and 1 cup water into a medium saucepan. Heat over medium-low heat, gently swirling the pan to help dissolve the sugar. When the syrup comes to a boil, cover the pan and cook until the sugar is completely dissolved, 2–3 minutes. Set the pan aside. Add the verbena leaves, cover, and let the syrup steep.

Blanch the peaches in a pot of gently boiling water for about 15 seconds to loosen the skin from the flesh. Quickly lift the peaches out of the water with a slotted spoon. Slip off their skins and put the skins into the syrup in the saucepan. Cover and set aside to steep for at least 15 minutes. The syrup will turn a pretty pink.

Slice the peaches in half and pull out and discard the pit. Put the peaches cut-side down in a deep dish in a single layer. Strain the syrup over them (it's fine if the syrup is still warm; it will bring out more of the fruit's perfume), and add a few of the verbena leaves. Let the peaches rest in the syrup for at least 30 minutes, turning them once or twice before serving. They will keep in the refrigerator, covered, for up to 2 days.

*White peaches*

## LEMON CURD WITH WHIPPED CREAM ☞ serves 4

This sweet-tart dessert pudding, filling, or sauce, is a staple at Canal House. Whipped cream is its counterpart. The curd can also be made with orange, lime, or Meyer lemon juice. It keeps, covered, in the refrigerator for up to two weeks, and freezes beautifully. Just pull it out of the freezer to defrost at room temperature. We serve it like a pudding, topped with a dollop of whipped cream; pour it while still warm into a pre-baked tart crust then let it cool to set up for a tart; spoon it onto warm buttered biscuits, instead of jam; alongside pound cake; as a garnish to fresh fruit; and over meringue piled with tropical fruits or fresh berries.

FOR THE LEMON CURD
2 large eggs
4 large egg yolks
4–6 lemons, washed and dried
1½ cups granulated sugar
6 tablespoons unsalted butter,
  cut into small pieces

FOR THE WHIPPED CREAM
1 cup cold heavy cream
2 tablespoons granulated
  sugar, optional

For the lemon curd, gently whisk the 2 whole eggs and 4 yolks together in a medium bowl then set aside. Finely grate the zest of 4 lemons into a medium nonreactive saucepan. Juice enough lemons to make about 1 cup of juice. Add the juice to the saucepan and whisk in the sugar.

Set the saucepan over medium-low heat and whisk in the beaten eggs. Cook the mixture, whisking or stirring with a wooden spoon constantly to prevent it from boiling, until it has thickened, 5–8 minutes.

Remove the saucepan from the heat and add the butter, a few pieces at a time, whisking until the butter has melted. Strain the lemon curd through a sieve into a plastic or glass container. Cover with plastic wrap pressed right on the surface of the lemon curd, then cover and refrigerate until cold and set, about 4 hours.

For the whipped cream, put the cream and sugar, if using, into a large mixing bowl and beat with a whisk until it just begins to thicken. Continue beating, but when the cream holds very soft peaks, stop beating. If it's still too loose, just before serving, whip the cream for one or two turns until the peaks just hold.

# THE CANAL HOUSE MESS ✑ serves 8

Make this only when the weather is dry because humidity prevents the meringue from becoming crisp and dry. Keep the completely cooled meringue in an airtight container if not using it right away.

FOR THE MERINGUE
4 large egg whites, at room
   temperature
1 pinch of cream of tartar
1 pinch of salt
1 cup superfine sugar
½ teaspoon vanilla extract

FOR THE RASPBERRY SAUCE
2 cups fresh raspberries
¼ cup sugar
2 teaspoons fresh lemon juice

FOR THE TOPPINGS
2 cups berries (raspberries,
   blackberries, hulled and
   halved strawberries, or a
   combination of berries)
2 tablespoons granulated sugar
1½ cups heavy cream
1 pint softened strawberry or
   vanilla ice cream

For the meringue, preheat the oven to 275°F with a rack set in the middle of the oven. Line a cookie sheet with parchment paper and set aside. Put the egg whites into the clean, dry bowl of a standing mixer fitted with the whisk attachment, and beat on medium-low speed until frothy. Add the cream of tartar and salt and beat on medium speed until very soft peaks form. Increase the speed to medium-high and gradually add the superfine sugar (1), beating in 1 tablespoon at a time. Increase the speed to high and beat the whites until they are smooth (rub some of the whites between your thumb and forefinger (2) to check if the sugar granules have dissolved). Continue beating until they are thick and glossy and hold stiff peaks (3). Fold the vanilla into the whites. Pile the meringue into the center of the parchment paper and gently smooth it out (4) to form a thick 9-inch circle. Bake the meringue for 1 hour.

Turn off the oven and leave the meringue inside to dry out and cool completely, 2–3 hours. The longer the meringue is left to dry out, the crunchier it becomes, so leaving it in the turned-off oven as long as overnight is fine, too. Peel off the parchment paper and put the meringue on a cake plate.

For the raspberry sauce, put the raspberries and sugar into the bowl of a food processor and pulse until the fruit is puréed. Strain the sauce into a bowl, pressing it through with a rubber spatula. Discard the seeds. Season the sauce with lemon juice.

For the toppings, toss the berries with the sugar in a bowl and set aside until the berries release their juices, about 30 minutes. Whip the cream in a bowl until soft peaks form.

Top the meringue with scoops of ice cream. Pile on the whipped cream. Spoon the berries and their juices on top, then drizzle the dessert with the raspberry sauce.

*Overleaf: The Canal House Mess*

1. FLOURS ⊙ All-purpose flour, though not the best choice for making chewy bread or cakes with a delicate crumb, is perfectly balanced for making terrific pie dough. Its moderate protein content (7–12 percent) yields tender pastry crust just sturdy enough to hold its shape when baked. We use unbleached, all-purpose flour because it is naturally bleached. *Naturally!*

2. WEIGHT VS. VOLUME ⊙ We are relatively intuitive, gadget-free cooks. But when it comes to baking, we rely on measuring our ingredients (particularly dry ones) by weight, not volume, for much more consistent results. Use a digital kitchen scale with measuring units that include ounces and grams.

3. DRY INGREDIENTS ⊙ More efficient than a sieve or flour sifter, we use a whisk for evenly blending dry ingredients like flour, salt, and sugar together.

4. FAT EQUALS FLAVOR ⊙ Butter gives pastry crusts great flavor. Vegetable shortening adds flaky tenderness. European-style butter with its high-fat content (at least 82 percent) makes a delicious dough that is easy to roll out.

5. GRATING BUTTER ⊙ It's easier to work the butter into the flour when it is cut into small pieces. Grating cold or frozen butter on the large holes of a box grater makes it especially so.

## ...NDER, FLAKY PASTRY DOUGH

3.

7.

8.

11.

12.

6. PASTRY BLENDER ☉ Use a pastry blender (or use two knives in a scissor fashion) to work the cold butter and shortening into the dry ingredients until the flour is flecked with pea-size pieces of butter.

7. ICE WATER ☉ To bind the flour with the fats, sprinkle in ice water while stirring with a fork until the mixture is moistened. It should hold together when pressed between your fingers.

8. RESTING THE DOUGH ☉ Press the mixture into a ball, shape into a disk, cover with plastic wrap, and refrigerate for at least 1 hour to relax the dough, make it easier to roll out, and reduce shrinking when baked.

9. ROLLING ☉ Bring the dough to room temperature. Working from the center, roll it out outwards with a rolling pin on a lightly floured, smooth work surface to a uniform thickness. Dust with more flour, if needed.

10. TRANSFERRING ☉ Loosely roll about half the dough around the rolling pin to move it to a cold baking steel, pizza stone, or pie or tart pan. Then gently unfurl the dough into place.

11. MAKING A GALETTE ☉ For a free-form tart, or galette, fold the edges over the filling, pleating the dough as you go.

12. GOLDEN CRUST ☉ Brush dough with heavy cream for a deep golden crust.

## CARAMELIZED APPLE GALETTE ✎ serves 6–8

Using cooked apples in this galette makes the filling particularly luscious as each apple wedge is transformed into a pillow of concentrated flavor. We like Honey Crisp, Cortland, Golden Delicious, Pippin, Gala, and Granny Smith apples—they hold their shape and keep their sweet tang as they bake.

FOR THE PASTRY DOUGH
1½ cups (180 grams) all-
   purpose flour, plus more for
   rolling out the dough
1 pinch of salt
4 ounces (8 tablespoons) cold
   unsalted butter, cut into
   small pieces
2 tablespoons cold vegetable
   shortening

FOR THE FILLING
8 apples, peeled, cored, and
   cut into thick wedges
½ cup granulated sugar
1 teaspoon ground cinnamon
3 tablespoons salted butter
½ vanilla bean, halved
   lengthwise
2 tablespoons heavy cream

For the pastry dough, whisk together the flour and salt in a mixing bowl. Work the butter and shortening into the flour using a pastry blender, two knives, or even your fingertips until the mixture resembles very coarse cornmeal with pea-size flecks of butter. Sprinkle in 5 tablespoons of ice water tablespoon by tablespoon, mixing it in lightly with your hands until the dough comes together (add a little more water, if needed). Press the mixture together with the heel of your hand until it forms a mass. Shape it into a flat disk; don't overhandle. Wrap the dough in plastic wrap and chill in the refrigerator for at least 1 hour.

For the filling, put the apples in a large bowl and toss with the sugar and cinnamon. Melt the butter in a large skillet over medium heat, add the vanilla bean, then arrange the apple wedges in a single layer and cook, turning occasionally with a fork, until the apples are tender, about 30 minutes. Scrape the seeds from the vanilla pod into the skillet and spoon the pan juices over the apples. Remove the skillet from the heat.

Preheat the oven to 375°F with a rack set in the middle of the oven. Roll out the dough on a lightly floured surface into a 14-inch round. Roll the dough around the rolling pin and unfurl onto a cold pizza stone, baking steel, or a large baking sheet.

Starting in the middle of the dough, arrange the apples in a circular pattern to about 3 inches from the edge. Spoon the pan juices over the apples. Fold the edge of the dough over the apples, pleating as you go. Brush the dough with the cream.

Bake until the crust is golden, about 45 minutes. Remove from the oven and allow to cool for 10 minutes before slicing.

## THE JERRE ANNE BAKE SHOPPE PECAN PIE ⇨ makes two 9-inch pies

These delicate pecan pies are centerpieces of both of our Thanksgivings. They have the perfect ratio of sweet goop to pecans. The recipe came to us by way of Geraldine Lawhon, proprietress of The Jerre Anne Bake Shoppe in St. Joe, Missouri. "Big G" took over from her aunt Afra Lineberry (Agee to her family), who opened the restaurant in 1930. They were especially known for their delicious pies. Sadly, The Jerre Anne is no more, but their reputation lives on in this treasured recipe.

FOR THE PASTRY DOUGH

1 1/2 cups (180 grams) all-purpose flour, plus more for rolling out the dough

1/2 teaspoon salt

4 ounces (8 tablespoons) cold unsalted butter, cut into small pieces

2 tablespoons cold vegetable shortening

FOR THE PECAN FILLING

1 1/2 cups light corn syrup

5 tablespoons butter, melted

1 cup light brown sugar (not packed)

1 pinch of salt

1/2 teaspoon vanilla extract

4 large eggs, beaten

3 cups pecan halves (not pieces)

For the pastry dough, whisk together the flour and salt in a mixing bowl. Work the butter and shortening into the flour using a pastry blender, two knives, or even your fingertips until the mixture resembles very coarse cornmeal with pea-size flecks of butter. Sprinkle in 5 tablespoons of ice water tablespoon by tablespoon, mixing it in lightly with your hands until the dough comes together (add a little more water if needed). Press the mixture together with the heel of your hand until it forms a mass. Divide the dough in half and shape into 2 flat disks; don't overhandle. Wrap the disks in plastic wrap and chill in the refrigerator for at least 1 hour.

Preheat the oven to 375°F with a rack set in the middle of the oven. Roll out one disk of dough on a lightly floured surface into an 1/8-inch thick round. Roll the dough loosely around the rolling pin and unfurl it into a 9-inch pie tin. Lightly press the dough into the tin. Trim the excess dough from the edge with a sharp knife or pair of scissors. Use your thumb and forefinger to crimp the edges. Repeat with the remaining dough.

For the pecan filling, mix together the corn syrup, melted butter, and brown sugar in a large bowl until the sugar has dissolved. Add the salt, vanilla, and eggs, mixing well after each addition. Arrange 1 1/2 cups of the pecans right side up in each unbaked pie shell, then gently pour in the filling. The pecans will float to the top.

Bake the pies for 40–50 minutes or until a knife inserted in the center comes out clean. Cool to room temperature.

WORKING WITH PUFF PASTRY: For the sake of convenience, we use commercial brands of puff pastry available in the frozen food section of the grocery store. The best have real butter; avoid those without a trace of the good stuff (they'll taste like flaky cardboard). Keep puff pastry frozen, then set it out on the counter to defrost while the oven preheats. The very nature of this famously flaky pastry is to puff up into leaflike sheets when baked. "Dock" or prick the dough all over the areas you want to stay flat (we use a fork), then cover with filling. Brush the edges of the pastry with heavy cream before baking for a shiny, deep golden brown crust.

## PUFF PASTRY ITALIAN PLUM & PRUNE TART  ⇀  serves 6–8

Baked puff pastry gets soggy when it sits for a while, so make this tart the same day you plan to eat it.

1 cup pitted prunes
½ cup brandy
½ cup granulated sugar
1 sheet (about 12 × 16 inches)
  puff pastry, defrosted
All-purpose flour
2 pounds Italian prune plums,
  halved lengthwise and pitted
4 tablespoons cold butter,
  cut into pieces
1 tablespoon heavy cream

Put the prunes, brandy, and ¼ cup of the sugar into a small saucepan and simmer over medium-low heat, swirling the pan often until the sugar dissolves. Remove the pan from the heat, cover, and let the prunes macerate for at least 30 minutes. Transfer the prunes with a fork to a bowl and set aside. Gently boil the liquor over medium heat until it is syrupy, 3–5 minutes. Set aside.

Preheat the oven to 400°F with a rack set in the middle of the oven. Roll the puff pastry out on a lightly floured surface to a ¼-inch thick rectangle. Slide the dough onto a parchment paper–lined baking sheet. Using the tip of a paring knife, lightly score a border about ½-inch from the edge of the pastry. Prick the dough inside the border all over with a fork to prevent it from puffing up too much during baking.

Arrange the plums cut-side up in the center of the pastry, then scatter the prunes on top. Drizzle the prune syrup over the fruit. Sprinkle the remaining ¼ cup sugar over the tart, dot with butter, and brush the ½-inch border with the heavy cream.

Bake the tart until the pastry is deeply browned around the edges (it's fine, even delicious, if the edges burn a little bit in places), and the plums are soft and jammy and their juices are bubbling and syrupy, 30–40 minutes.

## ROASTED RHUBARB SHORTCAKES ✏ serves 8

Remember the color of the stalks, which can range from green to deep red, will affect the color of the filling but not rhubarb's vibrant tart flavor, which is unaffected by hue.

FOR THE RHUBARB
2 pounds rhubarb, trimmed and cut in 1-inch thick pieces
1 cup granulated sugar
½ cup red wine
1 vanilla bean, split lengthwise

FOR THE BISCUITS
1 cup (120 grams) cake flour
1 cup (120 grams) all-purpose flour, plus more for the work surface
4 teaspoons baking powder
1 teaspoon granulated sugar
1½ teaspoons salt
3 cups cold heavy cream
4 tablespoons salted butter, melted

For the rhubarb, preheat the oven to 350°F. Combine the rhubarb, sugar, and wine in a medium baking dish. Scrape in the seeds from the vanilla bean, add the bean, and stir to combine. Roast the rhubarb until very tender and the juices are syrupy, 30–40 minutes, depending on thickness of stalks. Let cool. Discard the vanilla bean.

For the biscuits, preheat the oven to 375°F with a rack set in the middle of the oven. Whisk the cake flour, all-purpose flour, baking powder, sugar, and salt in a medium bowl to combine. Add 1½ cups of the cream and gently mix just until the dough holds together.

Transfer the dough to a lightly floured work surface and form it into a 9 × 6-inch rectangle about 1 inch thick. Cut the dough in half lengthwise, then cut crosswise three times to form 8 rectangular biscuits.

Arrange the biscuits on a parchment paper–lined baking sheet, spacing them about 1 inch apart. Brush the tops and sides of the biscuits with some of the melted butter. Bake the biscuits until golden brown, 18–20 minutes. Transfer to a wire rack to cool (biscuits can be served warm or at room temperature).

Beat the remaining 1½ cups cream in a medium bowl until soft peaks form. Split the biscuits and brush the cut sides with the remaining melted butter. Fill the biscuits with roasted rhubarb and serve with whipped cream.

## POUND CAKE ☞ makes 1 large cake

This cake is true to its name, made from an old recipe—a pound each of butter, sugar, eggs, and flour, all beaten together. It has a beautifully tender, tight crumb and lasts up to a week. We use our large tube pan to make an elegant, celebratory cake and serve it with berries or stewed fruit and mounds of soft whipped cream, or we make several smaller cakes in loaf pans. If you don't have pastry flour, use 2 cups cake flour plus 1 cup all-purpose flour.

1 pound (4 sticks) butter, at
    room temperature, plus
    1 tablespoon for the pan
1 pound (about 3 cups) pastry
    flour, plus 2 tablespoons
    for the pan
1 teaspoon salt
1 teaspoon baking powder
¼ teaspoon ground
    cardamom
1 pound (about 2 cups)
    superfine sugar
1 pound whole eggs
    (8–9 large eggs)
1 teaspoon vanilla extract
½ cup buttermilk
Citrus Syrup, optional
    (page 406)

Preheat the oven to 325°F with a rack set in the middle of the oven. Grease a 10-cup (preferably nonstick) angel food cake tube pan with the 1 tablespoon of butter and dust it with the 2 tablespoons of flour, tapping out any excess. Set the prepared pan aside.

Whisk together the flour, salt, baking powder, and cardamom in a medium bowl and set aside.

Put the butter in the bowl of a standing mixer fitted with a whisk attachment and beat on high speed until light and fluffy, about 5 minutes. Continue to beat as you gradually add the sugar to the butter, beating until creamy, about 5 minutes. Scrape down the sides of the bowl often with a rubber spatula. Add the eggs one at a time, incorporating each completely before adding the next. Add the vanilla and heavy cream and beat just until combined.

With the mixer on low speed, slowly add the dry ingredients to the wet ingredients while you continue to beat the batter until it is mixed well. Don't overbeat. Spoon the batter into the prepared pan and smooth the top with a rubber spatula. The batter should fill the pan no higher than 1 inch below the rim.

Bake the cake until golden and slightly split and a skewer comes out clean when poked into the center, about 1 hour and 15 minutes. Let the cake cool in the pan for at least 15 minutes on a wire rack, then run a small knife around the inside edges to help release the cake. Cover the pan with a serving plate, turn the pan over, and unmold the cake. Brush with Citrus Syrup (page 406), if using.

CITRUS SYRUP: Heat ½ cup fresh lemon or orange juice or a combination of both and ½ cup superfine sugar together in a small saucepan over medium heat, stirring until the sugar dissolves completely and the syrup thickens slightly. Remove the pan from the heat and let the syrup cool for a few minutes. Using a thin skewer, poke holes all over the top of the cake and brush it with some of the syrup. Let the cake rest and brush it with the remaining syrup shortly before serving.—*makes about ¾ cup*

## SHORTBREAD COOKIES ✍ makes 12

This recipe makes the classic Scottish shortbread cookie, buttery and not too sweet. They're made in a pan and cut into shapes after they have baked, so no fussing, just our kind of cookie.

2 cups (240 grams) all-purpose flour
½ cup (99 grams) granulated sugar
1 pinch of salt
1 teaspoon vanilla extract
½ pound (16 tablespoons) cold butter, cut into pieces
Powdered sugar

Preheat the oven to 350°F with a rack set in the middle of the oven. Put the flour, granulated sugar, and salt into a mixing bowl and whisk to combine. Stir in the vanilla, breaking up the bits with your fingers.

Using two butter knives, a pastry blender, or your fingers, work the butter into the flour until it is crumbly and has the texture of coarse meal. Spread the crumbly mixture out in an 8-inch loose-bottomed round tart pan or other 8-inch baking pan. Pat and press the mixture lightly so it is smooth on top and the crumbs are all lightly packed together. Using a fork, gently press a pattern into the pastry around the edge and over the surface of the shortbread.

Bake until pale golden brown, about 30 minutes. Remove the shortbread from the oven and cut into 12 wedges in the pan while it is still warm. Let the shortbread cool completely on a wire rack. Dust with powdered sugar. The shortbread will keep in an airtight container for up to 2 weeks..

## THICK & CHEWY BROWNIES ⟿ makes 16

Heating the butter and sugar together gives these brownies their distinctive taste and look—rich and fudgy, with a shiny, tissue-thin top crust. The perfect kind of brownie.

6 ounces (12 tablespoons) butter, plus more for greasing the pan

1 cup (120 grams) all-purpose flour, plus more for dusting the pan

2 cups granulated sugar

4 ounces semisweet chocolate, chopped

2 ounces unsweetened chocolate, chopped

1 teaspoon instant espresso powder

¼ teaspoon salt

4 large eggs

2 teaspoons vanilla extract

1 cup chopped walnuts, optional

Preheat the oven to 350°F with a rack set in the middle of the oven. Grease a 9-inch square baking pan with some butter, then dust it with some flour, tapping out any excess.

Melt the butter in a medium saucepan over medium heat. Add the sugar, stirring until it has the consistency of soft slush and just begins to bubble around the edges, 1–2 minutes. Remove the pan from the heat. Add both chocolates, the espresso, and the salt to the pan, stirring until the chocolate melts and the mixture is well combined.

Put the eggs in a large mixing bowl and beat with an electric mixer fitted with the whisk attachment on medium speed. Gradually add the warm chocolate mixture, about ¼ cup at a time, beating constantly until well combined. Stir in the vanilla. Add the flour and walnuts, if using, stirring until just combined. Pour the batter into the prepared pan.

Bake the brownies until a toothpick inserted into the center comes out clean, 45–60 minutes. Let the brownies cool in the pan on a rack, then cut into squares.

## THE CHOCOLATE CAKE ⟿ makes one 9-inch two-layer cake

New York City's Katherine Yang of Gigi Blue—Delectable Edibles, shared this recipe with us when we needed to make a very special chocolate wedding cake. She is the best baker we know and always generous with her knowledge to boot. We thank her with every bite of this cake, and you will too. It's moist and chocolatey through and through. When it comes to baking, Katherine advises measuring the ingredients by weight rather than volume for the most consistent results. The frosting may be made ahead and kept in the fridge. Just bring it to room temperature before spreading it on the cake (see page 410).

*continued*

FOR THE CAKE

Nonstick cooking spray

8 ounces (16 tablespoons) unsalted butter, at room temperature

2⅓ cups plus 3 tablespoons (508 grams) superfine sugar

1¼ cups (94 grams) extra-dark cocoa powder, sifted

2 large eggs

1 large egg yolk

1⅓ cups plus 4 teaspoons (200 grams) all-purpose flour

1½ cups plus 4 teaspoons (182 grams) cake flour

2 teaspoons salt

2¼ teaspoons baking powder

2 teaspoons baking soda

2 cups boiling water

½ cup canola oil

FOR THE FROSTING

1 cup granulated sugar

1 cup heavy cream

1 teaspoon vanilla extract

4 ounces unsweetened chocolate, chopped

4 ounces (8 tablespoons) unsalted butter, diced

3–4 tablespoons apricot or other jam, optional

For the cake, preheat the oven to 325°F with a rack set in the middle of the oven. Spray two 9-inch round cake pans with non-stick cooking spray. Line the bottom of each pan with a parchment paper round, spray again, and set aside.

Put the butter and sugar in the bowl of a standing mixer fitted with the paddle attachment. Beat on medium speed until light and fluffy, 5–8 minutes. Add the cocoa powder and beat until combined, 3–5 minutes, scraping down the sides of the bowl with a rubber spatula as necessary.

Whisk together the eggs and egg yolk in a small bowl. With the mixer on low speed, slowly add the eggs, mixing until well combined. Scrape down the sides of the bowl as necessary.

Whisk together both flours, the salt, baking powder, and baking soda in a large bowl and add to the butter mixture. Mix on low speed until the batter is combined.

Combine the boiling water and the oil in a bowl. With the mixer on low speed, gradually add it to the batter, mixing until combined. Divide the batter evenly between the prepared cake pans. Transfer to the oven and bake until a cake tester inserted into the center comes out clean, 35–40 minutes. Transfer cakes to a rack to cool completely. Peel off and discard the parchment paper.

For the frosting, whisk together the sugar, cream, and vanilla in a saucepan and bring to a simmer over medium heat. Add the chocolate and butter, and whisk constantly until melted and just about to boil. Strain into a bowl and cool to room temperature. Refrigerate until the frosting is just set but still spreadable (1).

To assemble, place one cake layer top-side down on a cardboard round (this makes it easier to slide the frosted cake onto a serving plate). Using an offset spatula, thinly spread the frosting on top. Spread the jam on top of the frosting, if using (2). Place the remaining cake layer top-side down on the bottom layer (3). Spread frosting on top, then frost the sides. Add more frosting in decorative swirls (4).

*Overleaf, left page from top: spreadable chocolate frosting; spooning apricot jam on the frosted bottom layer; placing top layer on the frosted bottom layer; decorating the top of the cake with swirls of frosting; right page: a piece of The Chocolate Cake*

1.

2.

3.

4.

# INDEX

# METRIC CONVERSIONS & EQUIVALENTS

## APPROXIMATE METRIC EQUIVALENTS

### WEIGHT

¼ ounce . . . . . . . . . .7 grams
½ ounce . . . . . . . . . 14 grams
¾ ounce . . . . . . . . . 21 grams
1 ounce . . . . . . . . . 28 grams
1¼ ounces . . . . . . . . 35 grams
1½ ounces . . . . . . . 42.5 grams
1⅔ ounces . . . . . . . . 45 grams
2 ounces . . . . . . . . . 57 grams
3 ounces . . . . . . . . . 85 grams
4 ounces (¼ pound) . . . 113 grams
5 ounces . . . . . . . . 142 grams
6 ounces . . . . . . . . 170 grams
7 ounces . . . . . . . . 198 grams
8 ounces (½ pound) . . . 227 grams
16 ounces
  (1 pound) . . . . . . . 454 grams
35.25 ounces
  (2.2 pounds) . . . . . . 1 kilogram

### LENGTH

⅛ inch . . . . . . . . . 3 millimeters
¼ inch . . . . . . . . . 6 millimeters
½ inch . . . . . . . . .1¼ centimeters
1 inch . . . . . . . . .2½ centimeters
2 inches . . . . . . . .5 centimeters
2½ inches . . . . . . .6 centimeters
4 inches . . . . . . . 10 centimeters
5 inches . . . . . . . 13 centimeters
6 inches . . . . . 15¼ centimeters
12 inches (1 foot) . . . 30 centimeters

### VOLUME

¼ teaspoon . . . . . . . . 1 milliliter
½ teaspoon . . . . . . .2.5 milliliters
¾ teaspoon . . . . . . . . 4 milliliters
1 teaspoon . . . . . . . . 5 milliliters
1¼ teaspoons . . . . . . 6 milliliters
1½ teaspoons . . . . . .7.5 milliliters
1¾ teaspoons . . . . . .8.5 milliliters
2 teaspoons . . . . . . . 10 milliliters
1 tablespoon
  (½ fluid ounce) . . . . 15 milliliters
2 tablespoons
  (1 fluid ounce) . . . . 30 milliliters
¼ cup . . . . . . . . . 60 milliliters
⅓ cup . . . . . . . . . 80 milliliters
½ cup
  (4 fluid ounces) . . .120 milliliters
⅔ cup . . . . . . . . . .160 milliliters
¾ cup . . . . . . . . . .180 milliliters
1 cup
  (8 fluid ounces) . . . 240 milliliters
1¼ cups . . . . . . . .300 milliliters
1½ cups
  (12 fluid ounces) . . .360 milliliters
1⅔ cups . . . . . . . .400 milliliters
2 cups (1 pint) . . . . .460 milliliters
3 cups . . . . . . . . .700 milliliters
4 cups (1 quart) . . . . . . .95 liter
1 quart plus ¼ cup . . . . . . 1 liter
4 quarts (1 gallon) . . . . . 3.8 liters

## OVEN TEMPERATURES

To convert Fahrenheit to Celsius, subtract 32 from Fahrenheit, multiply the result by 5, then divide by 9.

| Description | Fahrenheit | Celsius | British Gas Mark |
|---|---|---|---|
| Very cool | 200° | 95° | 0 |
| Very cool | 225° | 110° | ¼ |
| Very cool | 250° | 120° | ½ |
| Cool | 275° | 135° | 1 |
| Cool | 300° | 150° | 2 |
| Warm | 325° | 165° | 3 |
| Moderate | 350° | 175° | 4 |
| Moderately hot | 375° | 190° | 5 |
| Fairly hot | 400° | 200° | 6 |
| Hot | 425° | 220° | 7 |
| Very hot | 450° | 230° | 8 |
| Very hot | 475° | 245° | 9 |

## METRIC CONVERSION FORMULAS

| To Convert | Multiply |
|---|---|
| Ounces to grams | Ounces by 28.35 |
| Pounds to kilograms | Pounds by .454 |
| Teaspoons to milliliters | Teaspoons by 4.93 |
| Tablespoons to milliliters | Tablespoons by 14.79 |
| Fluid ounces to milliliters | Fluid ounces by 29.57 |
| Cups to milliliters | Cups by 236.59 |
| Cups to liters | Cups by .236 |
| Pints to liters | Pints by .473 |
| Quarts to liters | Quarts by .946 |
| Gallons to liters | Gallons by 3.785 |
| Inches to centimeters | Inches by 2.54 |

## COMMON INGREDIENTS AND THEIR APPROXIMATE EQUIVALENTS

1 cup uncooked rice = 225 grams

1 cup all-purpose flour = 120 grams

1 stick butter (4 ounces • ½ cup • 8 tablespoons) = 110 grams

1 cup butter (8 ounces • 2 sticks • 16 tablespoons) = 220 grams

1 cup brown sugar, firmly packed = 225 grams

1 cup granulated sugar = 200 grams

# ACKNOWLEDGMENTS

We thank heaven for the day we fell into the company of our extraordinary editor, Michael Szczerban. He has guided us with the surest yet lightest touch. Our heartfelt thanks for your wisdom and kind, sensitive manner. And most of all, for your deep belief in all that we do.

To our terrific agent, Doe Coover, who immediately understood our vision for this book and skillfully found just the right home for it. Thank you.

We are grateful to our copy editor, Valerie Saint-Rossy, whose foodcentric knowledge of English (and French, Italian, Spanish, Japanese, and Chinese) always makes our sentences more better. *Merci!*

To the lovely Teresa Hopkins, who is always ready to screenshare and jump into any technical situation we ask of her cheerfully and with wizardry. Girl power! Thank you.

Katherine Yang, whose baking knowledge and ability to perfectly balance sweet and salty is equal to her openhanded generosity. Thank you for sharing your fine taste with us.

Niloufer Ichaporia King makes even the simplest things taste divine. We are grateful for your unstinting friendship.

To Julia Lee, friend, colleague, and chowiest home cook we know, you still reign as the fry queen in our world.

To longtime friends Geraldine and Charla Lawhon, for sharing part of their family's legacy. A delicious gift. Thank you.

A great big thank-you to the wonderful Voracious / Little, Brown team: Ben Allen, Reagan Arthur, Lisa Ferris, Nicky Guerreiro, Lucy Kim, Juliana Horbachevsky, Kim Sheu, and Elora Weil. We couldn't have landed in a finer tub of butter.

Jim Hirsheimer, artist and enthusiastic amateur eater, thank you for your steadfast support and love.

To Hugh Cosman, who had the great idea to put a ring on it, with thanks and everlasting love.

To Henry, Lillie, and Nash Anderson, Amanda, Brandon, Brian, Frani, and Molly Beadle, Haden and Lucas Cosman, Olivia and Ryan Goldfarb, Eliot Hagerty, Madeleine Hamilton, Verity Liljedahl, Colman Andrews, Dorothy Kalins and Roger Sherman, and Peggy Knickerbocker and Robert Fisher. Our shared love for the everyday practice of cooking and the enjoyment of eating together with you are two of life's greatest pleasures.

To Bob and Leni, the studio dogs, for their sweet natures and constant companionship.

To all the kind and generous Canal House readers, followers, and friends, and to *The Canal House Kitchen Hour* listeners in radioland. We are hugely grateful for your enthusiastic support. Eat well, be happy. And remember, cook something delicious for yourselves, dear friends.

CHRISTOPHER HIRSHEIMER and MELISSA HAMILTON are cofounders of Canal House, a publishing venture in Milford, New Jersey, that combines a culinary and design studio. Their collaboration includes *Canal House Cooking*, a series of seasonal cookbooks, for which they do the writing, recipes, photography, illustration, design, and production. Their cookbook, *Canal House Cooks Every Day* (Andrews McMeel, 2012) received the 2013 James Beard Foundation award in the General Cooking category. Their blog, *Canal House Cooks Lunch*, is followed by thousands of devotees who get inspiration from their daily lunch ideas. They are the hosts of *The Canal House Kitchen Hour* on WDVR-FM, a one-hour radio program devoted to food, home cooking, and great tunes.

Christopher (CH) lives with her husband and Bob, the studio dog, in Bucks County, Pennsylvania. Melissa (MH) and her husband live in Hunterdon County, New Jersey, with Leni, the studio Redbone Coonhound.

To learn more about Canal House, visit thecanalhouse.com.

Eat well, be happy!